# NUECES BATTLE AND MASSACRE SOURCE DOCUMENTS

Compiled and Edited By
Wm. Paul Burrier, Sr.

Watercress Press
San Antonio, 2014

A *Watercress Press* book
from Geron & Associates
www. watercresspress.com


ISBN-13: 978-0-9897820-0-5
Library of Congress Control Number: 2014944077


Cover image by Wm. Paul Burrier, Sr.
Cover design by 3iii's Graphic Studios

# Table of Contents

# Preface

A large number of Germans settled the Texas Hill Country in the late 1840s and early 1850s. Most of these were farmers, stonemasons, craftsmen, and so forth. With the group was a small number of Freethinkers; someone who did not believe in the organized church. After the failed 1848-49 German Revolution several hundred of the radical leaders joined the earlier German arrivals in the Hill Country. These Forty-Eighters joined with the Freethinkers and attempted to organize a German political party. One of their goals was to establish a free state in Western Texas, which is now the Texas Hill Country. It was only at the start of the Civil War did they see an opportunity to do so. They organized an insurgency. In June, 1861, the political element was created. Today this political element is called the Union Loyal League, but the insurgents simply called it 'The Organization.' The insurgents believed that the Union was going to invade Texas with two forces. One would land at Galveston and the second would drive overland from Kansas. These two forces would link up at Austin, splitting the state in two along the Colorado River. The Free State of West Texas would be organized in the area west of the Colorado. In March, 1862, the insurgents organized the military element of the insurgency. It was battalion-sized with somewhere between three hundred and five hundred members. This battalion was a secret unauthorized military unit solely devoted to the creation of West Texas. When the Union invasion came this battalion would rise up, join with armed Unionist units in Austin, San Antonio, and Bandera, Comal and Medina Counties, and declare The Free State of West Texas. Meantime the insurgents would remain members of the local militia units. All white males in Texas above the age of eighteen and under forty-five were required to be a member of a militia unit. Bandera County had a Unionist company of about forty-five members and Medina County had Unionist control of a battalion of four companies with about three hundred fifty members.

The insurgent battalion began to organize and conduct guerrilla operations which culminated with the death of at least two secessionists. The Confederate military commander of Texas declared martial law over the entire state and sent regular Confederate units into the Hill Country to destroy the insurgency. With the arrival of regular Confederate troops a hard-core element of the insurgency, sixty-three in number, decided to flee Texas, go to Mexico, and make their way to New Orleans to join the Union Army. With this group were five Anglos who were also Unionists. All of the insurgent forces were deserters from either their militia units or the Confederate Army.

A hundred-man pursuit force overtook the insurgents on August 10, 1862, on the West Prong of the Nueces River. A hard-fought battle followed. The Confederates assaulted the insurgency camp three times and were forced back. Twenty-eight of the insurgents, to unclude four Anglos, gave up the fight and left their comrades. On the fourth assault the Confederates captured the insurgent camp. Nineteen insurgents were killed in the battle, including about seven who were executed. The Confederates lost six men killed outright or who later died from their wounds and another fifteen wounded, of whom at least five received medical discharges.

Almost everything written about the events leading up to the battle and the aftermath is incorrect; this became clear when the author began research for this book. It took almost twenty years to piece together the correct story of the events surrounding the Nueces fight. Myths had replaced facts and the few accounts of events were wrong or greatly biased. As the author was attempting to get the book published by a university press, the manuscript was sent to universities who sent it to well known Texas-German scholars for their comments. The experts didn't believe the version contained in the manuscript and no university press would publish the book. The author had to resort to using a private publisher.

Slowly the correct story began to unfold. Countless interviews with descendants were conducted. Some of the accounts were so sensitive that they would share only on the condition that the materiel would not be traced back to them. Others were very open and glad to have their story told. As one interview began, the interviewee started crying and said, "I have been looking for you all my life. When I was a small child at family events, all the men would go out and set under a tree while the old men told family stories. All my cousins got to play while my dad made me sit and listen. Now they are all dead. I am the only one who knows these stories. My children and grandchildren don't want to hear them. At last someone will tell the family stories." Individuals began to provide me with copies of letters, diaries, and a host of other data, almost all in German and not intended for general use. Many were written by Nueces battle participants. This and my military background enabled me to better understand what had happen. In one of my assignments it was drilled into me that "You never say what you thought you said and you never heard what you thought you heard. You must listen and read with the goal of hearing and reading what the person was trying to tell you."

This was especially true when it came to family stories, letters, and diaries most of which were written in German and translated into English. Every effort was made to verify stories and data by other accounts. On completion of the manuscript, the author wanted to share the source documents so that readers can see the origins of the data and the basis for the author's conclusions. This book is that result.

# Synopsis of Each Document

Document Number 1. *The Introduction to Battle of Nueces River* by John Sansom. Sansom's account set the tone for many other authors and researchers. The reader should remember that Sansom was not a member of the Union Loyal League and was only a witness to the Nueces battle – not the insurgency's other actions.

Document Number 2. The Texas Governor Proclamation of June 8, 1861. One of the major myths is that the governor issued a proclamation giving the Unionists thirty days to leave the state and the fleeing insurgents were travelling under the protection of the proclamation. This proclamation was the only one issued by the Texas governor pertaining to the Unionists.

Document Number 3. Charles Montague's Letter. One of the earliest accounts indicating that those not in support of the Confederacy were in fact organizing a military unit.

Document Number 4. President Davis' Proclamation of August 14, 1861. This proclamation gave all male citizens forty days to either take the oath of allegiance or leave the Confederacy. Unionists would later claim that the insurgents were travelling under this proclamation.

Document Number 5. The regulations regarding President Davis' Proclamation of August 14, 1861.

Document Number 6. In many published accounts of the "Nueces Event" much has been made of the belief that the Unionists and insurgents refused to take the oath of allegiance to the Confederate States of American because they did not want to violate their oath to the Unites States taken only a few years before when they became citizens. This list shows the names of many Comfort men who were insurgents or who joined the Union Army took the required oath when President Davis issued his August, 1861, proclamation.

Document Number 7. The required Confederate Oath of Allegiance.

Document Number 8. A. O. Cooley's letter. Letter from a Gillespie County attorney to the Texas Comptroller, complaining that Philip Braubach's home guard company – a Unionist unit – had done little against Indian attacks.

Document Number 9. Frank Van der Stucken's letter. Letter from a Gillespie County citizen claiming that the company which Jacob Kuechler was organizing for frontier protection contained only Unionists.

Document Number 10. David H. Farr's letter. Letter from a Kerr County citizen claiming that the company Jacob Kuechler was organizing for frontier protection contained only Unionists.

Document Number 11. A petition from thirty-eight Kerr County citizens claiming that the company Jacob Kuechler was organizing for frontier protection contained only Unionists. This petition also established that some thirty Gillespie County citizens had also sent a petition. The Gillespie County petition is missing from the State archives.

Document Number 12. A Gillespie County Rifles (a home guard company) resolution condemning the activities of four Unionists. It also contains the names of Gillespie County citizens who took the oath of allegiance to the Confederacy.

Document Number 13. Ernest Cramer's letter. He was the commander of the Kendall Company of the Union Loyal League's Military Battalion. The letter was written in German to his parents, still in Germany, telling about the activities leading up to the Nueces battle and the immediate aftermath. This is one of the 'smoking gun' documents.

Document Number 14. Colonel Henry McCulloch's letter of March 27, 1862. He was the Confederate military commander of the area containing the Hill Country. The letter outlines the threats of the Unionists and explains that action must be taken to destroy the "traitors."

Document Number 15. Colonel Henry McCulloch's letter of March 28, 1862. This is a letter to the Texas governor telling of an armed Unionist company in San Antonio and Col. McCulloch's belief that martial law must soon be declared.

Document Number 16. Colonel Henry McCulloch's letter of March 31, 1862. This letter explains that German written "notices" have appeared in San Antonio urging Unionists to do "all they can to injure" the Confederate cause. Enclosed with the letter is a copy of the notice.

Document Number 17. A petition from twenty-six Spring Creek citizens from western Gillespie County, asking to raise a home guard company. Almost all of these Anglos citizens were Unionists.

Document Number 18. General H. P. Bee's proclaimation of martial law in Bexar County.

Document Number 19. Fritz Tegener's letter. He was the military commander of the insurgency battalion. This letter gives the number of fleeing insurgents of August, 1862, as well as details of the Unionist meeting at Bear Creek and his election as commander.

Document Number 20. Extract from D. P. Hopkins's diary. He was a Texas State Trooper from Davis' Company A, Frontier Regiment, stationed at Camp Davis in western Gillespie County. The letter tells of activities at Camp Davis in the early days of August, 1862, including results of the Confederate pursuit and the execution of four Unionists at Spring Creek.

Document Number 21. Captain Charles de Montel's letter of March 16, 1862. He was the commander of Company D, Frontier Regiment, stationed in south Kerr and western Bandera Counties. The letter tells of the Medina County Home Guard battalion being made up of Unionists.

Document Number 22. Captain Charles de Montel's letter of May 31, 1862. The letter tells of the Medina Unionists organizing an express courier system between the area towns and contact by Unionists telling local men to be on the northern side.

Document Number 23. General P. O. Hebert's Proclamation of Martial Law on May 30, 1862, over the entire State of Texas.

Document Number 24. Captain James Duff's report. He was the commander of a Confederate company of Partisan Rangers sent to the Hill Country to declare and enforce martial law. The letter tells of him arresting several Unionists in Gillespie, Kendall, and Medina Counties

Document Number 25. Captain Charles de Montel's Letter of July 7, 1862. This letter tells of finding armed Medina County Unionists "in the mountain" and "armed to the teeth."

Document Number 26. List of Luckenbach Rangers or Buschwachers. This is the roster of Luckenbach insurgents hiding near Albert in eastern Gillespie County.

Document Number 27. Captain Henry Davis' request for Confederate Troops. Captain Davis was the commander of Company A, Frontier Regiment stationed in western Gillespie County. He urged Confederate troops be sent to the area as his scouts were finding armed insurgents in groups of twenty-five to forty – large enough to pose a threat to his camps.

Document Number 28. Colonel James M. Norris letter supporting Captain Davis' request for Confederate Troops. He was the commander of the Frontier Regiment. Colonel Norris stated that Confederate Troops were necessary "to effectually route and disperse the forces of Lincoln and rid the country of them."

Documents Number 29. Lieutenant Colonel Benton's report. He was the commander of a three-company task force sent to the counties of Burnett, Llano, San Saba, and Kimball to rid that section of Unionists.

Document Number 30. Article from the August 30, 1862 issue of the *San Antonio Weekly Herald,* reporting the result of Colonel Benton's expedition.

Document Number 31. General H. P. Bee's report of October 21, 1862 This report summarizes the actions of Confederate forces against the Texas Hill Country insurgents. One of the major items in the report is Captain James Duff's role. Bee says he appointed Duff "provost-marshal for the counties composing the disaffected district." Bee goes on to explain the relationship of Duff to the military force sent. The military forces were commanded by Captain John Donelson. James Duff was not the commander of the military force. Bee uses the word "control," which in military terms does not indicate command authority. Bee clearly says the four-company task force was "commanded" by Captain John Donelson, not James Duff. The report also states the mission of the task force was "to find and break up any such encampment and depots as had been reported to exist there, and to send the families and provisions back to the settlements." It also says there "were still many in arms who were determined to resist the government at all hazards." Lieutenant C. D. McRae overtook the insurgent force and "did their work most effectually."

Document Number 32. Henry Schwethelm's letter of 1913. The letter briefly tells Schwethelm's activities in the Nueces battle and names one of the Confederates who executed the wounded insurgents.

Document Number 33. A letter from Eduard Degener; the leader of the Union Loyal League. This was written to his father-in-law and a family friend back in Germany. It gives an overview of the situation in the Texas Hill Country.

Document Number 34. Post Return for Camp Pedernales for the month of August, 1862. It shows several major items: "The Post Near Fredericksburg" was established August 1, 1862, that Captain Donelson was the commander of the post and troops, and that about August 5, Captain Donelson dispatched Lieutenant McRae with ninety-four fresh men and horses after the fleeing bands of traitors. It contains the names of the officers stationed at Camp Pedernales. Captain James

Duff's name is not included. It also establishes that Captain Donelson entered upon the duties of provost marshal on August 21, 1862, and that Captain Duff and his company left on August 21, 1862.

Document Number 35. Post Return for Camp Pedernales for the month of September, 1862. It shows two major items: That Captain Donelson ". . . entered upon the duties of his office (provost-marshal) on August 21, 1862," and Captain Donelson was relieved at Fredericksburg on September 20, 1862, replaced by Captain Josiah Taylor.

Document Number 36. List of Men Deserted Belonging to Kerr County. These men deserted their militia unit or the Confederate Army. Many of them were in the fleeing insurgent group.

Document Number 37. Extract from *Die Deutsche Pioniere,* a German-language book about some of the events of the Nueces battle, written in 1894. One item was the role that a German by the name of Bergmann played.

Document Number 38. Letter from Julius Schlickum; he was a German from Kendall County who was arrested and tried by the Confederate Military Commission. He observed the organization of the Union Loyal League and its military battalion, but opposed the organization of the Union Loyal League because he saw the "futility of this undertaking. I knew too well that a few backwoodsmen could not lead war against the State of Texas."

Document Number 39. John W. Sansom's account of the Nueces battle. One of the first accounts published and used by later writers and researchers. While it contains much vital information it must be remembered that Sansom was not a member of the Union Loyal League and merely repeated what insurgents told him. He was a witness to the Nueces battle, but not all the other information is drawn from first-hand observation.

Document Number 40. R. H. Williams' account of the Nueces battle. Williams was a Confederate soldier in Duff's company with the pursuit force. Williams was very critical of Captain Duff. The reader must remember that Williams was a private and not privileged to the inner workings of the pursuit force. His details of the actual battle recounted here is very good, but his other accounts are highly exaggerated, especially when it comes to numbers. William's book, like the Sansom account, is one almost every writer and historian uses, but it needs to be remembered that he was only a witness of the actual battle.

Document Number 41. Edited Journal of Fritz Schellhase. One of the documents written in German for only family use. It is the author's opinion that the descendants who released the edited version left out many details.

Document Number 42. Usener Brothers' Story. An account of the Usener brothers in the Nueces battle.

Document Number 43. Schwethelm's interview with Albert Schutze. This document is often treated as a primary document, when it is in fact an interview with Henry Schwethelm, not an account as told by Schwethelm. The document contains much useful information, but the reader must remember it is told by Albert Schutze – not directly from Henry Schwethelm.

Document Number 44. August Hoffmann's Helen Raley Interview. This document, like the Schwethelm document, has often by treated as a primary document, which it is not. The document contains much useful information, but the interviewer added data she mistakenly believed was correct.

Document Number 45. John W. Sansom's Article of November 11, 1911. This is a primary document where Sansom tells more about when the infamous proclamation was written.

Document Number 46. Letter from August Hoffmann; this is indeed a primary document written by August Hoffmann, the last living survivor of the Nueces battle.

Document Number 47. A *Harper's Weekly* article published on January 20, 1866. This is good account of the Nueces battle as written by a Texas Unionist – or at least resulted from interviews done shortly after the events.

Document Number 48. Lieutenant C. D. McRae's Report. This was written by Lieutenant Colin D. McRae, commander of the pursuit force, and is a good Confederate account of the Nueces battle.

Document Number 49. Lieutenant McRae's list of Confederate killed and wounded. This is the first time this document has been published. Federal researchers located the document in 1997.

Document Number 50. List of Confederate Casualties from Nueces Battle. This list was compiled from several sources such as Lieutenant McRae's List of Casualties, names of Confederates killed and wounded contained in several newspaper articles, and from a very detailed search of the

Confederate Compiled Service Records of those soldiers dispatched to Fredericksburg.

Document Number 51. *Neu Braunfelser Zeitung.* German-language article written shortly after the Nueces battle. The article gives the names of several of the insurgents who participated, or were killed or wounded. Some of these were not otherwise known to have been in the battle.

Document Number 52. Letter from J. M. Seal;  he was a member of Captain Davis' Company A, Frontier Regiment and wrote of killing an insurgent survivor of the battle.

 Document Number 53  Jacob Kuechler's letter.  He was the commander of the Gillespie Company of the League's military battalion.  He wrote of his role in the Nueces battle.

Document Number 54. *The Old Dutch Battleground.*  A Uvalde local history article about a Uvalde citizen's trip to the battle site and recovery of a wounded insurgent.

Document Number 55.  Captain John Donelson's Letter of August 21, 1862. This letter establishes that Donelson was the provost marshal at Fredericksburg by August 21, 1862.

Document Number 56.  Letter by Leonard Pierce, Jr.  He was the U. S. Consult in Matamoras, Mexico.  His letter tells about the Nueces battle.

Document Number 57.  The Bonnet Brothers.  This is the most detailed article about the second group of insurgents crossing into Mexico and the resulting fight at the Rio Grande.

Document Number 58.  Extract from Mary McDonald and Charles Frank's story.  One of the most complete accounts about the four Unionists hanged at Spring Creek on August 22, 1862.

Document Number 59. Extract from Thomas C. Smith's diary. He was a Confederate trooper sent to Fredericksburg after the Nueces battle.

Document Number 60. Captain John Donelson's letter of September 8, 1862. An update on the activities around Fredericksburg.

Document Number 61. A letter from James M. Hunter; he was in Captain Davis' Company A, Frontier Regiment and second in command and assumed command when Davis joined the Confederate Army. The letter identifies one of the state troopers who killed the wounded insurgents.

Document Number 62. A letter from Howard Henderson; he was with the fleeing August insurgents. The letter claims to identify some of the men James Duff killed. The problem is that Duff was not in the Hill Country when these deaths occurred.

Document Number 63. Court Martial of Private James Duff. One of the many myths surrounding Duff is that he committed some horrible crimes while in the U. S. military. This shows his crime was being absent from his unit for about ten days, an offense which in the military of today is treated as company punishment.

Document Number 64. Letter – National Archives. One of the myths about Duff is that he received forty lashes on his back and was drummed out of the U. S. Army. This letter and attached Special Orders show that his sentence was remitted and Duff rejoined his regiment.

Document Number 65. Extract James Duff's U. S. Army Service Records. This shows that Duff was almost immediately promoted to corporal a few weeks after his sentence was remitted and was promoted to fifth sergeant and regiment commissary sergeant. Duff received an honorable discharge at Fort McIntosh, Texas, at the end of his five-year enlistment term.

Document Number 66. Article from the Austin *Texas State Gazette* of May 10, 1865. This article demonstrates the high degree of esteem Duff held among Confederate supporters.

# 1. Battle of Nueces River in Kinney County, Texas, August 1862[1] (Extract)

## By John W. Sansom[2]

Before going into the details of the battle, though, let me put on record a chapter of hitherto unwritten local history which may prove of interest to the descendants of the old-timers, and which will explain why it was the Unionists came to be where they were when attacked by the Confederates.

\* \* \*

That the wise counsel needed was not lacking, is demonstrated by the fact that shortly after the promulgation of the Ordinance of Secession, a "Union Loyal League" was organized in June, 1861, by representatives from the sections named.

\* \* \*

Only eighteen persons were present at the first and initial meeting, but these were the chosen representatives from as many different sections. Each of these bound himself by a solemn vow not to bear arms against the Federal Government, and each was appointed by the body as a Committee of one whose duty it was to persuade others to join the league and make the same pledge. Then the eighteen dispersed and went to work so diligently and with such success, that on July 4th, 1862[3], not less than five hundred male Unionists met on Bear Creek in Gillespie County, and proceeded to perfect the organization of three companies, to wit: the Gillespie County Company, Jacob Kuechler[4], Captain, Valentine Homan[5], Lieutenant; the Kendall County Company, E. Kramer[6], Captain, Hugo Degener[7], Lieutenant; and the Kerr County

Company, Henry Hartman[8], Phil G. Temple[9], Lieutenant. Having elected company officers, the three companies then elected Fritz Tegener as Major to command the battalion. In addition to the foregoing action, an Advisory Board of which Edward Degener[10], Esq., since a Member of Congress from Texas, and others of the members, was appointed and a joint meeting of the Advisory Board and the officers elected immediately held.

ENDNOTES
Sansom's Battle of Nueces River

01. *Battle of Nueces River in Kinney County, Texas, August 10, 1862* by John W. Sansom. Privatly published, San Antonio, Texas, October 1, 1905, Page 2-3.

02. John William Sansom was born on February 5, 1834, in Alabama. The Sansom family arrived in Texas in 1839.They first settled near Washington-on-the Brazos and later moved to Lavaca County. They next moved to the area of current Uvalde. In 1855 they moved to Curry's Creek in present Kendall County. John Sansom was captain of several ranger companies in the late 1850s. He married Victoria Helen Patton on December 13, 1860, in Blanco County. They were the parents of one daughter. Sansom was elected the first sheriff of Kendall County. Eduard Degener asked Sansom to guide the insurgent group to Mexico and he agreed. They were attacked on the morning of August 10, 1862, while camped on the West Prong of the Nueces River. Sansom returned to his home after the battle, but shortly left for Mexico and went on to New Orleans where on October 28, 1862, he enrolled in Company A, First Regiment [Union] Texas Cavalry. After the war Sansom commanded several Ranger companies. Sansom moved to Roswell, New Mexico, in 1880 and returned to Uvalde County in 1884 where he remained until 1893, at which time he moved to San Antonio where he died on June 19, 1920.

03. Other sources at the meeting state it was held as early as March, 1862. See Ernest Cramer's letter, Document #13 p. 33, and Fritz Tegener's letter, Document #19, p.105.

04. Jacob Kuechler was born about 1823 in Hesse-Darmstadt. He was a member of *Die Vierziger,* or 'The Forty.' Kuechler arrived in Texas in July, 1847, on the *St. Pauli.* The Forty list shows he was a forester. Kuechler moved to Gillespie County in the mid-1850s and became a surveyor. He married Mary Petri on May 31, 1856, in Gillespie County. They were the parents of three children. Kuechler was very likely a founding member of the Union Loyal League. In the spring of 1862 he was elected captain of Company E, 2nd Regiment [Gillespie County], 31st Brigade District. During this time he was appointed enrollment officer to raise a company for the Frontier Regiment. He organized a company composed entirely of Unionists. Governor Lubbock ordered the company disbanded. Kuechler then organized a Gillespie company for the League's military battalion of which he was elected captain. When Captain James Duff arrived at the end of May, 1862, he attempted to arrest Kuechler, but failed. Kuechler and others hid in the mountains until the decision was made to flee to Mexico, then to New Orleans to join the Union army. He commanded the Gillespie portion of the insurgent group. Kuechler

survived the Nueces battle and returned to Gillespie County. In mid-October, 1862 he led another insurgent group toward Mexico. They were overtaken on the banks of the Rio Grande and another seven Unionists were killed and several wounded. Kuechler hid in Mexico for the remained of the war. After the war he served as a surveyor and Texas Land Commissioner. Jacob Kuechler died on April 4, 1893.

05. Valentine Hohmann was born about 1829 in Saxony. He arrived in Texas on the *Neptune* from Kaltennordheim in 1845. Hohmann married Sophie Feuge on March 7, 1852, in Gillespie County. They were the parents of six children. Valentine was a sergeant in Braubach's home guard company from February, 1861, until February, 1862. He left with the insurgent group in August 1862 and survived the Nueces battle. He returned to Gillespie County where he joined Jacob Kuechler in another attempt to reached Mexico. Valentine Hohmann was killed on October 18, 1862, at the Rio Grande crossing battle.

06. Ernest Cramer was born on May 23, 1836, in Schweinfurt, Bavaria. He first arrived in Texas in 1853 and worked as a merchant. Cramer was the first lieutenant in Captain John W. Sansom's 1859 Ranger company  He returned to Bavaria in late 1859. I believe he is the E. Cramer who arrived in Texas on the *Iris* from Schweinfurt in 1860. By 1861 he was living in the Comfort area. On September 12, 1861, Cramer married Charlotte Apollon Bauer in Kerr County. They were the parents of six children. He was a member of Harbour's home guard company in February, 1861. Ernest Cramer was an early member of the Union Loyal League. He was in the process of being elected major of the 3$^{rd}$ Regiment, 31$^{st}$ Brigade District when voting was suspended in June, 1862. Cramer was in the fleeing insurgent group and survived the Nueces battle. He first returned to the Hill Country, but later fled to Mexico where he remained until the end of the war. Cramer was the Custom Officer in Eagle Pass in the mid-1870s. He moved to Santa Clara, California, in the mid-1870s. Cramer moved his family to Hailey, Blaine County, Idaho, in the early 1880s. Ernest Cramer died on July 10, 1916, at Boise, Ada County, Idaho.

07. Hugo Degener was born about 1842, very likely in Brunswick. He was a son of Eduard Degener. The family arrived in Texas in 1852 and settled at Sisterdale. Hugo was a second lieutenant in Kuechler's company of December, 1861. He fled with the insurgent group. He was a messmate of John Sansom. Hugo was seriously wounded during the Nueces battle. He crawled to Captain Cramer's position to bid him farewell and covered the insurgent withdrawal. He was executed by order of Lieutenant Lilly.

08. Henry Hartman was born about 1821 in Coshocton County, Ohio. The family came from Westmoreland County, Pennsylvania. Henry Hartman married Eliza [maiden name not known] about 1847, likely in Adams County, Illinois. His only known child was a son, Amon. Eliza died about 1851, likely in

Adams County, Illinois. The date he and Amon arrived in Texas and Gillespie County is not known, but it was likely in late 1860 or early Hartman married the widow Mary Mathilde McDaniel on October 26, 186i, in Gillespie County. According to deed records Hartman lived on North Creek in Gillespie County. On April 17, 1862 Hartman gave his livestock, which included sheep and goats valued at $1,300; his mule, wagon, and all the improvements on his 'rancho' to his son. After the Confederate crackdown, Hartman fled to Mexico. Because his son was a minor, the Gillespie County court appointed a guardian for him in August, 1862. Henry enlisted in Company A, First Regiment [Union] Texas Cavalry on October 29, 1862, in New Orleans. His enlistment papers say he was forty-one years old, a farmer, with gray eyes, black hair, and a dark complexion. He was five feet tall. The papers also show he was married with one child. Hartmann was promoted to company quartermaster sergeant on December 5, 1862. He resigned this position on August 20, 1863. On January 20, 1864, Major General Herron placed him on 'Secret Detached Service'. His Union service records show this was on 'recruiting duty' back into the Texas Hill Country. A note in his service records by Captain P. G. Temple, his company commander states, "H. Hartman was sent into Texas on Secret Service by order of Maj Genl Herron [on] January 25, 1864, and has never been heard of since. His horse however was seen in Laredo some time [in] July of 1864. Hence it is thought he was killed as he was a good trusty man, has a son who is a corpl in Co. 'A.' who is the nearest relative of Henry Hartman." Henry Hartman's widow married Samuel Gibson on April 21, 1864, in Gillespie County. Samuel Gibson was a pro-Confederate bushwhacker.

09. Philip G. Temple was born in March, 1826, in Ohio. He served as a private in Company E, 2$^{nd}$ Regiment Kentucky Infantry during the Mexican War. He arrived in Gillespie County in late 1860 or early 1861. Temple was a member of the 'Spring Creek' Home Guard in April, 1862. He fled Texas after the Confederate crackdown. Temple enrolled in Company A, First Regiment [Union] on October 27, 1862, in New Orleans. He was appointed first lieutenant on November 6, 1862, and made acting regiment quartermaster on September 18, 1863. On January 21, 1864, Temple was promoted to captain and appointed commander of the company. He was wounded in Rancho Las Rucias battle on June 25, 1862. Temple remained with Company A until the end of the war and he was mustered out of service on October 31, 1865, in San Antonio. He returned to Gillespie County after the war, where he lived until 1896 when poor health forced Temple to return to his family home in Ohio. Philip G. Temple died on February 28, 1903, in Clermont County, Ohio.

10. Eduard Degener was born on October 20, 1809, in Brunswick. Eduard married Maria Von Bernewitz about 1830 in Brunswick. They were the parents of four children. Degener was a Freethinker and a leader in the German Forty-Fight

Revolution. According to his bio and the *New Handbook of Texas* he was a member of the first German National Assembly in Frankfurt-am-Main in 1848. He was forced to flee and arrived in Texas about 1848 and settled in Sisterdale. Some accounts claim Degener was in Texas about 1838 and served as a Texas Ranger during the Mexican War, but this is likely an error, as it was his brother August who served in that capacity. Degener declared his intentions to become a U.S. citizen on August 8, 1850, in Gillespie County. Degener was a member of the Sisterdale *Der Freier Verein* in October, 1853, and a member of the *Freier Maenner/Freimaennerverein* in 1853. He was one of the major speakers at the 1854 San Antonio Convention in May, 1854, and elected a delegate to the national meeting of the *Freimaennerverein*. Degener conspired with Frederick Law Olmsted in the "Deep Water Plan" to separate West Texas and make it a free state. He obtained his U.S. citizenship on May 18, 1858. Degener was an original member of the Union Loyal League and headed its political element, which John Sansom calls the "advisory board." Two of his sons, Hilmar and Hugo, were killed at the Nueces. The Confederate military authorities arrested Degener for disloyal activities. The Confederate Military Commission found him guilty of being "hostile of the Government of the Confederate States" and sentenced him to enter into a $5,000 bond. Degener moved to San Antonio after the war and opened a wholesale grocery business. He served as a member of the Texas Constitution Conventions of 1866 and 1868-1868. He was a major supporter of the plan to split Texas into five states and create a German controlled West Texas. Degener was elected to the U. S. Congress and served from March, 1870, to March, 1871. He was a member of the San Antonio city council from 1872 until 1878. Eduard Degener died on September 11, 1890, in San Antonio.

## 2. Proclamation by the Governor of the State of Texas
## June 8, 1861

WHEREAS, There is now a condition of hostilities between Governments of the United States and the Confederate States of American; and whereas, the Congress of the latter Government has recognized the existence of war with all of the United States except the States of Tennessee, Missouri, Kentucky, Maryland and Delaware, and the Territories of Arizona, New Mexico, and the Indian Territories situated between Kansas and the State of Texas; and, whereas, the late intimate commercial and political association of the people of the State of Texas, as a member of the Confederate States of American, is now at war, might disregard the relations in which war between said Governments has place them; and whereas, I have received information that some of the citizens of Texas have already violated their duty in the remises, as good citizen.

Now therefore, I, Edward Clark, Governor of the State of Texas, do issue this my proclamation to the people of said State, notifying them that all communication of whatsoever character between them and the citizens of the States and Territories now at war with the Confederate States of America must be discontinued; that all contracts heretofore made between them are suspended, and all that may be made during the continuance of said war, and until treaties of reciprocity are establish, will be void. It will be regarded as treason against the Confederate States of American and against the State of Texas for any citizen of said State to donate, sell, or in any manner exchange any property or commodity whatsoever with any citizen or citizens of either said State or Territories now at war with said Confederate States, without special permission from proper authority.

It will also be treasonable for any citizen of Texas to pay any debts now owning by him to a citizen of either of said States or Territories, or to contract with them any new debts or obligations during the continuance of war.

The statute of limitation will cease to run, and interest will not accrue during continuance of war.

The Executive deems it proper especially to warn all persons from endeavoring to procure title, in any manner, to property situated in Texas, and claimed by persons who are citizens of either of said States or Territories now at war with said Confederate States, or who have until recently or many now be citizens of Texas, or of the Confederate States, or of any of the States or Territories not including among those making war upon said Confederate States, and who have joined her enemies, as the Legislature may hereafter deem it property to provide for the confiscation of such property.

If there be citizens of the State of Texas owning such debts, the Executive would suggest that they deposit the amounts of the same in the Treasury of the State, taking the Treasury's receipt therefore. The United States are largely indebted to the State of Texas, and it may be determined by the Legislature of said State at some future time, that such deposits shall be retained, until the United States has satisfied the claims now held by Texas against her.

Citizens of either States or Territories, now at war with the Confederate States will not longer be permitted to visit Texas during the continuance of such war without passports issued by authority of the Executive of the Confederate States, or of this State. And if such persons are now within the limits of Texas, they are hereby warned to depart within twenty days of this date or they will be arrested as spies; and all citizens of this State of Texas are warned from holding any friendly communications whatsoever with such persons.

The Executive has issued this proclamation, impelled by belief that public safety required it, and he relies upon the people to sustain him; and to aid him in discovering and bringing to justice and lawful punishment anyone who many disregard his duty as herein set forth.

In testimony hereof, I have hereunto signed my  name and caused the great seal of the State to be affixed, at the city of Austin, this the eighth day of June, A. D., 1861, and in the year of the Independence of Texas the twenty-six and of the Confederate States the first.


By the governor:
s/Edward Clark
Bird Holland, Secretary of State

## 3. Letter-- Charles Montague[1] to Governor Clark

Bandera County
19th July 1861[2]

To His Excellency
Austin

I am sorry to trouble your Honor about the affairs of our county, but I hope to be excused when I state that the most of our settlers paid no taxes this year, that a document was handed round to get signatures of a remodeling of this government, so as to form a Union of the Sates again. That no officer of the county took the oath of allegiance, but the clerk of the District County, and that a Polander [sic] who entertained the Honorable Judge Buckner[3] from two nights was cursed next day intertaing [intentionally] being a Secessionist, and that the judge's buggy wheel was stolen and his cushions and thrown in the river, that a resolution was passed at a meeting of theirs at the Mormons feeled [failed?] to hang Judge Buckner, Doctor Downs[4] and myself. About a fortnight since I sent a man round with a paper for signatures for the call of a meeting to organize a militia company and take the Oath of Allegiance of this State and the C. S. There was a pretty good attendance, but they positively refused to take the oath and would not enroll themselves as militia, but formed a home guard, which in case of invasion may prove of a dangerous character.

Will you Honor give me or any one else authority to enroll them as militia company, or give me such direction as your Honor may deem advisable under the circumstances.

Your Obedient Servant.
Charles Montague
Justice of the Peace

P.S.  Our Southern boys have almost all joined Captain Adams[5] Company and the Secessionists are in a minority in the county at this time.

P.S. 2nd   The postmaster in Bandera[6] (a German) has not taken the oath, and in a great union man.  Honable Judge Buckner dropped in the office [for] me and next day I got it and it was torn open in the office before I got it.  Can this remediated?

ENDNOTES
Charles Montague's Letter

01. Charles Montague was born on September 25, 1800, in Ireland. He arrived in the United States in 1822 and was in Texas by the 1840s. He married Susan Ann Newton about 1833 in South Carolina. They were the parents of six children. Charles Montague purchased a large farm/ranch about 5 miles north of Bandera City. He died on June 14, 1889, in Bandera County.

02. It is interesting to note that this letter was written at the same time the Union Loyal League was being formed up north in Gillespie and Kerr Counties.

03. Eliphalet Frazer Buckner was born in 1810 in Louisville, Kentucky. He arrived in Texas about 1853. Buckner married Jane Elizabeth Fox on February 3, 1833, at Raymond, Mississippi. They were parents of two children. When Bandera County was formed in 1856 he was elected the 18th Judicial District. Buckner was forced to flee Bandera County in 1862 to Kentucky where he died in the 1870s.

04. Dr Edmund [Edwin] M. Downs was born in August, 1816, in Caledonia County, Vermont. He arrived in Texas about 1858. Downs married Caroline Lathrop about 1840, likely in Wisconsin. They were the parents of at least eight children. The family left Bandera County about 1866 and moved Refugio County. They arrived in California about 1875. Dr. Downs died in 1879 in Los Angeles County, California.

05. Captain Adam's company organized on June 25, 1861, at Fort Inge. The commander was William C. Adams who was born about 1824 in Tennessee. The date the family arrived in Texas is not known. William C. Adams married Mary Ann Rife on April 6, 1861, in Uvalde County. They were the parents of six children. William C. Adams died October 26, 1880, in Bexar County.

06. The postmaster at Bandera City was August Klappenbach. He was born about 1818 in Prussia. He arrived at Galveston on June 25, 1850, and became a U. S. citizen in 1853. Klappenbach married Mina Kuhne on May 6, 1856, in Medina County. They were the parents of five children. August Klappenbach drowned in the Medina River above Castroville on April 2, 1883.

## 4. Proclamation by the President of the Confederate States of America

## August 14, 1861

Whereas the Congress of the Confederate States of America did by an act approved on the $8^{th}$ day of August, 1861, entitled 'An act respecting alien enemies' made provision that proclamation should be issued by the President in relation to alien enemies, and in conformity with the provision of said act – Now therefore I, Jefferson Davis, President of the Confederate States of America, do issued this my proclamation and I do hereby warn and require every male citizen of the United States of the age of fourteen years and upward now within the Confederate States and adhering to the Government of the United States and acknowledging the authority of same and not being a citizen of the Confederate States to depart from the Confederate States within forty days from the date of the proclamation. And I do warn all persons above described who shall remain within the Confederate States after the expiration of said period of forty days that they will be treated as alien enemies.

Provided however that this proclamation shall not be considered as applicable during the existing war to citizens of the United States residing within the Confederate States with intent to become citizens thereof, and who shall make a declaration of such intention in due form, acknowledging the authority of this Government; nor shall this proclamation be considered as extending to the States of Delaware, Maryland, Kentucky, Missouri, the District of Columbia, the Territories of Arizona and New Mexico and the Indian Territory south of

Kansas, who shall not be chargeable with actual hostility or other crimes against the public safety, and who shall acknowledge the authority of the Government of the Confederate States.

And I do further proclaim and make known that I have established the rules and regulations hereto annexed in accordance with the provisions of said law.

Given under my hand and seal of the Confederate States of America at the city of Richmond on this 14th day of August, A. D. 1861.


s/Jefferson Davis

## 5. Regulations Respecting Alien Enemies
## Confederate States of America
## August 8, 1861

The following regulations are hereby established respecting alien enemies, under the provisions of an act approved 8th August 1861 entitled 'An Act Respecting Alien Enemies.'

1. Immediately after the expiration of the term of forty days from the date of the foregoing proclamation it shall be the several district attorneys, marshals and other officers of the Confederate State to make complaints against aliens or alien enemies coming within the purview of the act aforesaid, to the end that the several courts of the Confederate States and of each State having jurisdiction may order the removal of such aliens or alien enemies beyond the territory of the Confederate States or their restraint and confinement, according to the terms of said law.

2. The marshals of the Confederate States are hereby directed to apprehend all aliens against whom complaints may be made under said law and to hold them in strict custody until the final order of the court, taking special care that such aliens obtain no information that could possible be useful to the enemy.

3. Whenever the removal of any alien beyond the limits of the Confederate States is ordered by any competent authority under the provisions of said law the marshal shall proceed to execute the order in person or by deputy or other discreet person in such manner as to prevent the alien so removed from obtaining any information that could be used to the prejudice of the Confederate States.

4. Any alien who shall return to these States during the war after having been removed therefore under the provisions of said law shall be regarded and treated as an alien enemy, and if made prisoner shall be at once delivered over to the nearest military authority to be dealt with as a spy or as a prisoner of war, as the case may require.

# 6. Names and Dates of Comfort Area Men Who Took Oath of Allegiance to the Confederacy

| # | Surname | Given Name | Date | Source |
|---|---------|-----------|------|--------|
| 01 | Boerner | Louis | Aug. 19, 1861 | KNR, p. 95-6 |
| 02 | Bohnert | Anton | Sept. 30, 1861 | KNR, p. 100 |
| 03 | Brinkmann | Alexander | Sept. 30, 1861 | KNR, p. 101 |
| 04 | Brinkmann | Charles | Jan. 27, 1862 | KNR, p. 107 |
| 05 | Brukisch | Charles | Sept. 30, 1861 | KNR, p. 99-100 |
| 06 | Brukisch | Theodore | Jan. 27, 1862 | KNR, p. 107 |
| 07 | Dietert, Sr. | Frederick | Dec. 30, 1861 | KNR, p. 104 |
| 08 | Dietert, Jr. | Frederick | Sept. 30, 1861 | KNR, P. 102 |
| 09 | Faltin | Augustus | Jul. 1, 1861 | KNR, p. 93 |
| 10 | Geisster | Wilhelm F. | May 24, 1861 | KNR, p. 94 |
| 11 | Hanisch | Paul | Sept. 30, 1961 | KNR, p. 94 |
| 12 | Heinen | Anton | Sept. 30, 1861 | KNR, p. 99 |
| 13 | Heinen | Hubert H. | Dec. 30, 1861 | KPR, p. 52 |
| 14 | Heinen | Wilhelm | Dec. 30, 1861 | KPR, p. 50 |
| 15 | Hilke | Charles | Sept. 30, 1861 | KPR, p. 48 |
| 16 | Karger | John | Dec. 30, 1861 | KNR, p. 106 |
| 17 | Jacob | Christian | Feb. 17. 1862 | KNR, p. 108 |
| 18 | Lange | Ludwig | Jul. 8, 1861 | KNR, p. 92 |
| 19 | Lieck | Edward | Sept. 30, 1861 | KNR, p. 103 |
| 20 | Ludwig | Otto | Feb. 17, 1862 | KNR, p. 107 |
| 21 | Maertz | Charles C. | Dec. 30, 1861 | KNR, p. 105 |
| 22 | Schierholz | Louis | Feb. 17, 1862 | KNR, p. 109 |
| 23 | Schmidt | Charles | Dec. 30, 1861 | KPR, p. 50 |
| 24 | Schultze | Ferdinand | May 20. 1861 | KNR, p. 93-4 |
| 25 | Schultze | Wilhelm C. | May 20, 1861 | KNR, p. 95 |
| 26 | Schwelthelm | Henry | Aug. 26, 1861 | KNR, p. 96 |
| 27 | Serger | Emil | Sept. 30, 1861 | KNR, p. 97-8 |
| 28 | Simon | Ferdinand | May 27, 1861 | KPR, p. 42 |
| 29 | Stecher | John | Dec. 30, 1861 | KNR, p. 106 |
| 30 | Stieler | Gottfried | Jul. 1, 1861 | KNR, p. 92 |
| 31 | Strohecker | Louis | Sept. 30, 1861 | KNR, p. 103-4 |

KNR – Kerr County Naturalization Records
KPR – Kerr County Probate Records

ENDNOTES
Names and Dates of Comfort Area Men Who Took Oath of Allegiance to
Confederacy

01.  Louis Boerner was born about 1834 in Hanover. The family arrived in Texas
     about 1856 and settled near Comfort. Boerner was a member of Kuechler's
     December, 1861, Company. He was a member of the Kendall Company of the
     League's military battalion. He deserted from Company E, Second Battalion,
     Third Regiment of the 31$^{st}$ Brigade District in the summer of 1862, was in the
     August insurgent group, and killed near the Nueces battle site.

02.  Anton Bohnert was born on January 12, 1829, in Ulm, Haslach, Baden.
     Katherine Huber and Moritz Bohnert were his parents. Bohnert arrived in
     Texas in the Comfort area in 1855. He was a member of W. E. Jones'
     Company of the Third Frontier District in February 1864, and served until
     June 1864, likely until the end of the war. Bohnert married Fredericke
     Schellhase Grollimund, the widow of Joseph Grollimund on January 25, 1868,
     in Kendall County. They were the parents of six children. Anton Bohnert died
     on January 1, 1903, in Kendall County.

03.  Alexander Brinkmann was born about 1837 in Prussia. He was a twin brother
     of Charles Brinkmann, below. His parents' names are not known. Brinkmann
     arrived in Texas on the *Mississippi* from Hauseberge, Hanover, in 1855 and
     settled in the Comfort area in 1858. He was a member of Harbour's Kerr
     County home guard company in February, 1861. Brinkmann was very likely a
     member of the Kendall Company of the League's military battalion. He was
     conscripted into Company B, 3$^{rd}$ Regiment Texas Infantry on September 1,
     1862, and likely served until the end of the war. Brinkmann married Regina
     Wechsler on December 25, 1866. They were the parents of at least three
     children. His death date is not known.

04.  Charles Brinkmann was born about 1837 in Prussia, the twin brother of
     Alexander Brinkmann, above. His parents' names are not known. He arrived
     in Texas on the *Mississippi* from Hauseberge, Hanover in 1855 and settled in
     the Comfort area in 1858. Brinkmann was very likely a member of the
     Kendall Company of the League's military battalion. He was conscripted into
     Company B, 3$^{rd}$ Regiment Texas Infantry on September 1, 1862. Brinkmann
     deserted on December 9, 1862, at Ringgold Barracks and in February, 1863,
     enlisted in Company C, First Regiment [Union] Texas Cavalry. He was
     captured on June 25, 1864, in the fighting at Las Rancho Rucias near
     Brownsville. Charles Brinkmann died at Chapel Hill, Texas, on October 15,
     1864, while a prisoner of war.

05.  Charles (Carl) Bruckisch was born about 1835 in Prussia. Carolina [maiden
     name not known] and William Bruckisch, Sr., were his parents. Carl was a
     brother of Theodore Bruckisch, below. The family arrived in Texas on the

*Friedrich Grosse* by way of New Orleans in 1852 and settled in Comal County. Carl Bruckisch enrolled in Company B, 3$^{rd}$ Regiment Texas Infantry in early 1862. No further data.

06. Theodore Bruckisch was born about 1838 in Prussia. He was a brother of Carl Bruckisch, above. The family arrived in Texas on the *Friedrich Grosse* from Prussia in 1853 and settled in Comal County. By 1861 the family was living near Comfort. Bruckisch was a member of the Kendall Company of the League's military battalion and fled with the August insurgent group. He survived the battle but Davis' company captured and executed him in early August, 1862 on Goat Creek in Kerr County.

07. Frederick Dietert, Sr. was born on February 14, 1801, in Prussia. His parents' names are not known. Dietert married Fredericka [maiden name not known] 1835 in Prussia. They were they were the parents of six children. The family arrived in Texas on the *Franziska* in 1854 and arrived in the Comfort area in 1856. Frederick Dietert, Sr. died on November 10, 1881, at Comfort in Kendall County.

08. Frederick Dietert, Jr. was born about 1836 in Prussia. Fredericka [maiden name not known] and Frederick Dietert, Sr., were his parents. Dietert arrived in Texas on the *Fransiska* in 1854. He married Fredericka Karger on February 2, 1863, in Kendall County. They were the parents of at least nine children. His date of death is not known.

09. Friedrick August Faltin was born on July 19, 1830, in Prussia. Wilhelmine Krueger and Frederick W. Faltin were his parents. He was orphaned in 1844, when he was 14 years old. Faltin married Clara Below on March 30, 1856, in Prussia. They were the parents of six children. Clara and August Faltin arrived in Texas on the *Auguste* in the spring of 1856 and went on to Comfort where he became a merchant. Friedrick August Faltin died on June 9, 1905, in Comfort in Kendall County.

10. Wilhelm F. Geissler was born about 1829 in Austria. The names of his parents are not known. The date Wilhelm arrived in Texas is not known. He arrived in the Comfort area in 1854. Geissler was a member of Kuechler's December, 1861, company, and a member of Kendall Company of the League's military battalion. He was conscripted into Company B, 3$^{rd}$ Regiment Texas Infantry on August 1, 1862. Geissler married Elizabeth Mangold on April 28, 1866, in Kendall County. They had no children. His date of death is not known.

11. Paul Hanisch was born about 1829 in Prussia. The names of his parents are not known. He was likely a Forty-Eighter. The date Hanisch arrived in Texas is not known. He arrived in the Comfort area in 1855. Hanisch was a pharmacist. He was a member of the Comfort Home Guard in February, 1861. It is believed in died in the Fredericksburg area about 1879.

12.  Anton Heinen was born about 1840 in Prussia. Ann [maiden name not known] and Johann Heinen were his parents. The date the family arrived in Texas is not known. They arrived in the Comfort area in 1855. Anton Heinen was a member of Kuechler's company in December, 1861. He fled Texas and joined Company C, First Regiment [Union] Texas Cavalry on February 5, 1861. Heinen married Johanna Allerkamp about 1867, location of marriage not known. They were the parents of at least two children.

13.  Hubert Heinrich. Heinen was born in October, 1838, in Prussia. Katharine Gertrude Nauen and Carl Wilhelm Heinen were his parents. The family arrived in Texas on the *Fortuna* in 1860 and settled in the Comfort area. Heinen was a member of the Comfort Home Guard in February, 1862, and was very likely a member of the league's militia battalion. He was one of the insurgents who fled to the mountains where he hid. On August 14, 1864, he married Wilhelmina Stieler in Kerr County. They were the parents of at least seven children. Hubert Heinrich Heinen died in 1914 in Kendall County, Texas.

14.  Charles Wilhelm Heinen was born in 1813 in Prussia. His parent's names are not known. Heinen married Katharine Gertrude Nauen about 1835 in Prussia. They were the parents of at least four sons. The family arrived in Texas on the *Fortuna* in 1856 and settled in the Comfort area. Carl William Heinen died in 1890 in Comfort in Kendall County.

15.  Very little is known about Charles Hilke. He arrived in the Comfort area in 1856 and enrolled in the 6th Battery, Texas Light Artillery. His date of enrollment is not known.

16.  Johann Karger was born on March 4, 1816, in Falkenberg, Schlessing. Prussia. He married Carolina Fieder about 1841 in Falkenberg, Schlessing, Prussia. They were the parents of at least nine children. The family arrived in Texas on the *Iris* in 1860. Johann Karger fled into the mountains. He died of pneumonia on March 8, 1862.

17.  No additional information was located on Christian Jacob.

18.  There were two Ludwig Langes living in Kendall County, a father and son. This was likely the senior Ludwig Lange, who was born on December 12, 1808, in Bruggen, Hanover. His parents' names are not known. Heinrich Christian Ludwig Lange, Sr. married Johanna Streuer about 1830 in Hanover. They were the parents of at least six children. It is believed he is the Lange who arrived in Texas with family on the *Marnet* in 1851. Heinrich Christian Ludwig Lange, Sr. died on June 10, 1886, near Center Point, Kerr County.

19.  Edward A. Lieck is believed to have been born on March 1, 1834, in Prussia. Sophia Augusta Hubertine Huppet and Gottlieb August Lieck were his parents. The date Lieck arrived in Texas is not known, but it was likely in the

mid-1850s. Edward A. Lieck is believed to have died on December 23, 1914, at San Antonio in Bexar County.

20. Carl Otto Ludwig was born on November 20, 1834 in Prussia. His parents' names are not known. Ludwig arrived in Texas on the *Miles* in 1854 and settled in Comal County. He married Josephine Lafrantz on September 10, 1858, in Bexar County. They were the parents of at least one child, a son named Kurt, born about 1864. Carl Otto Ludwig died on November 17, 1919, in Galveston.

21. Charles C. Maertz was born about 1800 in Prussia. His parent's names are not known. Charles married Dorethea [maiden name not known] about 1842 in Prussia. They were the parents of at least three children. Dorethea died either shortly before or after the family arrived in Texas. They arrived in 1858 on the *Iris*. Charles married Caroline Haack about 1859, likely in Texas. They had no children. Charles C. Maertz died about 1883 in Kendall County.

22. Louis Schierholz was born about 1833 in Hanover. His parents' names are not known. Schierholz was likely a Forty-Eighter and a Freethinker. He arrived on December 25, 1855, and arrived in the Comfort area in late 1855. Schierholz applied for citizenship on July 2, 1860, in Kerr County. He was a member of Kuechler's company of December, 1861. He was a member of the Kendall Company of the League's military battalion. Schierholz fled with the insurgent group and he was killed at the battle site.

23. Charles Schmidt was born on September 29, 1808, in Prussia. His parents' names are not known. Charles Schmidt married Magdelen [maiden name not known] about 1831, likely in Prussia. They were the parents of four children. Charles and Magdelen and family arrived in Texas in the mid-1850 and settled in Comfort. Magdelen Schmidt died in 1879 and Charles Schmidt died on December 16, 1896, both in Kendall County.

24. Ferdinand Schultze was born on January 21, 1827, in Magdenburg, Prussia. His mother's name is not known. Peter Schulze was his father. The date Schultze arrived in Texas is not known. He arrived in the Comfort area in 1855. Schultze married Louise Schmidt, the daughter of Charles Schmidt, on October 1, 1859, in Kerr County. They were the parents of at least nine children. He was very likely a member of the Kendall Company of the League's military battalion. Schultze was in the group that went to the battle site in August 1865 and recovered the bodies of the executed insurgents. On his deathbed Schultze told his family he was the man who drew the short straw and went to where the "spy" was living and killed him. It is generally believed this "spy" was Oscar Splittgerber who was killed in 1889 near Toyah in Reeves County. Ferdinand Schultze died on May 27, 1900, in Kendall County.

25.  Wilhelm C. Schultze may have been a brother of Ferdinand Schultze, above. Because of the similarly of the surnames of Schultze, Schultz, Schuetz, and Schulze it is hard to determine who this individual was. There was a Wilhelm Schulte, single, who arrived in Texas on the *Colchis* in 1845. He may be the William Schultz who is shown on the 1850 Comal Census as 29 years old, living in the Christian Loefler household. No other record of him has been located. It may be this William C. Schultze individual is William Schultz who was living in Comfort. He was born about 1823 in Prussia. He married Dorethea [maiden name is not known]. They were the parents of at least four children. The date this Schultze arrived in Texas is not known, but he arrived in the Comfort area in 1855. The 1860 Kerr Census shows this William Schultz and family living near Comfort. In May, 1862, this family was living near Sisterdale. A William Schultz enrolled in Duffs' Company E on November 1, 1862. John Sansom claims Duff executed this William Schultz, but this is not correct as he appears still in the company as late as April, 1863. The compiler was unable to locate this family on a later Texas Census. There was a William Schultz who enlisted in Company D, First Regiment [Union] Texas Cavalry on August 5, 1863, in New Orleans. His enlistment papers show he was born in Prussia. This individual deserted his company on May 17, 1864, in Brownsville, Texas.

26.  Henry Joseph Schwethelm was born on September 4, 1840, in Langst, a village just outside Dusseldorf, Prussia. Sybille Catharina Heinen and Ernst Schwethelm were his parents. The family arrived in Texas about 1850 and in the Comfort area in 1854. Schwethelm served with several ranger companies before the war. He was the second corporal in Harbour's Kerr County Home Guard in February, 1861. Schwethelm married Emelia Stieler on March 19, 1862, in D'Hanis. They were the parents of three sons. He was a member of the Kendall Company of the League's military battalion fled with the insurgent group and survived the battle. He went on to Mexico and to New Orleans where he inlisted in Company A, First Regiment [Union] Texas Cavalry. He deserted his unit in June, 1864, near Brownsville, Texas and hid in the mountains for the remainder of the war. Unionist Governor E. J. Davis appointed Schwethelm a ranger captain in 1867. Henry Joseph Schwethelm died on August 16, 1924 in Kerr County.

27.  Emil Serger was born on March 27, 1811, in Prussia. His parent's names are not known. Serger arrived in Texas about 1854 and in the Comfort area in 1856. He was likely a member of the Kendall Company of the League's military battalion Serger was in the group that recovered the insurgencies bodies in August, 1865. He married Marie Sittel about 1865, location not known. They were the parents of at least four children. Emil Serger died on June 25, 1900, in Kendall County.

28. Ferdinand Simon was born about 1826 in Hesse-Darmstadt. His parents' names are not known. Simon was a Freethinker and likely a Forty-Eighter. He is likely the Ferdinand Simon who arrived in Texas on the *Strabo* in He married Caroline Bauer, the sister of Leopold Bauer – another member of the insurgent group – on May 14, 1855, in Bexar County. They were the parents of at least four children. He was a member of the league's military battalion, in the group of insurgents who fled in August, and seriously wounded in the battle. A Confederate scout captured him nearby, about August 14. He was tried by the Confederate Military Company and sentenced to be hanged. However, before the sentence could be carried out, martial law and its regulations were cancelled. Simon remained in jail until the end of the war. Ferdinand Simon died in July, 1878, near Boerne, likely as a result of his wounds.

29. John [Otto?] Stecher was born about 1829 in Bavaria. His parents' names are not known. The date Stecher arrived in Texas is not known. It is believed he arrived in the Comfort area in 1854. Stecher was very likely a member of the Kendall Company of the League's military battalion. He was a corporal in W. E. Jones' Kendall Company of the Third Frontier District in February, 1864. The date and location of his death are not known.

30. Gottfried Stieler was born on August 22, 1817, in the duchy of Anhalt. He was the father of Heinrich who was a member of the August insurgent group and killed about ten days later. Gottfried Stieler married Wilhelmine Urban about 1843 in the duchy of Anhalt. They were the parents of five children. The date the family arrived in Texas is not known. They arrived in the Comfort area about 1856. Gottfried Stieler died on August 26, 1893, at Comfort.

31. William Louis Strohecker was born in July, 1832, in Württemberg. The names of his parents are not known. He arrived in Texas in 1853 and in the Comfort area in early 1860. He married Christiana Schladoer on October 7, 1860, in Kerr County. They were the parents of at least four children. He was a member of W. E. Jones' Kendall Company of the 31st Brigade in February, 1864. William Louis Strohecker died on March 6, 1917, in Kendall County.

## 7.  Confederate Oath of Allegiance

I do solemnly swear that I will faithfully and honestly support the Constitution and laws of the Confederate State of America, and I will faithfully and honestly render true allegiance to said Confederate States in all things and in every particular; and I further swear that I will not directly or indirectly, by talking, writing, or otherwise Seditiously or rebelliously attempt to excite prejudice in the mind of any person or persons against the existence, perpetuity, or prosperity of said Confederate States; Nor will I in any manner, directly or indirectly, aid, assist, encourage, or advise the United States, or any officer, agent, or adherent thereof, in the present war against The Confederate States.

## 8. Letter–A. O. Cooley[1] to Honorable C. R. Johns
### Comptroller of State of Texas

Fredericksburg
December 19th, 1861

Honorable C. R. Johns
Comptroller

Dear Sir:

Regard for the public interest constrains me to give you information concerning a claim on the State Treasure, to be presented by Ph [Philip] Braubach[2], Lieutenant of the Minute Company in the county. Our Chief Justice[3] informs me that said Lieut made out his account, and sworn to it for service during each and every day since the company was organized when, in fact, said Lieut has been in actual service only a few weeks during said time. The Chief Justice also says he refused to certify to the account for the reason that he knew only a few weeks of such service had been perform. Is there is any remedy in said cause, you can learn the facts from the Chief Justice or other prominent persons at the place: also that the company is useless, has done nothing, ect. It seems that money should best be drawn from the treasure: and hence I feel it a duty to advise you of such a well known attempt at impositions

Respectfully Yours
A. O. Cooley

ENDNOTES
Letter A. O. Cooley

01. A. O. Cooley was born about 1826 in New York. By 1850 he was living in Tennessee. The date Cooley arrived in Texas is not known. Cooley was elected to the Texas House in August, 1856, from Gillespie County. He served from November 2, 1857, until February 16, 1858. On April 21, 1858, Cooley was elected a school examiner. In October, 1863, he enrolled in Menges' "squad" of the Gillespie County Home Guard. The unit's muster roll shows his age as thirty-eight years old. A. O. Cooley died on September 26, 1899, in Gillespie County.

02. Philip Braubach was born on July 28, 1829, in Wiesbaden, Duchy of Nassau. Braubach arrived in Texas on the *Neptune* from Wiesbaden in 1850 and by the late 1850s was living in Gillespie County. He received his U. S. Citizenship on April 15, 1853, in Gillespie County. Braubach was elected Gillespie County sheriff in August, 1860. Braubach organized a 41-man home guard company in February, 1861, which served until February of 1862.The unit was composed mainly of Unionists. He was the first lieutenant in Kuechlers' Unionist company formed in December, 1861. Duff arrested Braubach in June, 1862, and he was tried and convicted of Unionist activities by the Confederate Military Commission in July of that same year. He escaped and fled to Mexico where he organized a guerrilla company that operated along the Rio Grande. On May 4, 1864, he joined the First Regiment [Union] Texas Cavalry and was elected captain of Company H. Braubach married Louise Schuetze the daughter of another Unionist, Louis Schuetze, on October 9, 1865, in San Antonio. They were the parents of at least seven children. Braubach was mustered out of service on October 31, 1862, in San Antonio. Philip Braubach died on June 30, 1888, in San Antonio.

03. The Chief Justice of Gillespie County was William Wahrmund, born on April 31, 1824, in Wiesbaden, Duchy of Nassau. William Wahrmund married Amalie Schildknecht shortly before arriving in Texas. They were the parents of ten children. William Wahrmund was one of four brothers to arrive with their parents in Texas on the *Talisman* from Wiesbaden in 1846. Ship records show William Wahrmund as married to Amalie Schildknecht. He was elected chief

justice in 1852 and served until August 18, 1862. William Wahrmund, Sr. was a member of Nimitzs' Gillespie Rifles Company in June, 1861. He took the Confederate oath of allegiance in February, 1862. He was appointed one of the men to draw up the resolution condemning Unionists for their activities in February, 1862. He signed the petition requesting Kuechler's company be disbanded. He was very likely the Gillespie Provost Marshal in May, 1862. Wahrmund was the first lieutenant of Locke's Company, Third Frontier District in January, 1864. The units' muster roll shows him as forty-eight years old. After Locke deserted and joined the Union Army, Wahrmund was elected captain. He served until at least October, 1864, and likely until the end of the war. William Wahrmund was elected chief justice several more times. William Wahrmund died on June 20, 1890, while serving as Gillespie County Chief Justice.

## 9. Letter–Frank Van der Stucken[1] to Texas Governor Lubbock

Fredericksburg, Texas
February 13, 1862

To His Excellency the Governor of the State of Texas

Sir,

Allow me to bring to your knowledge that state of affairs in this district in regard to the company for frontier protection. Mr Kuechler the enrolling officer has acted not openly but secretly in organizing this company and has not acted in good faith towards the State. Mr. K is a German and he has enlist[ed] no one but a German into his company. Now sir, the American population who are really to be frontier defenders have not been allowed to enter said company to my knowledge of fifty men came to his (Mr. K) place to be enrolled and was not to be found. I hear today that Mr. K. met in Comfort Kerr County and not a man from Hays did present himself, I suppose they have not been notified.

Hoping your Excellency will not allow such wrongs to be practice, and that all good men as well American as Germans will have a fair opportunity to serve the frontier.

Mr. K has even gone so far as to take Germans from Blanco County into his company. The appointment of an impartial man would give full satisfaction to the people of this district.

Your Obedient Servant
Frank V. D. Stucken

ENDNOTE

Van der Stucken's Letter

01. Frank Van der Stucken was born about 1831 in Belgium. He arrived in Texas about 1846 with Henry Castro. Van der Stucken settled in Fredericksburg in 1852. He married Sophie Schoenewolf on December 23, 1852, in Gillespie County. They were the parents of at least five children. Van der Stucken was a member of Nimitz's Gillespie Rifles in early to late 1862. He was a member of the committee to draft the resolution condemning activities of several Gillespie Unionists. Van der Stucken was on the 31st Brigade District Staff in early 1862. He raised a company which was mustered into Confederate service as Company C, 8th Battalion Texas Cavalry in May, 1862. On December 18, 1863, it became Company E, 1st Regiment Texas Cavalry. In August, 1864, Van der Stucken was elected Gillespie Chief Justice. In the spring of 1865, he and his family fled to Belgium to avoid Unionist reprisals.

# 10.  Letter–David H. Farr[1] to Texas Governor Lubbock

Governor F. R. Lubbock
Austin, Texas

Kerrs Ville, Kerr County*

Dear Sir,

I offer my respects today to you that we the citizens of Gillespie and Kerr Counties need justice and I know of no other to apply to get it only to your Excellency which I am satisfied you will grant under the existing circumstances when you have the facts set forth as following;

Mr. Cameron[2] of Fredericksburg came over here to inform me that the arrangement was made to meet (the) enrolling officer at the live oak mill 5 miles from the town of Fredericksburg on the 1 day of this month we met accordingly. Some our men meet him as they came to the mill and he said he knew no thing of the appointment and he set the 11 of this month to meet us again at the same place we met according to appointment and he did not shown then went to Fredericksburg to there and informed that the enrolling officer and his German friends had left town to organize the Fredericksburg or Gillespie squad and intended to meet the next day at Comfort another dutch town in Kerr County for the same purpose.

I have been informed by Mr. Cooley and Cameron of Fredericksburg that he was borrowing German names to enable him to organize so as to insure his election as captain and then to supply their places by substitute. I have it from a respectable man by the name of Land of Kerr County that he has enrolled six in Blanco County near Sisterdale and one of which is running for lieutenant by the name of Degener.

I also was informed by our mail rider that he had 19 or 20 enrolled at Comfort and Sisterdale. They are working so secretly that it is almost impossible to get any thing correct about them only by taking them off of their guard.

I have understood that said enrolling officer has been a violent union man and is thought to be a black republican and heard until yet for further particulars in this case apply to Mr Cameron partner of Frank V. D. Stucken of Fredericksburg, Lawyer Cooley and Lawyer Dennis[3] all of Fredericksburg.

I have not as yet been able to hear of him soliciting the first American man to join his company or even made him self known to one that he thought would join.

I write to you not through prejudice to the dutch but to inform you as near as I am able the condition of things in our county which I think is a duty I owe to my country.

I was informed by Mr. Cameron of Fredericksburg that questions had been asked him the enrolling office in regard to his political sentiments and he promised to answer them satisfactory and had failed to do it.

I suppose Mr Cameron will be pleased to answerer any interrogations from you.

Yours with respect this 13 February 1862
D. H. Farr

*\* All errors of grammar, punctuation, capitalization and spelling*
*are preserved as written. – Editor*

ENDNOTES
Letter David H Farr

01.  David Henry Farr was born about 1820 in Tennessee. The date he arrived in Texas is not known. Farr married Martha Ann Houston in Harrison County, Texas, on June 9, 1845. They were the parents of eight children. Farr moved to Kerr County about early 1861. He enrolled in Davis' Company A, Frontier Regiment on March 4, 1862. In February, 1864, he organized a company for the Third Frontier District. Farr's date and location of death is not known.

02.  Ewin Cameron was born about 1828 in Canada. The date Cameron arrived in Texas is not known. He enrolled in the Gillespie County Rifles on February 23, 1862, and took the oath of allegiance on that date. No further data.

03.  Nathan Mark Dennis was born in July, 1829, in Massachusetts. The date he arrived in Texas is not known. Dennis married Mary Armstrong on February 18, 1858, in Williamson County, Texas. They were the parents of at least five children. Dennis arrived in Gillespie County by 1860. He was an attorney and was the major speaker at the January, 1861, Gillespie County meeting discussing secession. Dennis was a member of Nimitz's Gillespie County Rifles in June-July 1861 and signed the petition requesting Kuechler's company be disbanded. He enrolled in Davis' Company, Frontier Regiment on March 4, 1862, and was elected the second sergeant. He re-enlisted in Davis' Company F, 14th Battalion on February 6, 1863, and appointed the first sergeant on June 22, 1863. He remained with the unit until the end of the war. After the war he moved to Parker County. Nathan Mark Dennis died about 1905 in Parker County, Texas, and is buried in the Oakland Cemetery.

## 11. Petition of Kerr County Citizens to Texas Governor Lubbock

Honorable F. R. Lubbock
Governor of the State of Texas

Your petitioners Citizens of Kerr County in behalf of their fellow citizens who has been at the expense of filing [sic] out for the frontier service would referent:

1st that the person appointed by your Honor as enrolling officer for his district has never gave any notice of said appointment.

2nd that the citizens of this county with some thirty American Citizens of Gillespie County meet twice for the purpose of getting enrolled and by their appointed and the other by the request of the enrolling officer in Gillespie County and on both occasions he managed to avoid them. They then went to the town of Fredericksburg and was informed by Mr. Stuckens a merchant of that place that the enrolling officer with his German friends had met at some other place.

3rd he has accepted men from Blanco County germans not giving the Americans any chance [to enroll].

4th we are informed that he has borrowed names so as to organizes and elect officers.

5th We believe on good authority that he has never sent any notice to Hays County of his appointment. Consequently that county has not been represented.

6th We don't think he has acted in good faith with the State of Texas as enrolling officer or just or fair with the people of this district.

Therefore we as citizens of this State feeling an interest in him welfare pray that the said enrolling officer be removed and that D. H. Farr of this county be appointed. I your Honor desires it we can furnish any amount of certificates of these facts from citizens of this and Gillespie County.

Believing you will do us justice.
We Remain Your Servants.

C. C. Quinlan[1]
Nathan Jackson[2]
Aaron W. Jackson[3]
E. A. Steel[31]
Isaac Lamb[4]
R. W. Freemon[32]
Hiram Lamb[5]
Freemon Myers[33]
John Lowrance[6]
Daniel Arnold[34]
Marcellon Dunham[7]
P. M. Stanford[36]
James Coleman[8]
George Holliman[37]
F. P. Click[9]
R. G. Farr[38]
E. Whitley[10]
J. E. Hampton[11]
J. L. Hudson[12]

A. C. Fairman[13]
J. H. Regges[14]
R. F. Camford[15]
A. J. Rogers[16]
M. A. Lowrance[17]
A. L. Williamson[18]
J. W. Rogers[19]
H. M. Burney[20]
P. O. Lowrance[21]
J. P. Stroops[22]
D. B. Lowrance[23]
J. D. Buchanan[24]
Scott Kell[25]
William Long[26]
E. W. Brown[27]
J. D. Brown[28]
Joseph Follord[29]
Seman Blevins[30]

Our list of petitioners is short but if time permitted could be extended to large numbers and we think the present emergency demands immediate actions [but?] is now therefore we submit it to your honor

The 14th February 1862.

ENDNOTES
Petition Kerr Citizens

01. Cornelius C. Quinlan was born about 1833 in New York. His parents' names
    are not known. Quinlan married Susan [maiden name not known] about 1855,
    likely in Texas. They were the parents of at least six children. He arrived in
    Kerr County about 1857. Quinlan was the Kerr County clerk from 1857 until
    1860. He was a member of Harbour's' Kerr Minuteman Company having
    enrolled in February, 1861, and served until February, 1862. On May 7, 1862,
    Quinlan enrolled in Duff's Company of Partisan Rangers. He was with the
    company when it arrived in Gillespie County in late May and early June 1862.
    Quinlan remained a member of Duff's Company when it was dispatched to
    Gillespie County in late July and early August, 1862, was very likely in the
    pursuit force, and took part in the Nueces battle. He returned to Kerr County
    after the war. Quinlan was elected Chief Justice in 1867. In the mid-1870s he
    and his family moved to Kansas City, Missouri. C. C. Quinlan died about
    1890, likely at Kansas City, Missouri.

02. Nathan Jackson was born December 18, 1833, in Stoddard County, Missouri.
    Susannah M. Sifford and Solomon B. Jackson were his parents. The Jackson
    family arrived in Texas about 1845 and settled in Bexar County. Nathan
    Jackson married Susan Jane Tinkle on January 8, 1862, at Comfort in Kerr
    County. He enrolled in Davis' Company, Frontier Regiment on March 4,
    1862, and served until December. 1862. Nathan Jackson died on January 15,
    1900, in Wilson County.

03. Aaron William Jackson was a brother of Nathan Jackson, above. He was born
    on March 2, 1838, in Stoddard County, Missouri. Aaron Jackson enrolled in
    Davis' Company, Frontier Regiment on March 4, 1862, and served until
    December 1862. On December 24, 1862 he reenlisted in James Hunters'
    Company, Frontier Regiment. He remained with the company until the end of
    the war. Aaron W. Jackson married Susan A. M. Arnold on November 3,
    1863, in Kerr County. They were the parents of thirteen children. Aaron
    William Jackson died on March 17, 1895, at Floresville in Wilson County.

04. Isaac Lamb was born about 1808 in Canada. His parents' names are not
    known. Lamb married Julia Frost about 1835, likely in New York. They
    were the parents of at least eight children, to include Hiram, below. The
    family arrived in Texas about 1855 and settled in Burnet County. Lamb was
    appointed Kerr County clerk in 1867. His date and location of death is not
    known.

05. Hiram Lamb was born about 1841 in Michigan. Julia Frost and Isaac Lamb
    were his parents. Hiram Lamb enrolled in Davis' Company, Frontier
    Regiment on March 4, 1862. He re-enlisted in the same company, now
    commanded by James Hunter, on December 24, 1862, and remained with it

until the end of the war. Lamb married Sara Belle Ridgeway on August 17, 1871. They were the parents of at least four children. Hiram Lamb died on August 12, 1908, in Coke County.

06. John Shelby Lowrance was born on January 6, 1840, in Shelby County, Tennessee. Susan Moose [Mussgenung] and Peter O. Lowrance were his parents. The Lowrance family arrived in Texas in 1859. John Shelby Lowrance had several wives. He enrolled in Davis' Company, Frontier Regiment on March 4, 1862, and re-enlisted in Hunter's Company on December 24, 1862, and remained with the unit until the end of the war. John Shelby Lowrance died on July 21, 1920, in Kerr County.

07. Marcellus Marcellies Dunham/Durham was born in January, 1844, in Texas. Jerushua [Jeruisa] was his mother. His fathers' name is not known. Dunham enrolled in Davis' Company, Frontier Regiment on March 4, 1862, and re-enlisted in Hunter's Company on December 24, 1862, and remained with the unit until the end of the war. It appears he married Amelia A. Wimberley on June 22, 1869, in Medina County. She must have died as on June 26, 1870, he married the widow Emilia Rosina in Comal County. They were the parents of at least seven children. Marcellus Dunham died about 1905 in Brown County, Texas.

08. No information has been located on James Coleman.

09. No information has been located on F. P. Click.

10. Elisha Franklin Whitley was born on September 21, 1827, at Perryville, Bond County, Illinois. Sarah Hudson Little and Sharp Whitley were his parents. The family arrived in Texas about 1840. Whitley married Emily A. Smith on May 17, 1847, in Walker County. They were the parents of at least eight children. Whitley enrolled in Davis' Company, Frontier Regiment on March 4, 1862. He was mustered of service on February 7, 1863. Whitley died on January 12, 1872, in Medina County.

11. Jordan E. Hampton was born about 1845 in Williamson County, Tennessee. It is believed Nancy R. Better and James H. Hampton were his parents. The date Jordan Hampton arrived in Texas in unknown, but it was before 1860. He enrolled in Davis' Company, Frontier Regiment on March 4, 1862. It is believed he was discharged on December 24, 1862. Hampton married Fanny Nichols on December 13, 1866, in Kerr County. They were the parents of at least five children. Hampton died about 1890.

12. James L. Hudson was born about 1822 in Connecticut. His parents' names are not known. Hudson married Roxella [married name not known] but the date and location of the marriage is also not known. Hudson was the Kerr County chief justice in 1866. No other information has been located.

13. August C. Fairman was born about 1817 in Mississippi. His parents' names are not known. Fairman married Margaret E. [maiden name not known] about 1849, likely in Leake County, Mississippi. They were the parents of seven children. The family arrived in Texas about 1855. August C. Fairman died about 1875.

14. No information on J. H. Regges has been located.

15. No information on R. F. Camford has been located.

16. Andrew J. Rogers was born about 1817 in Georgia. His parents' names are not known. Rogers arrived in Texas about 1855. He married Harriet A. [maiden name not known] about 1856, likely in Newton County, Texas. They were the parents of at least four children. The family arrived in Kerr County about 1861. Rogers was the first lieutenant in Harbour's Minuteman Company of February, 1861 – February, 1862. Andrew J. Rogers died before 1880.

17. Miles Abernathy Lowrance was born on January 11, 1827, in McNairy County, Tennessee. Susan Moose [Mussegenung] and Peter O. Lowrence were his parents. Miles Lowrance married Martha McCann about 1849, likely in Tennessee. They were the parents of two children. Martha McCann died about 1853 in Arkansas. The Lowrance family arrived in Kerr County in 1859. Miles A. Lowrance married Margaret Ann McCann on June 24, 1860, in DeWitt County. They were the parents of seven children. Lowrance enrolled in Davis' Company, Frontier Regiment on March 4, 1862, and served until February 7, 1863. At the expiration of his term of service, he next enrolled in D. H. Farr's Company, Third Frontier District on November 7, 1864, and served until the end of the war. Miles Abernathy Lowrance died on November 13, 1900, in Kerr County.

18. Augustus Leroy [Lee] Williamson was born on January 1, 1830, at Charlotte, North Carolina. His parents' names are not known. Williamson arrived in Texas about 1852 and Kerrville in 1856. He was the Kerr County sheriff from 1859 until 1860. Lee Williamson married Elizabeth C. Phillips Nelson [the widow of P. M. Nelson] on December 4, 1860, in Gillespie County. They were the parents of nine children. Williamson enrolled in Duff's Company B, 14th Battalion Texas Cavalry on October 1, 1862, and remained with the unit until the end of the war. Augustus Leroy [Lee] Williamson died on October 12, 1911, in Kerr County.

19. Jesse William Rogers was born on August 6, 1812, in Tennessee. His parents' names are not known. Rogers married Mary G. Middleton on August 7, 1832, at Tuscaloosa, Alabama. They were the parents of nine children. The family arrived in Texas about 1847 and settled in Travis County. Rogers enrolled in Davis' Company, Frontier Regiment on March 4, 1862, and served until February 4, 1863. Jesse William Rogers died on December 24, 1895, at Elmtown, in Anderson County, Texas.

20. Hance McClain Burney was born on May 12, 1826, at Guilford Courthouse, North Carolina. Lydia McCain and Robert H. Burney, Sr. were his parents. The Burney family arrived in Texas about 1852. Hance M. Burney married Mary Tatum on December 28, 1853. They were the parents of seven children. Hance M. Burney was the first Kerr County postmaster, a position he held for eight years. Burney enrolled in Harbour's Kerr County Minuteman Company in February, 1861, and was promoted to third corporal. Burney served with the unit until February, 1862. In February, 1864, he enrolled in D. H. Farr's Company of the Third Frontier District. Hance McClain Burney died on April 1, 1915, in Kerr County.

21. Peter Osborn Lowrance, Sr., was born on June 21, 1802, in Lincoln County, North Carolina. His parent's names are not known. Peter O. Lowrance married Susan Moose [Mussgenung] on July 3, 1824, in North Carolina. They were the parents of ten children. The family arrived in Kerr County about 1859 and settled near what is now Center Point. Peter Osborn Lowrance, Sr. died on July 15, 1890, in Kerr County.

22. John P. Stroope was born on July 10, 1827, in Arkansas. Olive Colbath and Henry Stroope were his parents. The family arrived in Bastrop County about 1848. Stroope married Sarah Jane Benson on November 15, 1855, in Gillespie County. They were the parents of five children. Stroope was a teacher and gunsmith. He was also the Kerr County Clerk in 1862 – 1863. John P. Stroope died on March 22, 1864, at Kerrville in Kerr County.

23. Daniel Boone Lowrance was born on April 1, 1829, in McNairy County, Tennessee. Susan Moose [Mussgenung] and Peter O. Lowrance were his parents. Daniel B. Lowrance married Leah Ann Thompson on February 24, 1855, in Montgomery County, Alabama. They were the parents of five children. The family arrived in Kerr County in 1859. Lowrance was a member of Harbour's Kerr County Minuteman Company in February, 1861, and served until February, 1862. Unionists shot and killed Lowrance on August 21, 1875 on the thirteenth anniversary of the day he turned two insurgents who had survived the Nueces battle, into Confederate authorities.

24. J. D. Buchanan was born about 1825 in Pennsylvania. The names of his parents are not known. The date he arrived in Texas is also not known. In 1860 he was a lawyer living in Bexar County. No further information.

25. Scott Kell was born about 1835 in Indiana. Elizabeth Field and James Kell were his parents. The Kell family arrived in Rusk County, Texas, in the mid-1840s. Scott Kell married Narcissa Moore on March 1, 1855, in Coryell County. They were the parents of three children. Kell enrolled in Davis' Company, Frontier Regiment on March 4, 1862. He reenlisted in Hunter's Company of the Frontier Regiment on December 24, 1862. Kell deserted Hunter's Company in August, 1863, and on December 3, 1863, he enlisted in

Company I, First Regiment [Union] Texas Cavalry at Brownsville. Kell died on January 15, 1864, at Brownsville of typhoid fever.

26. William Long was born on April 4, 1801, in North Carolina. His parents' names are not known. The date Long arrived in Texas is not known. By 1860 he was living in Kerr County. Long enrolled in Davis' Company, Frontier Regiment on March 4, 1862. He re-enlisted in Hunter's Company of the Frontier Regiment on December 24, 1862, and served until the end of the war. William Long died on October 1, 1892, in Kerr County.

27. Edward W. Brown was born about 1826 in Kentucky. His parents' names are not known. The date he arrived in Texas is not known. Brown married Franzia A. [maiden name not known] about 1857, likely in Texas. They were the parents of at least two children. Edward Brown enrolled in W. E. Jones' Company of the Third Frontier District in February, 1864, and served until at least June, 1864. No further data.

28. Joshua David Brown, the founder of Kerrville, was born around 1816 in Madison County, Kentucky. Anastasia Janey Campbell and Edward Brown were his parents. The family arrived in Texas in 1837. J. D. Brown served in the Cherokee Expedition in 1839, in the Woll-Somervell Campaign in 1842, the Salado Creek Battle in 1842 and in Ben McCulloch's spy company in 1846 during the Mexican War. Brown married Eleanor Smith on July 20, 1846, in Gonzales County. They were the parents of one child. Eleanor Smith Brown died in 1848 and he married Sarah Jane Goss on May 20, 1849, in Gonzales. They were the parents of seven children. Brown traveled up the Guadalupe River into the area that is now Kerr County, where he began making shingles. In 1855 Brown purchased a section of land and donated parts of it for the new town of Kerrville. He enrolled in Davis' Company on March 4, 1862, and served until February, 1863. Brown was the first lieutenant of D. H. Farr's Company, of the Third Frontier Battalion from February, 1864, until at least June of 1864. Joshua David Brown died on February 16, 1877, at Kerrville in Kerr County.

29. Joseph Follord was born about 1823 in North Carolina. His parents' names are not known. The date he arrived in Texas is not known. Follord married Fantomin [maiden name not known]. Date and location of marriage is not known. It is not known if they had any children. By 1860 they were living in Kerr County. He later served in Duff's Regiment. No further data.

30. Leroy Seaman Blevins was born about 1841 at Long Creek in Carroll County Arkansas. Delilla Meek and James M. Blevins were his parents. Leroy Blevins arrived in Texas in the mid-1850s and settled in Bexar County. Blevins enrolled in Davis' Company, Frontier Regiment on March 4, 1862. He re-enlisted in Hunter's Company, Frontier Regiment on December 24, 1862, and remained with the unit until the end of the war. Blevins married Elizabeth [maiden name not known] about 1863, location of marriage not known. They

were the parents of at least five children. Blevins was a member of the *Haengerbande*, a pro-Confederate vigilante group and took part in the March 4, 1864, raid on Unionist settlers along South Grape Creek. He was indicted for the murders of John Blank and William Feller. Leroy Seaman Blevins died on June 15, 1885, in Arkansas.

31. Elisha [Doc] Asbury Steel was born on July 23, 1839, in Tennessee. His mother's name is not known. His father was Henry Steel. The family arrived in Texas about 1845 and settled in what is now Wilson County. Steel arrived in Kerr County about 1861. He enrolled in Duff's Company in May, 1862. Steel may have been in the Confederate pursuit force. He remained with the company until the end of the war. In 1866 he married Matilda Skinner, a widow. They were the parents of two children. Steel was the Kerr County hide and animal inspector from 1880 until 1900. Elisha Asbury Steel died in February,1912, in Kerr County.

32. No information has been located on R. W. Freemon.

33. Freeman Myers was born about 1830. Location of birth is not known. Myers enrolled in Davis' Company, Frontier Regiment on March 4, 1862. He re-enlisted in Hunter's company on December 24, 1862 and remained with the unit until the end of the war. No further data.

34. Daniel Arnold was born about 1797 in North Carolina. The names of his parents are not known. He arrived in Kerr County by 1856, as he purchased the first city lot from Joshua Brown on August 15, 1856. Arnold was a member of Bladen Mitchell's Company of the Third Frontier District by February, 1863, and served until at least June, 1864. His date and location of death is not known.

35. Philip Minor Stanford was born about 1797 in Shenandoah County, Virginia. Judith Burroughs and James Stanford were his parents. Philip Stanford married Mary Boyd on October 24, 1816, in Warren County, Ohio. They were the parents' of at least seven children. Stanford and his family arrived in Kerr County in late 1860 or early 1861. He was a member of Harbour's company of Minutemen in February, 1861, and served until February, 1862. Philip M. Stanford died between 1870 and 1880 in Kerr County.

36. George Robert Hollimon, Sr. was born about 1826 in Tennessee. His parents' names are not known. Hollimon married Phoebe Fincher on August 26, 1841, in Osage County, Missouri. They were the parents of ten children. The Hollimon family arrived in Texas about 1852 and settled in Burnet County. He served in D. H. Farr's Company of the Third Frontier District from February, 1864, until at least June, 1864, and likely until the end of the war. George Robert Hollimon, Sr. died on November 13, 1884, in Kerr County.

37. Robert James Farr was born about 1848 in Texas. Martha Ann Houston and David Henry Farr were his parents. By 1860 the family was living in Burnet County. Farr enrolled in his father [D. H.] Farr's Company of the Third Frontier in February, 1864, and served until at least until June, 1864, and likely until the end of the war. He was the Kerr County district court clerk in 1867. Robert Farr married Martha Avant on April 15, 1869 in Kerr County. They were the parents of two children. Robert James Farr died about 1875 in Kerr County.

## 12. The Gillespie County Rifles Resolution

In a meeting of the Gillespie County rifles held in the town of Fredericksburg on the 23d day of Feby 1862. The company was called to order by the Captain C. H. Nimitz –

Herr John Hunter[1], Ewin Cameron, Chs Human[2], N. M. Dennis, Mr. Ransleben[3], applied for membership – on motion the usual mode of balloting was dispensed with and the aforesaid person were admitted members of the company by acclamation –

Several members having expressed their opinions with regard to those residents of the County whose loyalty to the Southern cause is, to say the least, extremely doubtful, on motion Wm Keidel[4], F. V. D. Stucken, Wm. Wahrmund, and John M. Hunter appointed a committee to draft take the matter unto consideration and draft resolutions, if they come to the conclusion that the public safety requires any measures to be adopted. The said committee having retired the following persons applied for membership and were accepted singly by acclamation – to wit, John E. Doss[5], Thos Smith[6], A. G. Foster[7], A Meinhardt[8], A. O. Cooley –

The oath was applied by the following order: E. Cameron, A. Kott[9], O Muller[10], L. Weiss[11], Dr. Keidel, J. E. Doss, John Hunter, Nimitz, E. Staus[12], Fresenius[13], E. Krauskopf[14], Ransleben, Meinhardt, Dennis, Lungkwitz[15], Schneer[16], E. Stucken[17], F. Stucken, Tatsch[18], Bassy[19], Foster, Js Hunter[20], Human, Kook[21], Wight[22], Waltersdors[23], A. Siemering[24], John Weber[25], F. Wrede,[26] W. Wahrmund, A. Weiss[27] –

A.Siemering a member of the company asked leave to present a memorial signed by Hon. Thomas J. Devine.[28]

Leave, being granted the said memorial was read, it expressed that the Judge having heard a report that the said Siemering when taking the oath of allegiance to the Conf. Government before him and said that he would break it whenever a fit opportunity afforded, wherefore the judge states in said memorial that said report is false –

The Captain ordered all who are not members of the Company to leave the room. The room being cleared H. Beckmann[29], a member of the Company was sworn –

The resolution Committee introduced the following resolution to wit: # Resolutions were amended by striking out the name of Mr. Siemering. They were then passed.

Election for 2d Lieut in order – Mr. John Hunter having received a majority of the votes cast was declared duly elected.

The State of Texas  }
County of Gillespie  }

On Sunday the 23d day of February A. D. 1862 at the meeting of the Gillespie Rifles the following resolution was unanimously adopted –

That, whereas there are now living in the town of Fredericksburg in the afore said County, four persons, to wit, Ph. Braubach, F. W. Doebbler[30], Radeleffe[31], and A. Siemering[32], who by their teaching have been, and are still openly and covertly demoralizing the people of said County, by endeavoring to demonstrate to them the weakness and instability of the Government of the Confederate States and in various other ways doing all in their power to organize encourage an opposition to the southern cause, who openly speak of their party as one opposed to southern rights and institutions, and whereas we deem the aforesaid men dangerous to our community. Therefore be it resolved that they be warned to desist from the course heretofore pursued by them, or else that measures will be adopted to prevent their doing further injury to our community.

And be it further resolved that the following persons officer of the Gillespie Rifles be and they are hereby appointed a committee to acquaint the said persons with the forgoing resolution –

Copy of Oath Taken by Gillespie County Rifles.

I _____ do solemnly swear or affirm that I will be faithful, and true allegiance be as to the State of Texas. So long as I may be a citizen thereof and that I will, to the best of my ability discharge the duties of a soldier for the period of twelve months and that I will preserve, protect and defend the Constitution of the State of Texas, and of the Confederate States against all enemies or opponents whomsoever, and that I will obey all orders of my superior officers, according to the Rules and Articles of War for the government of the armies of the Confederate States. So help me God.

The State of Texas } This is to certify that the foregoing oath has been admonished to all County of Gillespie } officers commissioned and noncommissioned and to all privates as named on the Muster Roll to which this certificate is attached.

Fredericksburg March 5, 1862
s/W Wahrmund
Chief Justice of G.C.

At a meeting of the Gillespie Cty rifles held on Sunday
the 27 day of March 1862 at the home of Capt C. H. Nimitz –
The Captain called the meeting to order. A. Mengers[33] and J.
Splittgerber[34] applied for membership and having been
respectively balloted for were declared duly elected members
of the Company –

The said members and also Louis Wahrmund[35] were then
duly sworn by W. Wahrmund Chief Justice. The Captain then
declared the election of an orderly sergeant in order. Mr. J.
Splittgerber was nominated for said position, and having
received a majority of all the votes cast was declared duly
elected. – The election of a corporal came next in order. John
Weber having received a majority of all the votes cast was
declared duly elected.

ENDNOTES
Gillespie County Rifles Resolution

01. John M. Hunter was born September 2, 1821, in Tennessee. He arrived in Texas by 1847 and settled in Fredericksburg. Hunter married Sophie Ahrens on March 9, 1848, in Gillespie County. They had no children. He was the first Gillespie County clerk and owned a mercantile store. John Hunter died on September 5, 1870, in Gillespie County.

02. Charles Human was born about 1818 in North Carolina. He and his family arrived in Texas about 1851. Human enrolled in Jacob Dearing's home guard company in April, 1862. His date and location of death is not known.

03. Julius Johann Ludwig Ransleben, Sr. was born on August 17, 1814, in Prussia. Ransleben married Maria Spannagel about 1834, likely in Prussia. They arrived in Texas in 1846 on the *Mathilde* and were some of the first settlers in Fredericksburg. He and Maria were divorced. On October 18, 1852, he married Josephine Klier, a sister of Wilhelm Klier, a member of the insurgent group and who was later captured. They were the parents of ten children. Ransleben was a member of Nimitz's Gillespie Rifles. Ransleben was able to convince the Confederates not to hang Wilhelm Klier. Julius Ransleben died on October 9, 1897, in Gillespie County.

04. Wilhelm Keidel was born in March, 1825, in Hildesheim, Lower Saxony. He received his medical degree from University of Göttingen. Keidel arrived in Texas in 1845 on the *Margaretha*. He was one of the ultra-radical leaders at the May, 1854, San Antonio Convention, but softened his views by 1860. Keidel was the first chief justice of Gillespie County and served until 1852. Dr. Wilhelm Keidel died on January 9, 1870, in Gillespie County.

05. John E. Doss was born on February 16, 1812, in Fluvanna, Virginia. Doss arrived in Texas by 1833. John E. Doss married Rachel Leathers about 1842, likely in Texas. They were the parents of at least five children. John E. Doss and his brother Thomas C. Doss founded a gristmill and distillery in northwest Gillespie County in late 1849 or early 1850. He was a member of Nimitz's Gillespie Rifles. Doss owned of ten slaves in 1860. He was killed during the Bushwhacker War sometime around 1863 by pro-Union vigilantes.

06. Thomas J. Smith was born about 1832 in Georgia. The date he arrived in Texas is not known. Smith was a member of Nimitz's Gillespie Rifles. He enrolled in Davis' Company, Frontier Regiment on March 4, 1862, and re-enlisted in Hunter's Company on December 24, 1862. In late 1863 and 1864 he was a member of the *Haengerbande* [Hanging Gang]. No further data.

07. No information was located on A. G. Foster and Edmond Albert.

08. Edmund Albert [August] Meinhardt was born about 1816 in Prussia. He arrived in Texas on the *Hamilton* in 1845. Meinhardt married Dorethea Wammel Pape on October 23, 1852, in Gillespie County. Meinhardt enrolled in Nimitz's Gillespie Rifles on February 23, 1861. Meinhardt served in Schuetze's Company, Third Frontier District in January, 1864. Many members of the unit were pro-Union bushwhackers. After Schuetze's company was disbanded he enrolled in Krauskopf's Company, Third Frontier District. Albert Meinhardt's date of death is not known.

09. August Kott was born June 22, 1822, in Saxony. He arrived in Texas on the *Elisa & Charlotte* from Ohrdruff, Gotha, Saxony in 1846. Ship records show him single and twenty-seven years old. August applied for his citizenship in Bexar County on June 16, 1852. At the time he stated he was thirty-one years old and born in Gotha. Kott married Karoline Menzel on January 15, 1854, in Gillespie County. They were the parents of seven children.Kott was a member of Nimitz's Gillespie Rifles in June-July 1861. He took the oath of allegiance to the Confederacy in February, 1862, and likely signed the petition requesting Kuechler's company be disbanded. August Kott was a member of Menges' October, 1863, "squad." The muster roll shows his age as forty-three years old. He was a member of Schuetze's company of January, 1864. That muster roll shows his age as forty-two years old. August Kott died on April 4, 1907.

10. Ottocar Mueller was born about 1814 in Prussia. Mueller married Elise [maiden name not known], about 1848, likely in Prussia. They were the parents of four children. The date they arrived in Texas is not known, but it was between 1849 and 1854, which likely means he was was a Forty-Eighter. Mueller was a member of Nimitz's Gillespie Rifles. He enrolled in Schuetze's company, of November, 1863. Many members of this unit were pro-Union bushwhackers. After Schuetze was killed Mueller enrolled in Locke's company of the Third Frontier District of January, 1864. Many member of this unit were also pro-Union bushwhackers. The unit's muster roll shows him as forty-three years old. Mueller died in Gillespie County, but the date of his death is not known.

11. Louis Weiss was born in 1829 in Nassau. He arrived in Texas on the *John Holland* in 1848. Ship records show he was twenty-seven years old. Weiss was a member of Nimitz's Gillespie Rifles in February, 1861, and served until at least until March, 1862. He enrolled in Davis' Company on March 4, 1862, at Fort Martin Scott and served as the company's farrier. Louis Weiss married Susana Rumpf on October 28, 1862, in Gillespie County. They were the parents of at least five children. Weiss re-enlisted in Hunter's Company of December 24, 1864. The unit's muster roll shows him as thirty-four years old and the company's farrier. He and his family moved to Bexar County by 1870. It appears that Louis Weiss died by 1900, likely in San Antonio.

12. No information was located on E. Staus.

13. Frederick Fresenius was born about 1826 in Prussia. The date he arrived in Texas is not known. Fresenius married Bertha Basse, the daughter of Pastor Henry Basse, on November 28, 1855, in Gillespie County. They were the parents of at least one child. He joined the Gillespie Rifles on February 23, 1862, and took the oath of allegiance to the Confederacy. Fresenius was elected the first lieutenant of the company. He very likely signed the petition requesting Kuechler's company be disbanded. Frederick Fresenius testified against the Unionists during the Confederate Military Commission in San Antonio. He may be the Fredericks Fresenius who was conscripted in mid-1862. This Frederick Fresenius received a parole on June 11, 1865, at San Antonio. The parole showed his place of resident was San Antonio. Frederick Fresenius died sometime between 1870 and 1880, very likely in Gillespie County.

14. Engelbert Krauskopf was born on August 21, 1820, in Bendorf, then part of the kingdom of Prussia. He arrived in Texas on the *Andacis* in 1846. Krauskopf married Rose Herbst on January 28, 1849, in Comal County. They were the parents of at least seven children. Krauskopf was an early gunsmith and during the War Between the States he manufactured ammunition. He was a second lieutenant in Nimitz's Gillespie County Rifles. In May, 1864, he re-organized Louis Schuetze's militia company, the Third Frontier District. Engelbert Krauskopf died on July 11, 1881, in Gillespie County.

15. Adolf Lungkwitz was born about 1819 in Prussia. He and his older brother, Hermann Lungkwitz, a famous painter, arrived in Texas in the early 1850s. Adolf married Elise Heuser on October 14, 1855, in Gillespie County. Adolf Lungkwitz enrolled in Schuetze's Company, Third Frontier District of January, 1864. Adolf Lungkwitz died in Gillespie County, but date not known.

16. Frederick William Schneer was born on October 20, 1823, in Frankfort am Main, Prussia. Schneer married Elizabeth Emma Schneider sometime around 1850, likely in Prussia. They arrived in Texas on November 15, 1855, and settled in Gillespie County. They were the parents of four children. Frederick William Schneer died on December 1, 1908, in Gillespie County.

17. George Emile Van der Stucken Van der Stucken was born on February 17, 1840, ln Belgium. He was a brother of Frank and Julius Van der Stucken, below. The date he arrived in Texas is not known. Emile was a member of Nimitz's Gillespie Rifles and took the oath of allegiance to the Confederacy on February 23, 1862. He signed the resolution requesting Kuechler's company be disbanded. He enrolled in Company C, 8$^{th}$ Battalion Texas Cavalry in May 1862. Van der Stucken remained with the unit when it became

Company E, 1st Regiment Texas Cavalry. He was discharged on June 16, 1863. Emile Van der Stucken was a member of Locke's Company, Third Frontier District of January, 1864. The unit's muster roll shows him as thirty-three years old. George Emile Van der Stucken married Wilhelmina Kordzik on September 11, 1865, in Gillespie County. They were the parents of at least six children. By 1880 Emile Van der Stucken was living in Menard County. George Emile Van der Stucken died on February 14, 1906, in San Angelo in Tom Greene County, Texas.

18.   Jacob Tatsch was born in August, 1829, in Koblenz, Prussia. He arrived in Texas on October 15, 1853, and settled at Fredericksburg. He enrolled in Nimitz's company in February, 1862, and took the Confederate oath of allegiance. He signed the Gillespie petition requesting Kuechler's company be disbanded. Jacob Tatsch never married. The date of his death in Texas is not known.

19.   Henry S. W. Basse was born October 6, 1804, in Prussia. He married Fredericke Charlotte Quintel on November 29, 1831. They arrived in Texas on the *York* in 1846 and were some of the first settlers in Fredericksburg. Basse was the pastor of the local church. Pastor Henry Basse died on January 10, 1865, in Fredericksburg.

20.   James M. Hunter was born in 1829 in Buncombe County, Tennessee. He was a younger brother of John Hunter. James Hunter married Philippine Keller on August 9, 1860, in Gillespie County. They were the parents of eleven children, but only seven lived to be adults. In March, 1862, Hunter enrolled in Davis' Company, Frontier Regiment and he was elected first lieutenant. In December, 1862, when the company was re-organized he was elected captain. In early 1864 he was appointed major and commander of the Third Frontier District. Hunter served as county judge of Edwards and Mason counties. He died on August 31, 1907, in Mason County.

21.   Wilhelm Koock was born on February 17, 1838, in Hanover. He arrived in Texas with his parents on the *Magarette* in 1846. Koock married Wilhelmine Jordan on October 29, 1868, in Gillespie County. They were the parents of at least seven children. They settled in Mason County and established the community of Koockville. William Koock was killed in a fall from his horse on May 14, 1890.

22.   Levi Lamoni Wight was born March 1, 1836, in Clay County, Missouri. The family arrived in Texas in 1845 as part of the Mormon settlement. He married Sophia Leyland on September 4, 1856, in Bandera County. They were the parents of six children. Wight enlisted in Van der Stucken's company on May 7, 1862, and remained with the unit until the end of the war. He died on May 14, 1918, in Nolan County, Texas.

23. Albert Wathersdorff was born about 1833, likely in Saxony. The date he arrived in Texas is not known. Wathersdorff married Louise Runge on December 8, 1861, in Gillespie County. It is not known if they had any children. Wathersdorff enlisted in Van der Stucken's company in May, 1862. He re-enlisted in the 5$^{th}$ Artillery Battery later in the war. Louise Runge Wathersdorff died about 1865. After the war ended Wathersdorff married Alphonsine [maiden name not known] about 1870 in Louisiana. They were the parents of at least three children.The family returned to Gillespie County for a short time where he was employed of the state-supported school. He applied for citizenship on October 30, 1878, in Bexar County. Albert Wathersdorff died about 1886, likely in Travis County.

24. August Siemering was born on February 8, 1828, or 1830 in Brandenburg, Prussia. Siemering was both a Freethinker and Forty-Eighter who had to flee Prussia. He arrived in Texas on the *Republic* from Hahlhausen, Prussia in 1851. On May 29, 1862, at New Braunfels in Comal County, August Siemering married Emma Boehme who had arrived on the same ship in 1851. He was a major participant in the 1854 San Antonio Convention. Emma Boehme Siemering either died or they were divorced as on June 12, 1859, he married Clara Schuetze, the daughter of Louis Schuetze, another original member of the League in Gillespie County. They were the parents of eight children. Siemering was a member of Nimitz's Gillespie Rifles in June – July 1861. He was one of the Unionists original condemned by the Rifles in February, 1862, but whose name was removed after he appeared before the group. Siemering was a member of Kuechler's company of December, 1861. He enrolled in Van der Stucken's company in May, 1862 and was elected junior second lieutenant. Siemering resigned on March 4, 1864. August Siemering was appointed Gillespie Chief Justice in 1865. In 1865 Siemering established the German language newspaper *Freie Presse fuer Texas*. August Siemering died on September 19, 1883, in San Antonio.

25. John George Weber was born on April 6, 1817, in Nassau. The names of his parents are not known. Weber married Catharina [maiden name not known] about 1844 in Nassau. They were the parents of six children. The family arrived in Texas on the *Arminius* in 1845 and settled in Gillespie County. He was a member of Nimitz' Gillespie Rifles in June-July 1861. Weber took the oath of allegiance to the Confederacy on February 23, 1862, and likely signed the petition requesting Kuechler's company be disbanded. John George Weber died on April 7, 1865, in Gillespie County.

26. Friedrich Wilhelm Von Wrede, Jr. was born on December 31, 1820, in Hessen. His family first arrived in New Orleans on the *Manko* on January 5, 1836. Ship records shows Wrede Jr.'s age as fifteen. His mother died of yellow fever in December 1837. He and his father traveled to East Texas, St. Louis,

and New York. Wrede and his father returned to Germany in 1843. In 1844 he was appointed secretary to Prince Carl of Solms-Braunfels and arrived with him in Texas. Wrede accompanied John O. Meusebach to the San Saba River when he established his treaty with the Comanches. Indians killed his father on October 24, 1845. From 1851 until 1859 Wrede was Gillespie County Clerk. Friedrick Wrede represented Gillespie County in the Eighth Legislature as a member of the House of Representatives from November 7, 1859, until April 9, 1861. Friedrich von Wrede married Sophie Bonzano about 1850. They were the parents of four children. Wrede very likely signed the petition requesting Kuechler's company be disbanded. He testified against the Unionists during the Confederate Military Commission in San Antonio in July – August 1862. In the spring of 1865 because of his pro-secessionist views, Wrede and his family returned to Wiesbaden, where he remained until 1871. The date and location of his death are not known.

27. Adolph Weiss was born about 1821 in Nassau. He was a brother of Louis Weiss. He arrived in Texas on the *John Holland* in 1848. Adolph married Lisette Schub on October 25, 1852 in Gillespie County. They were the parents of at least nine children. Weiss enrolled in Nimitz's company in February, 1861, and took the Confederate oath on February 23, 1862. He signed the petition requesting Kuechler's company be disbanded. Adolph Weiss died in Gillespie County sometime between 1900 and 1910.

28. Thomas Jefferson Devine was the judge of the Confederate Western District of Texas. He was born on February 20, 1820, in Nova Scotia. He attended Transylvania University in Kentucky where he received his law degree. He moved to Texas in 1838. Devine was a member of the Secession Convention and a member of the Committee of Public Safety that supervised the surrender of federal troops in Texas in February, 1861. After the war he fled to Mexico, but returned a short time later. Federal authorities arrested him and twice indicted him for high treason He was pardoned and his citizenship restored on June 17, 1867. Thomas Devine died at San Antonio on March 16, 1890.

29. Herman Beckmann was born on April 13, 1843, in Hanover. He arrived in Texas on the *Juno* in 1853 from Oberg. His name appears on the 1855 Gillespie school rolls, living in his parent's household. Beckmann enrolled in Nimitz's Gillespie Rifles on February 23, 1862, and took the oath of allegiance. He very likely signed the petition requesting Kuechler's company be disbanded. Beckmann enrolled in Hunter's Company, Frontier Regiment on August 8, 1863. Herman Beckmann died on June 3, 1922, in Gillespie County.

30. Friedrich Wilhelm Doebbler was born on March 26, 1824, in Luckenwalde, near Berlin, Prussia. He was both a Forty-Eighter and a Freethinker. F. W. Doebbler married Henriette [maiden name not known] about 1849, in

Prussia. They were the parents of at least five children. The family fled Prussia in 1851 and settled in Gillespie County. He was an original member of the Union Loyal League and ran a "beer hall" first in Fredericksburg and later in Grape Town. Doebbler wrote several newspaper articles for northern newspaper critical of the Confederacy. He was an early member of the Gillespie Rifles but was forced to leave due to his northern sympathies. Captain Duff arrested him in June, 1862. He was tried by the Confederate Military Commission and found guilty of "disloyalty." Doebbler escaped from the San Antonio jail, fled to Mexico, and waited out the war. Friedrich Wilhelm Doebbler died on December 23, 1913, in Gillespie County.

31.    J. Rudolph Radeleff was born about 1829 in Holstein or Denmark. He was very likely both a Forty-Eighter and a Freethinker. Radeleff arrived in Texas about 1857 and settled in Fredericksburg. On October 11, 1859, he declared his intentions to become a U. S. citizen, which was not granted until January 6, 1868. Radeleff was a partner with the Hunter brothers before the war. He enrolled in Nimitz's Gillespie Rifles on January 30, 1861, and was elected first lieutenant. Radeleff left the Gillespie Rifles by late 1861. On March 6, 1862, he was elected captain of 1st Company in Gillespie Precinct Number 2, 1831. Radeleff was a member of the Gillespie Company of the League military battalion. Captain Duff arrested him and he was convicted for Unionist activates and banished from the Confederacy. Before Radeleff left he gave Friedrich Lochte his power of attorney. He spent the remainder of the war in Mexico. After the war he returned to Gillespie County and he was elected justice of the peace. In 1870 Radeleff was elected as presiding justice [county judge] of Gillespie County and he was reelected in 1872. J. Rudolph Radcliff died in Gillespie County but the date is not known.

32.    See endnote 24, p.67 for a biography of August Siemering..

33.    Braubach, Doebbler, Radeleff, and Siemering were all very likely original members of the Union Loyal League. As August Siemering explains in his article his name was stricken from the resolution. James Duff arrested the other three in June, 1862, during his first trip to Gillespie County.

34.    John Anton Menges was born about 1821 in Niederelbert, Nassau. He married Catherine [maiden name not known] about 1842. They were the parents of at least eight children. The family arrived in Texas on the *Rega* in 1845. Menges enrolled in Nimitz's Gillespie Rifles on March 23, 1862, and took the Confederate oath of allegiance on the same date. He organized a squad of home guards in October, 1853, and was elected first lieutenant. He was a member of Schuetze's home guard company of November, 1863. In April, 1864, he was a member of William Wahrmund's Company, Third Frontier District and served until the end of the war. The date and location of his death is not known.

34. Julius Theodor Splittgerber was born April 23, 1819, in Prussia. He graduated from Breslau University in 1836 and was commissioned a second lieutenant in the Prussian army on September 18, 1842. King Friedrich Wilhelm IV signed Splittgerber's orders to be assigned to the Adelsverein on August 10, 1845. Splittgerber arrived in Texas on the *Arminius* on October 22, 1845. He was assigned command of the Adelsverein militia detachment that accompanied the wagon train which established Fredericksburg in June, 1845. Julius Splittgerber married Sophie Dorothea Miehe in 1848. Splittgerber was Gillespie County sheriff from August, 1862, to August, 1864. Julius Theodor Splittgerber died on November 14, 1897, in Menard County.

35. Louis Wahrmund was born about 1821 in Nassau. He arrived in Texas on the *Talisman* in 1846. He was one of four Wahrmund brothers to settle in Gillespie County. Louis Wahrmund married Susanna Ressmann. The date and location of their marriage is not known. He was a member of Braubach's company from February, 1861, until February, 1862. He then joined Nimitz's Gillespie Rifles where he took the oath of allegiance to the Confederacy on March 27, 1862. He was a member of his brother William's company of the Third Frontier District from April until the end of the war.

## 13. Letter–Ernest Cramer

Monterey, Mexico,
Oct. 30, 1862

My Beloved Parents:

At last I have found the opportunity to write to you. I must take advantage of it even though I know of nothing pleasant to relate to you. Fate has dealt very harshly with me. It is beyond belief to think that any human being could come under such conditions of sorrow and misery.

I had to leave Texas very hurriedly without the time to properly provide for my family. Also I live in a state of constant fear for their lives. My poor wife and small daughter[1] are still in Comfort with my sister-in-law, Mrs. Simon.[2] My wife's parents are on my farm. Mr. Simon[3] is in prison in San Antonio – in constant danger of being hanged. He may already have lost his life, for it is two months since I have heard anything of him. Leopold[4], my wife's brother, is dead – killed in a battle we had during our flight to Mexico. I live in such a state of anxiety that I can hardly collect my thoughts sufficiently to picture to you the life that I have been forced to lead the last few years.

I never thought that this disastrous war could last so long, and bring us all such grievous circumstances.

I was married on the 17th of September in 1861 to Charlotte Bauer. I have already told you about her. I had a prosperous business – lived happily and contentedly – until towards the end of the year. Then military laws were enacted and every man between the ages of 18 and 45 was subject to conscription in the Confederacy.[5] All of our friends in San Antonio as well as in our small town of Comfort – in fact – we felt that all of the West was in sympathy with the North. And then came the first apprehension when we were threatened to be forced into the service of the South.

In February a Frontier regiment was organized of men who lived in our county and in the surrounding counties. It was for the purpose of protection against the Indians and only to be used in the service of the state of Texas.[6] The young men of the counties joined and an intimate friend of men by the name of Kuechler (of Darmstadt) was elected Captain. He soon had a company together all Germans.[7]

Now a party formed themselves in Freidrichsburg, composed of Americans mainly, and appealed to the Governor at Austin, declaring that our company was not legally organized and that they had not been given the opportunity to join.[8]

Our company had been formed of men gathered together with the understanding that as soon as the Northern troops would come within reaching distance, we would join them. But it followed that our plans were overthrown in a most lamentable manner.[9]  Most of those in our company, rather than be forced into the service of the South, swore that they would never enter into any service again.[10]

Up to this time Simon and I had taken no active part. We had been appointed to collect the property and war taxes for the counties of Kerr and Kendall and in consequence had not been interfered with or molested.

But as the agitation became stronger and stronger, we had to definitely take a stand for one side or the other.  We resigned our positions and naturally joined our friends in support of the North.

The forbearance of the people seemed at an end. The Union flag was hoisted and the outbreak of a revolution was momentarily expected. On the 24th of March a meeting was called at a well named the *Barenguelle* between Freidrichsburg and Comfort.[11] Unfortunately at just this time the Northern troops attacked at Galveston.[12] That raised our hopes and gave us the surety and confidence that the North would bring us help. The 'Hurrah' for the Union echoed from all corners. Companies were organized and Officers for the different districts were elected.[13]

My Company, composed of 80 men, elected me Captain for the Comfort district.[14]

The next day [March 25th] I was ordered to go to San Antonio for the purpose of joining our forces with the others from the different districts.[*] I found everything well prepared there.[15] But the spirit and enthusiasm that we had in our original organization was not there. I was told to await further orders. In my heart I knew that without help from the Northern forces we were helpless. I cannot deny that in San Antonio I lost much confidence. However, I did not allow myself to become disheartened. I did begin to realize however that in what I had undertaken I had placed much too much faith and trust in people. The others from the various districts who had been called at the same time that I had, returned to their homes with the same feeling of hopelessness. And so we all came to the decision to maintain peace and quietness. It was no small thing to do. Every evening we met but delayed action from one day to another.[16]

---

[*] See Letters of Colonel H. E McCulloch, document numbers 14, 15, and 16, pp.90-94

At last on the 15th day of April we were informed that the Union party in Austin had been forced to disband. Our hope had been built on the strength of the party there. When that failed our only hope was to be able to reach Mexico. It was a great blow to us all. We were very apprehensive. We had taken our stand but all our plans had to be abandoned. Our hope so inconceivably lost – we could not await the outcome.[17]

Now San Antonio and 8 days later our whole district was put under the laws of the Confederacy. Everyone must appear before the "Provost" within ten days and take the oath to support and be true to the Comfort division of the Confederacy on penalty of losing all properties.[18] Then it was that I began to really know people. Excepting a very few, all took the oath, and also betrayed their officers. All Officers had to immediately flee for their lives. If anyone had told me eight days before that such a thing could be possible, I could conscientiously have shot him.[19]

Simon then also took the oath so that he could remain with his family. I took my wife to him. I had prudently sold my property to my father-in-law sometime before. And now, with a number of my friends I departed into the mountains. There was Kuechler – two brothers by the name of Degener[20] about my own age. They were sons of a very cultured and well-educated man who had to leave Germany in '48. Franz and Moritz Weiss[21] – Ernest Beseler[22] – Wilhelm Telgman[23] – Emil Schreiner[24] – all educated young men of fine families.

We formed a hunting party, hunted in the mountains, and were hunted and chased by soldiers. But we knew the country and every secret path and hiding nook too well to allow ourselves to be caught.

Early in July I had to go home.[25] We were expecting a child. I arrived on the morning of the 10th, and on the following day we were blessed with the birth of a small daughter. It was then that I felt my circumstances bitterly. I could not sit quietly for one instant. I had to conceal myself as though I were a thief. Because I knew that had I been caught I would surely have been hanged. I stayed at home for eight days and then went eight miles from Comfort to a well [spring] where I met my companions again.[26]

Simon was under constant suspicion and his life at home was very unsafe – exposed to constant risk – so he decided to come with me. Immediately thereafter all men up to the age of 35 were called. A death penalty if they did not appear. That made it livelier in our mountains. One by one we were joined by acquaintances until we numbered 20.

We decided than that as there were 600 men in the Confederate troops surrounding us,[27] and as we wanted to uphold the law, we would go to Mexico where there might be a chance for us to join the Northern troops. On the 2nd day of August we started out.[28] Leopold, my brother-in-law, provided our family with means for their livelihood for one year and went with us. At the well [spring or water hole] of Guadeloupe we met 40 more men.[29] Five Americans also joined us and that brought our number to 68.[30]

On the 9th [31] [8th] of August, late in the evening, we came to a narrow "draw" heavily covered with cedar growth. We stayed there, though without food for our horses. The next morning after riding barely two miles, we came to an open space – a meadow with fine grass and plenty of water. Not a stream but springs that seemed to sink again. Here and there were groups of small cedars. It was an outer arm of the

Nueces. We figured that Fort Clark was about 50 miles to the Southwest and that we were about 45 miles from where the San Felipe joined the Rio Grande. Our horses being hungry and tired we decided to rest there for the day and the next morning to continue on our way to the Rio Grande.

We proceeded to make our camp under the first group of cedars nearest the water. On this evening we were all quite cheerful, not having any omen that this place would be the grave for most of us. We sang and declaimed until late in the night.

About an hour before sunrise we heard one shot that awaken us.[32] Immediately after came another and another. We leaped to our feet and were met with a volley of about 100 shots. Leopold fell dead and four others were wounded.[33] Then all became quiet. We held a consultation and decided to fortify ourselves as well as we could. That was quickly done and then followed a deadly stillness that was almost unbearable. I had given my word to Hugo Degener, the older of the two brothers, to cover the right wing and was fully determined to stay and die at my post if need be.[34] The chances to make escape seemed impossible. The soldiers greatly outnumbered us, had just a good position as we had and had at least 100 to 200 men available from Ft. Clark. And to add to our despair, the men who had joined us at the Guadeloupe deserted their posts one by one. At the end of the day, of the 68 men we had only 32 were with us.[35] And now the soldiers charged. Three times they assailed us and each time we drove them back. Hugo and Hilmar, his brother, fell. Hugo's back was shattered by two bullets. He came to me, crawling, to bid me farewell. W. Telgman had been shot through the body sometime before, but kept his place bravely and continued to fight.

We rested about one hour and a half. But after another attack we realized that we could not continue to hold our position.[36] Kuechler, Moritz Weiss, and I were the only ones that were not wounded. Of my close friends Simon had a shot through the ribs. Franz had a shot through the heel and one through the lower part of the leg. I had a shot through my pants and a shot had torn away the entire front of my shirt, but did not touch my skin. Of the others six were severely wounded.[37]

Now we went forward up the valley very cautiously so as to leave no trace that could be followed.[38] We had not traveled two miles when we met six or eight of those men who had deserted us.[39] They were lost and did not know which way to turn. They begged to be allowed to join us and as bitterly as we felt towards them we still could not refuse them & leave them there. We journeyed on until noon and still not the first trace of water. The wounded were exhausted so we made a camp for them in a sheltered place. Kuechler and Moritz remained with them. I started out again with a companion to search for water. About 4 o'clock we returned having found no water. As we came to the sport where he had left our companions we found no one there.[40] We were too tired and weak to hunt for them. After resting for a while we proceeded to walk back to the battlefield. About two hours after dark we came to the water. As soon as we had satisfied our thirst we felt ourselves strong again. We emptied our powder horns and filled them with water. We meant then to continue our search for the wounded. Just then ten men appeared. They had been to the water but had hidden themselves on our approach. As the soldier were still not more than 150 steps away – I suggested that we empty and clean every article that could be used to hold water and asked several of the men to hunt for the wounded and take the water to them. I wanted to go four or five miles further to try to get a deer at dawn. Everyone seemed satisfied with that plan because all were hungry. I left them without feeling any anxiety. Weber[41], who had been my companion all through the day, joined me. We were not fortunate in finding any game and came to the place where we had planned to meet about 10 o'clock. All of the wounded were there excepting Simon. He had become too weak to continue with them. I was almost frantic – was too anxious about him to be able to take any rest. So, dangerous as it was, I started out in the evening. It was a bright moonlight night and I hunted for him throughout the whole night. I had no success – he was nowhere to be found. I felt convinced that he was dead.[42] I came back to our camp in the morning completely exhausted. I had had nothing to eat for three days and the anxiety and worry and strain was enough to exhaust the strongest man.

On the 4th day the soldiers withdrew.[43] Then I went back to the battlefield to search for my friends and perhaps to see them once again. The sight was horrible beyond description. They had been stripped of their clothing and the bodies had been piled up one over the other in a large heap. Those who were still living when we were forced to leave them had been lined up and used as targets. Their faces and bodies completely riddled with bullets. It was heartrending and I could not linger there.

The next day[44] with four others, I started back to my home to get provisions. On the 7th day we arrived in the outskirts of Comfort.[45] It was a terrible day for me. I stayed in the thickest about a half a mile from my home and dared not go to my Lottchen. I could not face her with the news I had to tell of Leopold's death and Simon's.

The next day[46] I went 18 miles further to the home of a friend to beg him to break the sad news to my sister-in-law and to the others. By the time that I reached my friend's home in Boerne I had a high fever. For four days I was delirious. Had hardly recovered from illness when I heard that Simon had been captured and taken to San Antonio. How it all happened I do not know to this day.

It was too dangerous for me to attempt to go home. Everyone was under suspicion. If anyone had even been suspected of giving aid to one of us they would have been taken and hanged. One hundred people had been hanged in less than that many days.[47] Relatives of those who had been with us were especially watched. And so how it happened that Simon was still living, I do not know.

In six days after I arrived in Boerne[48], I went to Leon Springs. There I found the opportunity to speak with my sister-in-law. She had visited Simon in San Antonio and was very anxious about him. She begged me to be careful and for me to try to get to Mexico as I was the only one left for them to depend upon. Kuechler during this time had returned with the wounded. I did not have the time to look for him.

Through an earlier companion, Richard Brotze[49], I managed to secure a horse with the understanding that I leave immediately for the Rio Grande. He insisted on that and I could not blame him for had I been seen with his horse he would immediately have been hanged. I still had many dangers to face before I could get to the Mexican border and heard the whistle of many a bullet.

Kuechler left again shortly after I did, together with Moritz and Franz and ten other good friends of mine. They had no trouble until they reached the Rio Grande. Just at the river they were attacked and under heavy fire had to leave their horses and ammunition behind. They had to swim the Rio Grande. Franz was shot and Moritz went to his aid and both were downed. Four others were killed while swimming.[50] Kuechler is now the only one of my intimate friends that is left. He is safe here.

Since speaking to my sister-in-law I have heard nothing of my family. I think, however, that no harm has come to them. If Texas is still in the hands of the Confederacy in the spring I feel that I must bring my family here. Our families are defenseless, against attacks of Indians as well as at the mercy of all marauders. Because now all between the ages of 16 and 45 are called. Death and confiscation of their property, the penalty.

I am in great need of money and wish to draw on you for $100 hoping that the unfortunate and unhappy position in which I find myself with excuse it. I need money to equip myself and straighten out my affairs so that I can return to Texas. I must return within four or six weeks so that I can make some effort to rescue my property. Through my father-in-law I hope to trade my cattle and Simon's for heavy freight wagons and bring them down here. Freight wagons command a high price here. I am waiting now for some businessmen from San Antonio who will cover my draft and give me the money, so I beg of you to honor the same.

I think that I will be in no danger on the expedition because I know the way so well now. Am sure that I can find safe ways of traveling. Should, however, I be unfortunate and be killed, then, of course, the money will be lost to you.

Also I beg of you to leave $1000 to my wife and child in case of my death. I am certain that you will do that. It would be so terrible for my poor wife who has already had so much to bear to be left in poverty and want.

The outlook seems very favorable that the Confederacy in Texas will soon be played out. We are told that the Northern troops are on the coast. If that is true we do not know positively, but the Proclamation of Lincoln not to divide the Union would suggest that the North is in earnest. And we think that Texas would be the first state to be taken over. As long as Texas is not in the hands of the Northern troops, it places the Confederacy in easy communication with the whole outside world.

A great deal of cotton is sold here. Exchanged for powder, clothing and other necessities. I have no idea how conditions are in the Union states. In fact I know nothing of the whole political situation. Since the blockade I have seen no newspaper. Here all the news of the states is withheld. I will write once again before returning to Texas.

Meanwhile I hope that you are all well. Please write to me. For you cannot know how much that would mean to me. To hear from you – how things are with you – the dear grandparents – brothers and sisters and the Franckes. No day passes that my thoughts are not with you.

s/Ernest Cramer

Monterey, Mexico
Addr. Sigm Dresely
    Schwemian

ENDNOTES
Letter Ernest Cramer

01. Cramer's wife was Charlotte Bauer. She was born about 1845 in Prussia. Her parents were Christine Ostenberger and Gottlieb Bauer. Her brother Leopold was also a member of the August insurgent group. Charlotte and Ernest Cramer obtained a marriage license in Kerr County on September 12, 1861. Their daughter was Catherina Louisa Longa, born on July 11, 1862.

02. Cramer's sister-in-law was Caroline Bauer. She was born about 1836 in Darmstadt. Caroline married Ferdinand Simon on May 14, 1855, in Bexar County. She died in mid-1878 at her home near Boerne.

03. Ferdinand Simon was born about 1826 in Hesse-Darmstadt. It is believed he arrived on the *Strabo* in 1845. The 1860 Bexar Census shows him as thirty-four years old, a merchant, living near Leon Springs. He was a member of the August insurgent group, wounded in the Nueces battle and captured about three days afterwards. He was tried by the Confederate Military Commission and sentenced to death, but before the sentence could be carried out, martial law was revoked. Simon spent the remainder of the war in prison. He died in July, 1878, at his home in Boerne.

04. Leopold Bauer was born about 1839 in Prussia. He was in the August insurgent group and killed in the opening shots of the Nueces battle.

05. The Confederate Conscription Act was passed on April 16, 1862. It stated that all free white males between the ages of eighteen to thirty-five were subject to conscription into the Confederate army. This age limit was raised to forty-five on September 27, 1862.

06. On December 21, 1861, the Texas Legislature approved a bill creating the Frontier Regiment. It was made up of volunteers from the frontier counties. One company was authorized from Kerr, Gillespie and Hays Counties. At the time of the bill, Kendall County had not been created. The men from Comfort were to be in the Kerr County group.

07. The muster roll shows there were seventy-four members in Kuechler's company. All but five had German surnames. These members were: Jacob Kuechler, Captain; Philip Braubach, First Lieutenant; Moritz Weiss, Second Lieutenant; Hugo Degener, Second Lieutenant; Theodore Bruckisch, First Sergeant; August Duecker, Second Sergeant; Friedrich Sauer, Third Sergeant; Louis Boerner, Fourth Sergeant; Johann Becker; First Corporal; Gottlieb Sauer, Second Corporal; A. J. Nixon, Third Corporal; Josiah Reagan, Fourth Corporal; Jacob Remeck, Farrier; and Privates Heinrich Behrend; Ernst Beseler; Carl Brinkmann; Adam Blucher; Arthur de Cloudt; Benjamin Coffey; Hilmar Degener; Pablo Diaz; Joseph Dengel; Joseph Elstner; Christian Feuge;

Casper Fritz; Jacob Gold; Peter Gold, Senior; Peter Gold, Junior; E. H. Freeman; W. T. Geissler; August Graft; Carl Herbst; Rudolph Hartbeck; Heinrich Neumann; Anton Heinen; John Hertzberg; Wilhelm Juenke; Frank Jung; John Jung; Alfred Kapp; Carl Karder; George Kallenberg; Wilhelm Klier; Wilhelm Kuehne; John Klein; John Adam Klein; Joseph Leyendecker; Anton Lott; J. Niemeyer; Otto Nieuberg; George Ottmers; Adolph Pfeiffer; Albert Quitzow; Ulrich Rische; John Reigner; Louis Schierholz; Frederick Schladoer; Christian Schaefer; August Siemering; Heinrich Stevens; Olford Striegler; Arthur Striegler; O. W. Striegler; Carl Schwartz; Jacob Schneider; Wilhelm Tellgmann; Peter Tatsch; Ludwig Usener; Gottlieb Vetterlein. Friedrich Weber; Franz Weiss; John Walter, Joseph Weiner; and Edward Westphal.

08. Kuechler enrolled only Unionists from Blanco, Kerr, and Gillespie County. No men from Hays County were enrolled. Area citizens who were not Unionists were not notified of where and when to report for enrollment. At least two men, David Farr of Kerr County and Frank Van der Stucken of Gillespie County, wrote the governor complaining that they and others were unable to enroll. There were two petitions also sent to the governor. One was from Kerr County. It contained thirty-eight signatures. They were: C. C. Quinlan; Nathan Jackson; Isaac Lamb; Hiram Lamb; John Lowrance; James Coleman; Marcellon Dunham; A. P. Paul; F. P. Click; E. Whitley; P. E. Hampton; J. A. Hudson. A. J. Rogers; A. C. Farmann; J. H. Regges; R. F. Camford; M. A. Lowrance; Scott Kell; A. L. Williamson; J. W. Rogers; H. M. Barney; R. G. Farr; P. O. Lowrance; J. P. Stroops; D. B. Lowrance; J. D. Buchanan; William Long; E. W. Brown; J. D. Brown; Joseph Follord; Semon Blevins; E. A. Steel; R. W. Freemon; Freemon Myers; Daniel Arnold; P. M. Stanford; Aaron W. Jackson; and George Hollimon. The second petition was from Gillespie County. A copy of that petition has not been located. There are conflicting reports about how many men signed this petition. Charles Nimitz said in his testimony before the Confederate Military Commission there were twenty-eight signatures. One researcher says he saw the petition and there were seventy-four signatures. The men who signed are very likely the same as those shown as members of the Gillespie Rifles.

09. This is proof that Kuechler's company was organized as a purely Unionist company and reveals the real purpose of the company.

10. Very shortly after this meeting on March 3-4, 1862, the insurgents met on Bear Creek and organized the secret, unauthorized insurgent battalion.

11. This statement established that the insurgents met on or about March 24, 1862, and organized the battalion at Bear Creek.

12. The editor was unable to locate any reference to the Union attacking Galveston at this time. It is known that the frigate *U.S.S. Santee* appeared off the Galveston port several times and fired a few rounds into the city. Known dates it fired included November 10, 1861, and again on May 17 and 19, 1862. *It may have been* that the Union blocking force fired on Galveston sometime in late March or early April, 1862.

13  The insurgent battalion had three companies: Gillespie, commanded by Jacob Kuechler with Valentine Hohmann as lieutenant; Kendall, commanded by Ernest Cramer with Hugo Degener as lieutenant; and the Kerr (or American Company), commanded by Henry Hartman with Phil G. Temple as lieutenant.

14. Cramer claims his company numbered eighty men. Likely this is the correct number. A comparison of the known Unionists in the Comfort area and the 1860 Census shows that the number *could have been* as high as 104.

15. This establishes the fact that the Hill Country insurgent group (the Union Loyal League) met with other area Unionist leaders in San Antonio on March 25, 1862. These other Unionist groups likely included the: Austin Unionist company of at least 89 men; the Medina Battalion was made up of at least 170 men; the Bandera Company with at least 35 men; giving the total Unionist force at least 539 members, plus the San Antonio *Turnvereine* companies – a very impressive force.

16. This seems to imply that an element in the Hill Country insurgent organization wanted to take immediate action.

17. The *San Antonio Herald* of March 29, 1862, reported the breakup of the Austin Unionist Party. It also establishes that the Hill Country insurgent group was looking to the Austin Unionists for guidance and leadership.

18. Confederate Brigadier General H. P. Bee declared martial law in Bexar County on April 24, 1862. All individuals living in Bexar County were given ten days to take the oath of allegiance to the Confederacy of all the bounds of the South.

19. On May 30, 1862, Confederate Brigadier General P. O. Hebert declared martial law over all of Texas. It was after the May 30, 1862, declaration of martial law that many of the Hill Country residents took the oath. To announce martial law in the Hill Country General Bee sent Captain James Duff and his Partisan Rangers to enforce the proclamation. At this time many of the insurgent officers fled to the mountains.

20. The two Degener brothers were Hugo and Hilmar. Their father was Eduard Degener, a Forty-Eighter who was the political leader of the insurgent groups.

21. The Weiss brothers were as Cramer states, Franz and Moritz. Franz was born about 1843 in Prussia. Moritz was born about 1836 also in Prussia. Their father had died and their mother married Oskar Roggenbucke, one of the most radical Unionists. Both survived the Nueces battle but were killed on October 18, 1862, when another insurgent group was engaged at the Rio Grande.

22. Ernest Beseler was born about 1842 in Wesel, Prussia. The family arrived in Texas on the *Franziska* in 1848 and settled in the Comfort area. Ernest Beseler was a member of Kuechler's December, 1861, Unionist company and was a member of the Kendall Company of insurgents. He is identified as the individual who shot and killed Basil Stewart on July 5, 1862. Beseler was in the August insurgent group and on guard on the night of the attack. He was the second insurgent killed at the battle.

23. William Tellgmann was born about 1831 in Brunswick. William and his brother Charles arrived in Texas in 1852 and settled in the Comfort area. William Tellgmann was a member of Kuechler's Unionist company of December, 1861. He was a member of Cramer's Kendall Company of the insurgent group and was in the August insurgent group. He was seriously wounded in the battle, but "Kept his place bravely and continued to fight." Tellgmann was one of the insurgents whom Lt. Lilly ordered shot.

24. Amil Schreiner was born about 1839 in Riguewihr, France. He was a brother of Charles Schreiner, also an insurgent. They arrived in Texas in 1852 and Kerr County about 1857, settling on Lower Turtle Creek. Amil was a member of the Kendall Company of the Hill Country insurgent group and in the August insurgent group. He died early in the Nueces battle, leading a counter-charge.

25. The daughter was Catherina Louisa Cramer, who was born on July 11, 1862. She married a man with the surname of Johnson, about 1882, likely in California or Idaho. Louisa Cramer Johnson died in late 1915 in Ada County, Idaho, and is buried in the Morris Hill Cemetery.

26. This meeting was off Turtle Creek on a small creek now known as Bushwhack Creek.

27. There were in fact about 500 Confederate and Texas state troops looking for the insurgents.

28. It is not clear exactly what date the insurgents left. Here Cramer states it was August 2nd. Based on the fact that his account was written in October of 1862 it is likely it was on August 2, 1862, that they left from Bushwhack Creek and went to the insurgent's base camp on the south fork of the Guadalupe River and departed from there on August 3, 1862.

29. Here Cramer is confirming the insurgent group left the assembly on Bushwhack Creek and met up with a larger insurgent group on the south fork of the Guadalupe River.

30. The five "Americans" who joined included John W. Sansom, who left Bushwhack Creek with the insurgent group. The other four were Tomas J. Scott and his brother Warren B. Scott as well as Howard Henderson and William Hester, bringing the total to 69.

31. It was late on the evening of August 8th that the insurgents made this dry camp. The next day, August 9, they arrived on West Nueces.

32. The Confederate plan was to captured any insurgent guard and thus not alert the camp. Leonard Bauer and John W. Sansom walked into Lieutenant Harbour's group of Confederates who immediately shot and killed Bauer and shortly thereafter Ernest Beseler. These opening shots alerted the insurgent camp and they were ready for the Confederate assault when it came at daylight.

33. According to Cramer's numbers only Leopold Bauer was killed in the opening shots, and four others were wounded. At least one other insurgent, Ernst Beseler, was killed in the first volley. Fritz Tegener, the insurgent leader was one of the four wounded. In additional a small group of insurgents made a counter-charge at the Confederates, resulting in Amil Schreiner being killed and an unknown number wounded.

34. Here Cramer tells us the insurgent leaders held a "consultation" and decided to stay and fight and die if "need be."

35. Accounted to Cramer's numbers, thirty-six insurgents left the battle site after the opening shots and before the Confederate ground assault. All five of the Anglos left, leaving somewhere about sixty-three or sixty-four German insurgents. At least twenty-eight German insurgents also "left early," including some of the wounded, leaving no more than thirty-six. This difference between Cramer's number of thirty-two and thirty-six likely means that about four other insurgents infiltrated out of the camp.

36. From Cramer's account it is plain that the Confederates made three charges on the camp and they were forced back each time.

37. The wounded included Gottlieb Vetterlein, Fritz Tegener, Franz Weiss, Ferdinand Simon, Henry Kammlah, William Vater, Karl Itz, Adolphus Zoeller, and an unidentified insurgent.

38. The survivors went up a deep draw to the northeast of the camp.

39. These men likely included August Hoffmann and some of his group who left because they had run out of ammunition.

40. The reason Cramer did not find the group is that Jacob Kuechler had moved further up the draw.

41. Phillipp Heinrich Weber was born on April 4, 1835, in Sulzbach, Nassau. He arrived in Texas on the *Washington* in 1845. Weber married Maria Elisabetha Christine Lanitz on February 12, 1860, in Kerr County. They were the parents of at least six children. He survived the battle, returned to Comfort, and hid until the end of the war. Phillipp Heinrich Weber died on January 12, 1920, at Comfort.

42. Confederate scouts captured Ferdinand Simon about August 13, 1862, and took him to Fort Clark. He died in the mid-1870s in Comfort.

43. This means the Confederates left the battle site on August 14, 1863.

44. Cramer began his journey back to Comfort on August 15, 1862.

45. Cramer arrived back in the Comfort area on August 22, 1862.

46. It was on August 23 when Cramer reached Boerne.

47. Cramer greatly exaggerates the number hanged; it was not close to a hundred men. Perhaps up to ten insurgents had been executed.

48. Cramer arrived in Leon Springs on August 29, 1862.

49. Richard Brotze was born about 1831 in Luzen, Germany. He arrived in Texas about 1849. Brotze was elected Kendall County sheriff on August 27, 1862, two days before he loaned Cramer the horse. He died about 1898, likely in Bexar County.

50. The other four were Joseph Elstner, Edward Felsing, Valentine Hohmann, and Henry Hermann.

## 14.  Letter – Col. H. E. McCulloch to Headquarters Department of Texas

March 27, 1862
Headquarters Sub-Military District of Rio Grande

Colonel Samuel Boyer Davis,
Acting Assistant Adjutant-General

Sir:

I find that many of the most notorious among the leaders of the opposition, or Union men, are leaving the country, principally in the direction of Mexico. Some of them, I have no doubt, are going simply to avoid the draft, and under its operations a participation in the present struggle with the North, while others are going to co-operate with a considerable number that have already entered Mexico, and are now at Monterrey and other points, doing all they can to prejudice our cause with the authorities of that country, and prepare the minds of the common people to take part against us in case there ever is a time when they dare call on them to do, and to act in concert with men of like feeling about Austin, this place, Fredericksburg, and other points were they are still living among us.

I have said, and I repeat, that there is, in my opinion, a considerable element of this character in this section that will have, ultimately (if the war becomes any more disastrous to us), to be crushed out, even if it has to be done without due course of law, or this county – the section in which I am stationed to protect and in which my family reside – will suffer.

In view of these things I have taken steps to prevent as far as possible the passage of these men out of the country into Mexico, by instructing the military under my command not to let any man go unless he is known to be our friend, and not then unless he can produce satisfactory evidence that he is not going to avoid the draft with which the State is threatened and which will come upon it.

I am fully aware of the responsibility of the step I have taken, and how much it perils my reputation as an officer, and how much it exposes my person and my domestic interest – my home, my wife and little ones – to the malignant acts of these cowardly traitors, but I believe it my duty to my country, and in here case I am willing to peril my all.

The force that I will have congregated here in a few days more will be sufficient to enable the State authorities to enforce the draft or do anything else that a military force may be required to do, and while I assure you that I shall take no step rashly or without reflection, I shall use it for the benefit of my country upon traitors at home if needs be.

Most respectfully, &ct.
H. E. McCulloch
Colonel First Regiment Texas Mounted Rifles,
C.S.P.A., Commanding District.

## 15. Letter–Col. H. E. McCulloch
## To Governor F. R. Lubbock

Headquarters Military District of Rio Grande
San Antonio, Texas, March 28th 1862

His Excellency
F. R. Lubbock Governor of Texas

Sir:

I have written you hitherto informing you that in my opinion the day was not distant when a necessity for martial law would present itself at this place and possibly at Austin, that day has about or nearly arrived. I have just been informed that the Germans in one quarter of this city have an organized a company of 73 men will armed with shot guns, rifles and pistols and plenty of ammunition who are connected with the Austin Party. These men intend watching their time and take the arsenal powder house and if they are forced to give them up will apply the match and blow up both. I have forces sufficient to prevent this and will as [act?], but these people are banding themselves together for mischief and it seem to me that their plans ought to be broken up. Nothing less then Martial Law will reach them and it ought to be declared. I am not opposed of the responsibility and would do it as every hazard but I desire to do what you might regard as an interferece with the operation of the civil laws and hence I unite [with] you again hoping to hear from you.

I am satisfied arrangements are making to resist the draft. I shall be ready to sustain it if necessary.

Your Obedient Servant
H. E. McCulloch
Colonel Commanding District

# 16. Letter–Col. H. E. McCulloch to Headquarters Department of Texas

March 31, 1862
Headquarters Sub-Military District of Rio Grande

Colonel Samuel Boyer Davis,
Acting Assistant Adjutant-General

Sir:

Inclosed you will find a copy of a notice stuck up in a prominent place in this city, written in a German hand, and showing plainly that it was written by a foreigner.

It may have been by some to array opposition to the character of the population, but it speaks the sentiments of a large portion of the population here, many of who are doing all they can to injure our cause secretly, and would do so openly if they dared.

Many Germans and some Americans are leaving here to avoid a participation in our struggle. I have directed the troops to permit none to go to Mexico, unless they have a pass from me, or can product evidence that they are our friends, and not leaving to avoid doing their duty to the country.

I have indicated plainly on other occasions that I deemed it *advisable to declare martial law here at some time, and I think the time has about arrived* [emphasis added] when it will have to be done.

I have force sufficient in the vicinity to enforce it if I declare it; and if I could know that it would not displease the commanding general if would be declared to-day.

Most respectfully, your obedient servant,
H. E. McCULLOCH,
Colonel 1$^{st}$ Regiment Texas Mounted Rifles, C.S.P.S.,
Commanding S.M.D. of Rio Grande

[Enclosure]

## NEWS

German brothers, are your eyes not opened yet? After rich took every picayune away from you, and the paper is worth only one-half what you so hard earned, now that have nothing left, now they go about and sell you, or throw you out of employment for Dunhauer, who left his wife and children, wants to do the same with you to the poor you might leave. Now is the time to stay [slay?] the heads of Dunhauer, Maverick, Mitchel, and Menger to the last bone. We are always ready. If the ignorant company of Newton fights you, do as you please. You will always stay the God damn Dutchman. Do away with that nuisance, and inform everybody the revolution is broke out.

It is a shame that Texas has such a brand. Hang them by their feet and burn them from below.

[Endorsement]

This was found sticking up since the letter was written; it was in German, and this is the translation.

McCULLOCH

# 17. Petition – Citizens of Spring Creek

The State of Texas
and County of Kimbal
April 22$^{nd}$ 1862

To his Excellency F. R. Lubbock – Governor of the State of Texas.

The undersigned citizens of Kimbal County, and Precinct No VI of Gillespie County ouring (sic) to the great danger to which we are exposed from the inclusions of our savage enemies and owing to the fact that most of us live entire by above the line of Posts lately established on the frontier, and the great necessity of having more effectual means of defense, so that this portion of the frontier will not be abandoned, have formed ourselves into a company of minute men to be mustered _____ and governed by the same rules regulations of the minute companies of 1861.

We further promise in case of an invasion for our cruel enemies of the Lincoln Government, we will do all we can to repel them, though our circumstances are such that it will not be in our power to go far from our homes being all of us men of families, and over and under, age and several of us having the families of those who are in the service to provide for and being scattered over so large a scope of Country, all of which circumstances combined will give your Excellency an idea of the amount of service we are able to render. We can do but little, but we feel anxious to be up and doing what we can in defense of our bleeding, and suffering country.

We therefore ask your Excellency to accept us as a company of minute men to act in the defense of our frontier.  _____ loyal petitioners will every pray ect.

## Names of Petitioners

R. A. Gibson (Captain)[1]
Thomas McDonald (1st Lieutenant)[2]
Martin McDonald (2nd Lieutenant)[3]
John Banta (Orderly Sergeant)[4]

| | |
|---|---|
| Joseph McDonald[5] | J. W. Locke[16] |
| Elijah Lacey[6] | Jesse Starr[17] |
| A. P. Lacey[7] | Andrew Starr[18] |
| John Lacey[8] | Frederick Harris[19] |
| Eli McDonald[9] | Wm Johnston[20] |
| A. B. Lacey[10] | J. N. Johnson[21] |
| John Joy[11] | P. G. Temple[22] |
| Rufus McDonald[12] | Bird Clements[23] |
| Robert P. Gibson[13] | Adam Clements[24] |
| J. A. McDonald[14] | T. T. Taylor[25] |
| Collins Lacey[15] | M. M. Taylor[26] |

P. S.  This list does not embrace all the names in the county and precinct above written and we are certain if we get an order from you for organizing this company that we can get as names as forty men to enlist.

Yours truly,
R. A. Gibson

Endorsement

Answer – that the Legislature having determined upon & fixed the manner of defending the frontier. I do not feel at liberty to accept the jurors? of company unenlised? of the Frontier Regiment which is very large & I trust will prove efficient.

That of course should any \_\_\_\_\_ _____ I might feel compelled to call out men but if I do so it would for action \_\_\_\_\_ and hunt, and kill Indians.

Allow(?) to the current law & say if in my power the people in the frontier shall be mustered.

ENDNOTES
Spring Creek Petition

01. Robert Alexander Gibson was born about 1814 in Knox County, Tennessee. He married Elizabeth Lackey about 1836, likely in Arkansas. They were the parents of at least ten children. The family arrived in Texas about 1843 and settled in Fannin County. During the war between the United States and Mexico, Gibson enlisted in Captain Robert H. Taylor's Company B, Michael Chevalier's Battalion, Texas Mounted Volunteer on February 24, 1847, in Fannin County. He was mustered out of service on June 30, 1848. By 1860 the family was living in Burnet County, and by early 1861 had moved to the Spring Creek area. Sometime in May of 1862 pro-Union bushwhackers raided his farm and burn his fences. After Captain James Duff left Gillespie, Gibson moved to eastern Gillespie County near the current community of Stonewall, where pro-Union bushwhackers again raided his farm. In retaliation Robert Gibson became a major leader of the *Haengerbande* [hanging gang]. He was in the raid that captured and hanged Louis Schuetze in February, 1864, and was part of the March 9, 1864, raid on South Grape Creek. He was one of nineteen men who "forted up" at Camp Davis in late March, 1864. Gibson was in the group which fled to Piedras Negras, Mexico, to avoid capture. Mexican authorities arrested the group and held them for Texas authorities. The circumstances of his death are not clear. According to John W. Samson, Gibson was killed in the escape attempt in June, 1864. However, according to August Siemering, Gibson was killed between Boerne and Fredericksburg in 1875. This second version is likely correct.

02. Thomas McDaniel McDonald was born on June 4, 1803, in Chatham County, North Carolina. He married Rachel Axley on June 14, 1827, in Monroe County, Illinois. They were the parents of at least eleven children. The family arrived in western Gillespie County about 1855. He testified that pro-Union bushwhackers burned the fences of Nixon's and that Warren Cass, a pro-Union bushwhacker, had shot at a Negro near the Nixon home. Thomas McDaniel McDonald died in 1870 in Harper in Gillespie County.

03. Louis Martin McDonald was born on September 29, 1835, in Jefferson County Illinois. By 1855, he was living in Gillespie County. Louis M. McDonald married Hester Ann Elizabeth Taylor on September 7, 1856, in Gillespie County. They were the parents of nine children. McDonald was likely a member of the Kerr [American] Company] of the Loyal League and was a pro-Union bushwhacker. By 1900 the family moved to Arizona. Louis Martin McDonald died May 22, 1924, in Douglas, Cochise County, Arizona.

04. John Walker Banta was born on February 22, 1833, in Princeton, Indiana. The family arrived in Texas in late 1839 and settled in Lamar and Fannin Counties. By 1850 the family was living in Hunt County. John Walker Banta married

Rebecca Angelina McDonald on January 22, 1860, in Gillespie County. They were the parents of at least eleven children. John W. Banta enlisted in Davis' Company, Frontier Regiment on March 4, 1862, and reenlisted in Hunter's Company, Frontier Regiment on December 24, 1862. He was appointed or elected the second sergeant. Banta remained with the company until the end of the war. John Walker Banta died on April 17, 1914, in Mason County.

05. Joseph McDonald was born in 1816 in Williamson County, Tennessee. He married Elizabeth Ester Taylor on March 22, 1832, in Monroe County, Illinois. They were the parents of six children. Elizabeth Ester Taylor McDonald died about 1847 in Illinois. Joseph McDonald married Rhoda Jane Nelson on February 15, 1849, in Jefferson County, Illinois. They were the parents of seven children. The family arrived in Gillespie County about 1851. Joseph McDonald was very likely a member of the Kerr [American] Company] of the League's battalion. He was one of thirteen men who "forted up" at Spring Creek in late March of 1864. Joseph McDonald died about 1890 in Gillespie County.

06. Elijah Lacey was born in 1804 in Livingston County, Kentucky. Ann Rankin and Lionel Lacey were his parents. The Lacey family moved to Madison County, Illinois, in 1807 and later to St. Clair County. On August 21, 1828, Elijah Lacey married Ruth McDonald Locke, the widow of Gerald Locke. They were the parents of eight children. In 1854 Lacey moved his family to Texas and by the early 1860s were living in western Gillespie County. Elijah Lacy was very likely a member of the Kerr [American] Company of the League's military battalion. Elijah Lacey died in 1885 in Tippecanoe County, Indiana.

07. Asa Phelps Lacey was born on May 18, 1830, in St. Clair County, Illinois. Asa P. Lacey married Rosanna England on July 26, 1849, in Marion County Illinois. They were the parents of eight children. By 1850, they were living in Jackson County, Illinois. The family arrived in Gillespie County about 1854. Asa P. Lacey was a member of the Kerr [American] Company of the League's military battalion. Lacey enrolled in Hunter's Company, Frontier Regiment on August 8, 1863, at Camp Davis. He was one of thirteen men who "forted up" at Spring Creek in late March, 1864. He fled the Hill Country and on May 1, 1864, enlisted in Company A, First Regiment [Union] Texas Cavalry in Brownsville. He was court-martialed on March 27, 1865, for leaving his quarters without a pass and fined $5.00. Lacey remained with the company until the end of the war and he was mustered out of service on October 31, 1865, in San Antonio. Asa Phelps Lacey died on July 3, 1913, in Asher, Pottawatomie County, Oklahoma.

08. John Bunyon Lacey was born about 1843 in Illinois. The family arrived in Texas in 1854 and living in Gillespie County by 1855. John B. Lacey was very likely a member of the Kerr [American] Company of the League's

military battalion. He enrolled in Hunter's Company, Frontier Regiment on July 10, 1863, at Camp Davis. He was a member of Locke's, Company, Third Frontier District on January, 1864. Lacey was the first lieutenant of Wahrmund's Company, Third Frontier District on April, 1864. He was one of nineteen men who "forted up" at Camp Davis in late March, 1864. John B. Lacey married Lucy Ann Dunn, on September 16, 1866, in Gillespie County. No further data.

09. Eli McDonald, Sr. was born about 1837 in Illinois. The family arrived in Texas in 1854 and living in Gillespie County by 1855. He married Caroline Taylor on November 28, 1856, in Gillespie County. They were parents of at least four children. Eli McDonald, Sr. was very likely a member of the Kerr [American] Company of the League's military battalion. Eli McDonald, Sr. and two of his children were killed by Indians on August 8, 1864, in Gillespie County.

10. No information location on this individual.

11. John William Joy was born on July 8, 1832, in Sebastian, Bloomington County, Arkansas. John W. Joy married Nancy War in 1852 in Arkansas. They were the parents of at least fourteen children. The family arrived in western Gillespie County in late 1850s. They first settled in Doss Valley, then at Spring Creek. During the Gillespie court term of the fall of 1859, John W. Joy was indicted for the September 27, 1859, robbery of William G. Thomas. He was a member of the Kerr [American] Company of the League's military battalion. He enrolled in Wahrmund's company of the Third Frontier District on April 15, 1864. He is shown as deserted in August, 1864. John W, Joy was indicted for the August 22, 1864, theft of two horses from William Wahrmund and one from Fritz Wilke. He claimed he was a member of the Union "Special Service" as a private from December 27, 1864, until May 31, 1865. He was a pro-Union vigilante. He died on June 19, 1921, in Kimball County. His tombstone shows he was a private in the U. S. Army.

12. Isaac Rufus McDonald was born about 1838 in Illinois. He was a son of Joseph McDonald above. The family arrived in Texas about 1851. McDonald married Polly Jane Lockhart on November 13, 1860, in Gillespie County. They were the parents of at least eight children. McDonald was a member of Locke's Company, Third Frontier District of January, 1864. He was of thirteen men who "forted up" at Spring Creek in late March, 1864. McDonald enrolled in Wahrmund's company on April, 1864. He remained with the company until the end of the war. Isaac Rufus McDonald died on May 16, 1905, in Kimble County and is buried in the Harper cemetery.

13. Robert Peal Gibson was born on May 28, 1847, in Fannin County. The family arrived in Gillespie County in 1861. Pro-Union bushwhackers raided his

father's farm and burned his crops. In retaliation the senior Gibson and Robert P. Gibson became pro-Confederate bushwhackers. Gibson enrolled in Hunter's Company, Frontier Regiment on August 12, 1863. Gibson took part in the capture and hanging of Louis Schuetze and Warren Cass, in February, 1864. He was one of those who raided the South Grape Creek settlement which killed John Blank and William Feller on March 9, 1864. Robert P. Gibson was arrested but he escaped in June, 1864. He returned to Hunter's company where he remained until the end of the war. Robert P. Gibson married Penina (Nina) Pollen [maiden name not known] known. They were the parents of at lease three children. Robert Peal Gibson died on January 25, 1933, near Montell in northwest Uvalde County.

14. No information on this individual.

15. Joshua Collins Lacey was born on March 5, 1842, in Jefferson County, Illinois. The family moved to Texas about 1854 and settled in Gillespie County. He was very likely a member of the Kerr [American] Company of the League's military battalion. Lacey fled Texas and enrolled in Company A, First Regiment [Union] Texas Cavalry on October 28, 1862, in New Orleans. He was wounded on October 1, 1863, and captured on October 4, 1863. He escaped from the Confederate Hospital at Alexandria and returned to duty on December 20, 1863. Lacey was mustered out of service on October 31, 1865, at San Antonio. On December 25, 1867, Lacey married Cloe Irena Elizabeth Fairchild in Gillespie County. His wife's father had been hanged by pro-Confederate bushwhackers. Cloe and Joshua Lacey were the parents of nine children. He was a Texas Ranger in 1872. Lacey moved his family to Lincoln County, New Mexico, where he died on January 25, 1901.

16. William Jackson Locke was born on November 27, 1828, in Illinois. He married Mary England on September 9, 1848 in Marion County, Illinois. They were the parents of eight children. The family arrived in Texas about 1854. Locke was a member of the Kerr [American] Company of the League's military battalion. He was elected captain of the Gillespie Company, Third Frontier District on January 27, 1864. Locke fled to Mexico and on March 4, 1865 he enlisted in Company B, Second Regiment [Union] Texas Cavalry. He resigned on July 7, 1865, and returned to the Hill Country. William Jackson Locke died on October 13, 1911, in Bexar Country.

17. Jesse Star was born about 1846 in Pulaski, Missouri. He was a brother of Andrew Starr, below. The family lived in Camden County, Missouri, in 1850 and 1860. The date he arrived in Texas is not known, but it was by April of 1862. He was very likely a member of the Kerr [American] Company of the League's military battalion. Starr fled Texas to Mexico and on to New Orleans where he joined Company A, First Regiment [Union] Texas Cavalry

on March 30, 1863. Starr deserted at White Rancho near Brownsville on August 4, 1864. Texas Rangers killed him in the fall or spring of 1864/1865.

18. Andrew Hamilton Starr was born on January 16, 1828, in Jackson County, Ohio. He was a brother of Jesse Starr, above. The family lived in Camden County, Missouri, in 1850. Andrew Hamilton Starr married Charity Mason Talley on March 20, 1855, likely in Camden County, Missouri. They were the parents of at least ten children. By 1860 they were living in Bastrop County, Texas, and by April, 1862, in the Texas Hill Country. Starr was a member of the Kerr [American] Company of the league's military battalion. He died on December 16, 1889, likely in Atascosa County.

19. Frederick Harris was born on March 9, 1837, in Dallas County, Missouri. By 1850, the family was living in Pope County, Arkansas. Frederick Harris married Catherine Starr in Dallas County, Missouri, on January 6, 1857. They were the parents of at least four children. Harris arrived in the Hill Country by April, 1862. He was very likely a member of the Kerr [American] Company of the League's military battalion. Harris fled Texas and on May 17, 1864, enlisted in Company A, First Regiment [Union] Texas Cavalry. He remained with the company until the end of the war and he was mustered out of service on October 31, 1865, at San Antonio. Catherine Starr Harris died in Williamson County, Texas in 1865. Harris married Mary Amanda Manis on January 3, 1867, in Burleson County. They were the parents of at least eleven children. Frederick Harris died on January 11, 1918, in Knox County, Texas.

20. No addition data located on this individual.

21. James N. Johnson, Jr., was born on October 7, 1843, in Indiana. Johnson arrived in the Hill Country by April, 1862. He was likely a member of the Kerr [American] Company of the League's military battalion. Johnson fled Texas and on October 27, 1862, he enlisted in Company A, First Regiment [Union] Texas Cavalry. He was promoted to corporal on January 1, 1864, and mustered out of service on October 31, 1865, at San Antonio. Johnson married Mary Elisabeth Smyth on November 8, 1866, in Kerr County. They were the parents of at least five children. Johnson was a Kerr County commissioner in 1867 and from 1871 until 1873. James N. Johnson died in El Paso on Mach 17, 1922.

22. Philip G. Temple was born in March 1826 in Ohio. He served in Company E, 2nd Regiment Kentucky Infantry during the Mexican War. Temple arrived in Texas about 1858 or 1859 and in the Hill Country by early 1862. He was the first lieutenant of the Kerr [American] Company of the League's military battalion. He fled Texas in late 1862, and enrolled in Company A, First Regiment [Union] Texas Cavalry on October 27, 1862, in New Orleans. He was appointed first lieutenant on November 6, 1862. Temple was wounded in

the Rancho Las Rucias battle on June 25, 1864. He remained with the company until the end of the war. After the war Temple returned to the Hill Country. Due to illness he returned to his family home in Clermont County, Ohio, in 1896. Philip G. Temple died on February 28, 1903, in Clermont County, Ohio.

23. Bird Clements was very likely a member of the Kerr [American] Company of the League's military battalion. He was likely a brother or father/son of Adam Clements, below. No further data.

24. Adam Clements was very likely a member of the Kerr [American] Company of the League's military battalion. He was likely a brother or father/son of Bird Clements above. No further data.

25. Thurman Thompson Taylor was born on December 14, 1825, in Monroe County, Illinois. He was the son of Matthew M. Taylor, below. The family arrived in Hunt County, Texas by 1850. T. T. Taylor married Elizabeth Catherine Alexander on April 27, 1852, in Hunt County. They were the parents of at least eleven children. By April, 1862, the family was living in the Texas Hill Country.Taylor was a member of Harbour's Kerr County Minuteman Company of February, 1861, and very likely a member of the Kerr [American] Company of the League's military battalion. The Confederates arrested Taylor; on October 2, 1862, he was tried by the Confederate Military Commission. He was acquitted and agreed to enroll in Hunter's Company of the Frontier Regiment and did so on December 24, 1862, at Camp Davis. In early 1865 Taylor deserted and on February 2, 1865, he enrolled in Company A, Second Regiment [Union] Texas Cavalry in New Orleans and was mustered out of service on November 10, 1865, in Brownsville. He returned to the Hill Country. Taylor died in Hidalgo County, New Mexico, in 1912.

26. Matthew Modglin Taylor was born on January 25, 1802, in Williamson County, Tennessee. He married Hannah Smith Axley on October 1, 1822, in Monroe County, Illinois. They were the parents of at least eight children. The family arrived in Texas about 1848 and settled in Hunt County. By 1860, they were living in Kerr County. Matthew Modglin Taylor died on August 1, 1880, at Harper in Gillespie County.

# 18. General Bee's Proclamation of Martial Law in Bexar County

Headquarters
Headquarters of Sub Military District of Rio Grande
San Antonio, April 28, 1862

General Order No 5

In power of my appointment as brigadier general in the Provisional Army of the Confederates States and as commanding officer of the Sub-military District of Rio Grande, I hereby order that the military jurisdiction of the camp of the Confederate soldiers in Salado, Bexar County, be further expanded so that it includes the city of San Antonio and Bexar County, and that martial law be declared within the these boundaries.

Every white male older than 16 years, who resides temporarily or otherwise within the above mentioned boundaries, either as citizen of the Confederate States or as a stranger, should report within six days of publication of this order to the office of the marshal of San Antonio, register his name, and give particulars, what is demanded of him.

The ones which claim to be citizens shall sign an unconditional oath of faith to the Confederate States; the ones which claim to be strangers should swear that they submit to the laws of this state and the Confederate States as long as they are permitted to stay and under no circumstances to inform our enemies with regard to the military and political matters of this country.

Person which since the 21$^{st}$ of May 1861 arrived from any state which is at war with the Confederates, into the above described jurisdiction to satisfy the authorities about the purpose of their coming and the reasons for staying, which if satisfactory, will be issued a permit to remain here. This permit shall be signed by the commanding officer general or the county provost marshal and the time for which such permit is granted be determined and be subject to renewal from time to time through an endorsement, which determines the extension period.

All orders which are issued by country provost marshal in the duty of his office will be immediately obeyed; every disobedience against these orders will entail a trial and all officers commanding troops are hereby instructed to immediately submit to every claim which is made by the country provost marshal in matters of help and aid.

All places for the sale of liquor shall be closed from eight at night until six in the morning. Every transgression of this order shall entail the closing of his business forever.

Every attempt to devalue the standard (currency) of the Confederate States will be considered an act of aggression and will be punished. This is the medium with which the nation leads the war and any refusal to support the circulation thereof by devaluing the nominal worth weakens our government. This will not be done by loyal men and shall not be done by our enemies. Nobody shall be permitted to engage in business or trade who will not accept Confederate money at its full value.

Our country requires the services, the support, and the sympathy of all her sons and while all of these are offered at free will, we will not allow that non-loyal people, which are corrupted by the gold of the enemy or driven by wicked dislike or fanatism (sic), destroy the fruits of patriotism; in that we say that those step into the way of our preparations by word or deed or thwart our measures which are necessary to secure the success of our good cause.

To free our country of those, martial law is declared.

No involvement into the rights of loyal citizens will be permitted if not needed for their preservation or for execution of this order. The usual way of business will not be interrupted and the governing civil authority of the law disturbed.

J. R. Sweet has been appointed county provost marshal.

On order of Brigadier General H. P. Bee.


E. F. Gray
Major, and A.A.A.G.

## 19. Letter–Fritz Tegener

Austin, August 23, 1875

Herr August Duecker[1]
Gillespie Co., Texas

Old Friend:

You are probably wondering why, after such a long time, you are hearing from me. I like for you to do me the favor of collecting all signatures in your county of all our friends which took part in the fight at the West Nueces on August 10, 1862, and ask them for me to sign the attached statement. The reason for that is the following: The *Galveston Post* published in the Nr 39[2] issue of this year a description of the fight at the Nueces. Some of it was described correctly, some of it was not. I intend to correct the article. It came from a notice in the *Freie Presse*[3], where it said that not Fritz Tegener, but Jacob Kuechler[4] was the leader at the Nueces, and that the *Freie Presse* will be publishing in the near future a detailed description of the fight. This description then was indeed published in the Nr. 7 issue of the *Freie Presse* on Saturday, August 14, 1875.[5] This description says that there were 68 men under the leadership of Mr. Jacob Kuechler. However, we where not 68 men but 65[6], and were not under the leadership of Mr. Kuechler but that of Mr. Fritz Tegener, because I remember the list, for I had all the names of our people in a pocket notebook in order to assign the guards for each evening.[7] You and all the others who were with us at the Nueces will probably remember that you made me the leader (major) at Bear Creek Spring, which I remember well. It was the assembly at Bear Creek in the beginning of May, 1862[8], where we chose at the same time Kuechler as captain for

Gillespie Co.[9], Hartman as captain of the Americans[10], and Cramer, who then lived near Comfort at the time, as captain of the Union Army from Comfort and surrounding area of Kendall Co.[11], and that there was never a second election as long as we were together, and that my orders were followed as far as the volunteers were concerned, who all clothed and armed themselves, and who did not receive or expect any payment for their service.

In order to truthfully correct these wrong statements, I am asking you to present our old comrades from the Nueces in your county with these facts and possible try to get a hold of the issue of the *Freie Presse* which carried the article, so that you may be familiar with the statements. In the end it does not matter who was the leader anyway. But if the *Freie Presse* or Mr. Siemering try to change historical facts on purpose, it is our duty as the survivors to honor the ones that died, by attacking such lies and at the same time correcting them.

Therefore, my old fellows from 1862, I am pleading with you to sign the attached writing after you have read my reasons for it, so that armed in such a way, I can confront these remarks.

With all my best regards to all of you who shared the dangers with me.

I remain your old friend.

s/Fritz Tegener

Immediately return the attached statement as soon as it is signed by our friends, because I have to give a response to Mr. Siemering as soon as possible.

Your s/Fritz Tegener

ENDNOTES
Letter Fritz Tegener

01. August Duecker was born in 1828 in Prussia. Duecker was very likely a Forty-Eighter. The family arrived in Texas on the *Texas* in 1853. August Duecker married Louise Feuge on June 11, 1854, in Gillespie County. They were the parents of four children. He received his U. S. citizenship on May 20, 1858. Duecker was a member of Braubach's home guard company from February, 1861, until February, 1862. He was the second sergeant in Kuechler's company of December, 1861. He was a member of the Gillespie Company of the League's military battalion. He was also a member of the "Luckenbach Bushwhackers" and a member of the fleeing insurgent group. He survived the Nueces battle and returned to Gillespie County where he hid in the family attic. Louise Feuge Duecker took ill and died on January 1, 1863. In order to escape imprisonment he agreed to be a teamster for the Confederates. However, Captain Frank Van der Stucken arrested him in mid-1863. He was held in jail in Austin. Oral accounts state he escaped and returned to Gillespie County. On February 22, 1866, August Duecker married Wilhelmine Knetsch Lindemann, the widow of widow of John A. Lindemann in Comal County. They were the parents of seven children. August Duecker died on April 19, 1894, in Gillespie County.

02. A copy of this edition has not been located.

03. A copy of this edition has not been located.

04. For biographical information of Jacob Kuechler see endnote number 4 in Document #1, p.19.

05. A copy of this edition has not been located.

06. This is additional proof that sixty-five insurgents left the Hill Country in August of 1862 for Mexico.

07. This notebook was captured after the Nueces battalion. It has not been located.

08. Tegener is incorrect regarding the date the insurgents met on Bear Creek. It was in March, 1862. See Endnote 11 of Document #13, p.83.

09. For the names of the officers of the Gillespie Company see Document #1, p.17.

10. For the names of the officers of the Kerr [American] Company see Document #1, p.17.

11. For the names of the officers of the Comfort [Kendall] Company see Document #1, pp. 17-18.

## 20.    Extract - D. P. Hopkins'[1] Diary

I left San Marcos on Wednesday morning at 9:30 o'clock (sun time), the 26th day of February 1862, with many sorrowful thoughts and forebodings to our dear Southland; for I must tell you right now that I voted against secession, but the thing [is] inevitable, so I though of the girl I left behind, and whistled to keep up my drooping spirits (the best brand), I am a member of the Sons of Temperance so do not make any mistake as to the kind of sprits I am talking about.

* * *

**FEBRUARY 27.** Arose early; felt lonesome; had a light breakfast and was soon on the road again. I forgot to state for future information my horse's name was Thomas Jefferson, in honor of the great patriot of that name, but Thomas J., don't know it. About 12 o'clock we arrived in the City of Pittsburg (now Blanco), as we were informed by the one citizen that lived there. In honor of our arrival, our boys sang "Run, Yank or Die." It was here we got a glimpse of the first Confederate flag since we started. Camped and rested our horses until 4 o'clock in the evening; saddled up and traveled until 6 o'clock, camped for the night in the mountains. There I witnessed the most beautiful sight I ever say (except my girl). The grass had been set on fire, burning in serpentine rounds, around and up the mountain declivities, it was indeed a beautiful sight. Staked Thomas J. out. Was awful lonesome; retired early and though of _____ and fell asleep.

**FEBRUARY 28.** Didn't get off until 8 o'clock. I discovered that some of the other boys were lonesome as well as myself. Traveled until 12 o'clock and stopped on small creek for dinner, rations were getting short, but we were all so lonesome we did not mind that. Half past one we were on the march again, and about 4 o'clock arrived at old "Fort Martin Scott," two miles south of the German town Fredericksburg. The old fort was built in 1848, and was named for Col. Martin Scott of United States Army, but had been abandoned many years and was in a complete state of dilapidation and decay for want of care and attention. Camped in clump of bushes near the old fort and during the night a cold norther sprang up, and I thought I would freeze before we could get a fire started.

\* \* \*

**TUESDAY, MARCH 4.** All hands and the cook were ordered to town to be mustered into service. I felt like I was bidding farewell to earth, liberty sweetheart and everything else; but I said nothing and thought of the girl I left behind. In due time we were lined up, ninety-six strong, facing a blue norther, the dust nearly blinding us. There being a surplus of men from Gillespie County, it became necessary to draw lots for the numbers that should be entitled to join the company. The first man to draw was the captain of the German Company. He drew a blank whereupon the whole German outfit became indignant, and backed out, which caused much rejoicing among our San Marcos boys as that gave our surplus a surety of getting in (this was a volunteer company). I should explain that Col. J. M. Norris had been ordered to raise a regiment of ten companies of 100 men to each company to be taken from the counties named in their order, one-third each. Our company was to be made up of one-third each from Hays, Gillespie and Kerr; and we had about sixty men, so when the Germans got knifed and backed out, our boys had a sure thing. After the excitement and the big talk had simmered down, we were sworn in hard and fast. We were sworn in bunches, five at a time, which I thought was a piece of foolishness, when we were facing a cold norther and long past the dinner hour. The company then proceeded to organize. It was foregone conclusion that Henry Davis was to be captain. He was duly elected without any opposition.

\* \* \*

**FRIDAY, MARCH 14.** We were early on the march and late in the evening went into camp on the mouth of Johnson's Creek, which empties into the Guadalupe River in Kerr County; where we expected to remain for six weeks if not longer, or until further orders; to make a permanent camp. We are now waiting for the general staff to put in an appearance as follows: J. M. Norris, colonel commanding; James E. O'Benchain, lieutenant colonel; James E. McCord, major; Alexander Conly, adjutant. We are now without ammunition and in an Indian country and should they attack us wouldn't we be in a box! No, we wouldn't be in a box; for there would be some of the tallest running done that was ever heard of.

\* \* \*

**SUNDAY, MARCH 16.** This day I record the arrival of James M. Hunter, first lieutenant and quartermaster, which would naturally indicate that he had bought something to eat, but the indications did not pan out. He didn't bring a thing, and not much of that. The company was now divided, one-half under the immediate command of Captain Davis, and the other half under the command of Lieutenant Harbour, known as the first and second detachments, but the captain had the general supervision. After the second detachment had left for their station, Captain Davis departed for Austin. What he went for, no one appeared to know; and Lieutenant Hunter went in search of something to eat. We had good grass and plenty of water, so our horses fared well. Right here I would remark our company had been treated shamefully. Our field and staff officers were appointed before our company was mustered into service and they knew the day and place of meeting, our destination, and not a thing to eat–ordered to the frontier at once (with empty guns)–no ammunition and plenty of Indians. We were promised twenty-five dollars a month in Confederate money, but that was only a promise.

\* \* \*

**WEDNESDAY, APRIL 2.** Today we raised the confederate flag over our camp, sang "Dixie" and things looked military. When I saw the flag hoisted, it did not appear to me like the old "Stars and Stripes" and I did not cheer. I seemed as if some foreign power had invaded our soil, and dared to raise their flag.

\* \* \*

**SATURDAY, APRIL 6.** We were drilling when the wagons came to haul our plunder to the new camp on White Oak Creek, and the boys were so elated with the news and the fact of moving that they broke ranks, not waiting for orders and nearly run over the captain; but, golly, wasn't he mad! After considerable hurrying and fussing around we bade farewell to the old camp, and took up the line of march to the new camp on White Oak Creek. The men were ordered to fall in line and march in regular order, but long before we reached the new camp (about twenty miles) the men were scattered out of sight, front and rear; but before night set in they were all in camp. We have a beautiful camp situated on a high bluff of the creek, with a dense growth of fine postoak timber on the camp side, and in the valley on the opposite side about ten thousand acres of prairie and fine grass and a spring of good water (now the Morris ranch). Quite an excitement was caused by the boys jumping up a fox in camp. The shooting sounded something like a small battle; but the fox escaped.

\* \* \*

**THURSDAY, APRIL 24.** Today a German came in camp all out of breath and reported Indians in the vicinity in large numbers, but we did not believe a word of it; as they were guilty of such reports so as to harass and annoy the troops. You know the Germans were bitterly opposed to the war.

\* \* \*

**SUNDAY, MAY 4.** General inspection – out in our new uniforms; I forget about the new uniforms – jacket and pants – the cloth was made in the Texas penitentiary of pure white wool. When the company got in line they looked like a young snow storm, except the orderly sergeant, he flamed out in the new blue jacket the captain had given him, had yellow stripes on both sleeves – that was me.

\* \* \*

**FRIDAY, JULY 18.** Capt. Frank van der Stucken's company of soldiers passed through town, making complete fools of themselves, just because they had on brass coats with blue buttons. (sic)I very much doubt their loyalty.

\* \* \*

**THURSDAY, JULY 31.** Shucked off my coat and started for the woods, with chopping ax in hand, indicating what was going to be done. On my arrival at the creek bottom I saw on the opposite side of the creek one of Duff's men making some queer motions. As I could not tell what the performance was going to be, decided to wait and see. He pulled off his coat, rolled up his sleeves, made a fire and put on a pot of water, and it then occurred to me that he was going to cook something to eat. I was on the point of moving forward at once and secure an introduction, when I saw him pull off his shirt and put it in the pot. My hopes of something good to eat were dashed, and I knew at once that he was one of the gang that had but one suit of clothes. I did not remain for further information.

\* \* \*

**SUNDAY, AUGUST 3.** Only four men in camp all told. Sunday evening our captain called on Capt. James Duff. Duff camped about one mile below us. They must have had a good time, for Duff was rich and had everything he wanted that money could buy.

\* \* \*

**MONDAY, AUGUST 4.** Some of the scouts having returned, a new detail was made, and we resumed work on the commissary building. About 9 o'clock George Glasscock came into camp with four large wagons, six yokes of oxen to each wagon, loaded with shelled corn and oats, to the great joy of the men, as grass was getting short. The remainder of the men in camp, not in the commissary, were detailed to unload the corn. A slight observation of the men unloading the wagons only went to prove what I have said before. A majority of the men in camp were too darned lazy to be healthy; but this may have been caused by the high altitude or the thin atmosphere in this section of the country.

\* \* \*

**TUESDAY, AUGUST 5.** As our regular scouts came in today they found a man hanging right over the trail with his throat cut from ear to ear. Learned his named was Howell, and hung over our trail by some of Duff's men, for two purposes. First, to leave the impression that our boys had done it; and second, we would have to burry (sic) him. D---- scoundrels. And sure enough came the order for our boys from old Duff for our boys to bury the dead man. Don't you think there were not lots of Sunday school lesions (sic) said about it? Poor man, his troubles were over in this world.

\* \* \*

**SUNDAY, AUGUST 10**. No inspection today. In fact, we have had no inspection since we were under command of Jim Duff. He keeps our men on the jump. He and his men lay in camp and drink good whiskey and smoke the best of cigars. He has the appointment of provost marshal for this district, upon the recommendation of General Bee and Governor Lubbock.

\* \* \*

**WEDNESAY, AUGUST 13**. More honor in the family. The commissioned officers all being absent, by order of Captain Duff, and I being the ranking non-commissioned officer, was of course in command–actually in full command of a military post in time of war; and it was so sudden, too. Actually, I could hardly eat my breakfast – forgot to curry Thomas J. – failed to make out the morning report. I hardly knew which one of the boys I was – to see how rapidly I had risen (in my own estimation).

\* \* \*

**FRIDAY, AUGUST 15**. Camp nearly deserted. I have become somewhat accustomed to being commanding officer in camp. Why, I can even entertain distinguished company with considerable ease and comfort. The guests sit and talk while I do the cooking.

\* \* \*

**SATURDAY, AUGUST 16.** A fellow citizen came into camp, and reported that our scouts up the country, had had a fight with the bushwhackers, losing one man on our side killed, and forty of the enemy killed. About 8 o'clock p. m. an order came from Captain Duff (to me, the commanding officer of the camp!) to send a squad of men at once to intercept fourteen of the men who had escaped in the fight and were reported coming this way. When this was done, I ordered the camp to be placed on a war footing at once. I sent out pickets, in case of a sudden attack – only three men in the camp. If the camp was attacked I had figured out how I could escape.

\* \* \*

**THURSDAY, AUGUST 21.** Arose early – in fact, did not do anything but rise all night, trying to keep the hogs from eating us up. Got some corn from the mill and fed our horses. Did not eat any breakfast – the hogs had got in ahead of us. Went to town. Saw the conscripts. They had long faces, and some of the good old German women had longer faces. Some of them sobbed as if their hearts would break. O those dear old mothers, wives and sweethearts – I did certainly sympathize with the sweethearts, for I had not forgotten the girl I left behind. From there I went to the hotel for dinner. Waited until away after dinner, and no dinner appeared. I got mad, and asked the landlord why he did not bring on dinner, when he began talking German to me. I gave him a cussing – no breakfast; no dinner. The wagon being loaded at 4 o'clock, we started for our camp. About five miles from town, another heavy raid fell. Golly, how the rain did come down. I think in three minutes the water was feet deep in the road. It is needless to say we got soaking wet. Arrived at Pedernales about 9 o'clock into the night so dark we could not see a black cat. Drove into the creek and found it nearly swimming. Came near being washed away. Stalled and had to unload 1,500 pounds of flour and meal. After much labor, we got the wagon out; reloaded and started for camp; but soon discovered that we were lost – hollered, and whooped and yelled until we were hoarse but not a thing could we hear but the occasional yelp of a wolf or hoot of an owl; but we were not hunting for them at that time. After wandering about for apparently a week, running against a tree every semi-occasionally, we reached camp at 1 o'clock in the morning, completely exhausted. I do not want to be an escort for the wagon any more.

* * *

**FRIDAY, AUGUST 22.** Our big scout got in from the bushwhackers fight on Nueces River. The men on our side were made up from the different companies of our regiment, and part of Duff's independent company, commanded by Major A. J. Donelson, an adopted son of Gen. Andrew Jackson (Old Hickory). There were two men killed and eighteen wounded on our side; and thirty bushwhackers killed. A number of prisoners were taken; but all got away, so the boys said; and I knew they would not lie about a little thing like that. We are having tough times in this neck of the woods these times. I counted seven men hung on one limb; cut down and thrown over the bluff into Spring Creek. One old gray-headed man, named Nelson, 80 years old, was among the number. When the body rose to the top of the water some women lifted him out in a sheet and buried him. Speaking of the fight, while our men were fighting like tigers, Duff's men were gobbling up the six-shooters and valuables. There came near being trouble over it, as our boys would not stand for it.

* * *

**SATURDAY, AUGUST 23.**  One of the wounded men died today; and three each had an arm cut off.  My book is full.  I have written the last page.  Here ends my diary.

## 21. Captain de Montel's Report[1] – March 16. 1862

Camp Ives
March 16, 1862

Colonel:

I have the pleasure to inform you that I have on the 14th instant called in the difference detachments from Blanco County and upper Medina and on the 15th took up the line of march to occupy my respective stations on the line according to the orders of Colonel Norris[2]. I have for the present left Lieut Gates[3] with 25 men to occupy the secio pass and confidently believe that he will succeed in intersecting the Indians who are raiding us [and] killing several head of cattle on their way down some 5 or six days ago. I hope this move will not interfere with the formation of the line. My command being divided in two detachments on the Secio and one on the Nueces which stations I will still occupy with the only difference of a smaller force in each the distance between my stations on the Frio and that of Cap Davis on the West Prong of Medina being 40 miles and too far and inpractible for Scouts to pass over in one day–by placing the Command in Lieut Gates I am able to keep up daily connection and better ground to travel over. We had considerable sickness in Bandera Camps the measles broke out among the men and I had to engage medical assistance. The men of my company subscribed one dollar each to pay Dr.Fowler in case the State should refuse to pay him.

*I wish (illegible) you and inform his Excellency that Medina County has organized 3 of the Militia companys 9/10 of which are not only Black Republicans by principle but quite a number of are abolitionists. They have elected the men of their own stamp to command them calculate to keep all together when they are ordered out and join the enemy the 1^{st} opportunely they get.[4] The men P. Kiefer[5] and Jacob Haby[6] from Castroville as will as Richarz[7] from the Secio are bitter enemies to the South I consider it my duty to give this information but pray not use my name in anything that may be done so my wife and children are down there among them unprotected and I fear they would burn my property some night.* [Emphasis added]

To:
Colonel J. Y. Dashiell
Adj & Insp General at Austin.

I remain very respectfully
your most obedient servant,
Charles de Montel
Captain Comg Company of Frontier Regiment

Editorial note: Every effort has been made to keep the original spelling and grammar on the source document. There where several case where the original word could not be clearly determined. An effort has been made to insert what is believed to be the original word, followed by (sic). In those cases where the word could not be determined at all, a blank _____ is inserted.

120

*Wm. Paul Burrier*

ENDNOTES
Captain de Montel's Report March 16, 1862

01. Charles Alexander de Montel was born Charles Scheidemontel on October 24, 1812, in Koenigburg, Prussia. Montel first immigrated to Pennsylvania and then to Texas in 1837. He was a guide and surveyor for the Henri Castro colonies and accompanied the first settlers when they established Castroville in September, 1844. Charles de Montel married Justine Pingenot on November 13, 1845, in Castroville. They were the parents of nine children. de Montel was the first Medina County clerk. In 1852, he and John James surveyed Bandera County and Montel was appointed a commissioner to hold the election for the new county. de Montel was a Medina County delegate to the Texas Secession Convention and in January of 1861 he signed the Declaration of Secession. In February of 1862 he was appointed enrollment officer and captain of Company D [G], Frontier Regiment and later the Bandera and Medina Counties' provost marshal. After a year with the Frontier Regiment de Montel was commissioned a naval commander and placed in command of the steamer *Texas*. In early 1864, he returned to Bandera and Medina Counties and on March 1, 1864, raised a twenty-one-man volunteer company for Colonel John S. Ford's "Cavalry of the West." Charles A. de Montel died on August 3, 1882, in Bandera County.

02. James Madison Norris was born on November 13, 1819, in Greenville District, South Carolina. He married Sophronia Elizabeth Robinson about 1839, likely in South Carolina. They were the parents of five children. He and his family arrived in Texas about 1840, and first settled in the vicinity of Burleson and Brazos Counties. By 1860, they were living in Coryell County. Governor Lubbock appointed him commander of the Frontier Regiment in February, 1862. He served until February of the following year. After the war Norris and his family lived in McLennan County where he died on April 21, 1874.

03. Amos Valentine Gates was born on August 29, 1825, in Texas. He married Martha V. Johnson on September 17, 1852, in Washington County. They were the parents of at least two children. Martha V. Johnson Gates died in 1857. Amos V. Gates married Margaret Harrison on May 25, 1858, likely in Blanco County. They were the parents of eight children. Gates enrolled in Blackwell's Blanco County Minuteman Company in May, 1861, and served until January, 1862. Gates served as chief justice of Blanco County from November, 1861, until March 20, 1862, at which time he enrolled in de Montel's Company, Frontier Regiment. He was elected second lieutenant and served until February 9, 1863. Gates was again elected Blanco's chief justice on June 25, 1866, but was removed by the Texas Reconstruction government. Amos Valentine Gates died on November 5, 1912, in Kendall County.

04. This "independent battalion" was authorized in the law passed in December of 1861, when all the precincts and counties were placed in a military brigade district to provide for defense of the state in case of a Union invasion. The majority of the citizens in Medina County were Unionists or at least Unionist sympathizers. Instead of organizing a secret military unit, they used the authorized Medina state unit, and controlled the battalion leadership and the four companies through elections.

05. Blasins Kieffer was born about 1835 in France. The date he arrived in Texas is not known. Kieffer married Adeline Halerdier on January 12, 1859, in Medina County. They were the parents of at least six children. Kieffer was a member of the Castroville Castle of the Knights of the Golden Circle. He was the commander of Company C, Medina County Independent Battalion of the 31$^{st}$ Brigade District. He was one of the Medina County men arrested by Duff in June, 1862. The Confederate Military Commission dismissed the charges and released him on July 28, 1862. Kieffer was elected a Medina County commissioner in August, 1862. Andrew Jackson Hamilton, military governor of Texas, appointed Kieffer as justice of the peace on August 24, 1865. Adeline Halerdier Kieffer died about 1866. Kieffer appears on the 1867 Voter Rejections as "imprisoned and driven out of the country by the Rebels, good Union man." Kieffer married Louisa Schule on February 25, 1870, in Medina County. No further data located on Blasins Kieffer.

06. Jacob [Jacque] Zacharie Haby was born about 1823 in Oberentzen, Alsace. The date Haby arrived in Texas is not known. He arrived in Medina County in 1851 and helped established the Haby Settlement, just north of Castroville. Haby married Catherine Mann on December 31, 1851, in Medina County. They were the parents of eight children. Haby was the commander of Company D, Medina County Independent Battalion of the 31$^{st}$ Brigade District. Jacob Haby died in 1899, in Medina County.

07. Henry Joseph Richarz was born on September 8, 1823, in Prussia. He married Josephina Schaufhausen about 1847 in Prussia. They were the parents of nine children. Richarz was a Forty-Eighter. The family arrived in New Orleans in 1850, and continued on to Medina County. He was the D'Hanis postmaster in 1860. He was elected the major and commander of the Medina County Independent Battalion. Duff's company arrested him in June, 1862, but the Confederate Military Commission released him in July, 1862. Richarz was elected as Medina County justice in August, 1862. Richarz was later a Texas Ranger captain. Henry Joseph Richarz died on May 21, 1910, in Medina County.

## 22. Captain de Montel's Report – May 31, 1862

Camp Verde
May 31, 1862

Colonel:

I am informed by Col Norris that the wagons, Camp Equipment, Mules etc, etc are on hand at Austin for the regt. And have sent 4 men and one officer to receive them and bring over [to] my portion. We need those articles very much and in fact I planned [to] start out as the large scout which I considered making to the Devils River and perhaps the Rio Grande to attack the Indians in their main camps where the[y] keep their families and horses without pack animals, etc;

I suggest the propriety of sending the balance of ammunition to which we are entitled by the wagons.

I had written a letter before I started to Camp San Saba to the Gen. Court Martial in regard to the Parties joined by Camp Davis, but on my return from there yesterday found the letter still in camp for the want of post office stamps or 10 cents in silver. I send it now with _____ . Colonel I have been informed by Capt Norris while at Camp San Saba that his Excellency the Governor is constantly besieged with petitions to _____ from the practices and employ the petitioners to protect them from ___ besides that a number of Complaints are pouring in against different Companies of this Regiment

I am convinced that you are fully acquainted with the Character and the motives of these croakers and complainants

– so I will only say that as far as my part of the line is concerned that the Indians did not in a single instance succeed in getting off their their spoils since I occupied it with my company and that any complaints that may reach headquarters are fabrications and falsehoods I beg you that in case any more such documents should he send you, you will for the sake of justice send me the Complaint and its author.

*There is even now a movement going on amongst those persons, which I have not been able to see through as yet- owing to my recent return – but shall know a little more about before many days.    I know however sufficient to give the military commanders as will as the Committee of Vigilance & Safety of San Antonio a warning!  During the last few days the enemies of the South shown considerable activity, expresses are kept up between Castroville, Dhanis, Comfort, Bonre [Boerne], Fredericksburg etc and enough and to satisfy me that the[y] are attempting to unite their forces – one of this expresses address a German of my company as follows;*

> *"I hope you belong the good cause we are organizing to have a chance to join our friends and make ready now and be united."*

*On asking what side he belong to the said the good side the North!   They even have in among the U. S. prisoners.* [Emphasis Added]

I hope they are known sufficiently well at headquarters at Austin to allow the authorites to judge them correctly and keep an eye on them.

To Colonel
J. Y. Dashiell

Adj & Insp General
At Austin

I remain very respectfully
your most obedient servant,
Charles de Montel
Capt Comg. F.R.T.R.


P.S.  No Indian troubles lately.


Editorial note: Every effort has been made to keep the original spelling and grammar on the source document.  There where several case where the original word could not be clearly determined.  An effort was been made to insert what is believed to be the original word, followed by (sic).  In those cases where the word could not be determined at all, a blank _____ is inserted

## 23. General Herbert Proclamation of Martial Law

CONFEDERATE STATES OF AMERICA
Headquarters Department of Texas
Houston, May 30, 1862
GENERAL ORDER NO. 15

I. The following proclamation is published for the information of all concerted.

### PROCLAMATION

II. I P. O. Hebert, Brigadier General Provisional Army Confederate States of American do proclaim that Martial Law is hereby extended over the Sate of Texas.

Every white male person above the age of sixteen years, being temporarily, or otherwise within the aforesaid limits, shall upon a summons issued by the Provost Marshal promptly present himself before said provost marshal to have his name, residence and occupation registered, and to furnish such information as may be required of him. And such as claim to be aliens shall be sworn to the effect that they will abide by and maintain the laws of this State and the Confederate States as long as they are permitted to reside therein and that they will not convey to our enemies any information whatever or do any act injurious to the Confederate States or ___ to the United States.

Provost Marshals shall order out and remove from their respective districts all disloyal persons and all persons whose presence is injurious to the interest of the county.

All orders issued by the Provost Marshal in the execution of their duties shall be promptly obeyed. Any disobedience of summons emanating from them shall be dealt with summary punishment.

Any attempt to depreciate the currency of the Confederate States is an act of hostility; will be treated as such and visited summary punishment.

No interference with the rights of loyal citizens, or with the usual routine of business, or with the usual administrative of the laws, will be permitted, except when necessary to enforce the provisions of this proclamation.

By order of Brigadier General
  P. O. Hebert, P. Army C. S.
  Commanding Department of Texas
  Samuel Boyer Davis, Capt. & A. A. G.

HEAD QUARTERS, SUB. MIL DIST OF THE RIO GRANDE
San Antonio, July 21$^{st}$, 1862

By virtue of General Order No 7, from the Head Quarters of the "Trans. Miss. Dist. South of Red River" bearing date July 8, 1862, as follows:

Head Quarters, Trans. Miss. Dist
South of Red River
San Antonio, July 8$^{th}$, 1862

GENERAL ORDER
No. 7.

1. Brig. Gen. H. P. Bee, is charged with the execution of Martial Law thro' out the State of Texas.

2. He will appoint such Provost Marshals as he may deem proper and establish all necessary regulations for their guidance.

3. Provost Marshals will report by letter to Brig Gen. Bee, at San Antonio for instruction, when in doubt as to their duties of jurisdiction.

By order of
    Brig. Gen. P. O. Herbert.
    C. M. Mason, Capt. & A. A. Gen'l

The Provost Marshals throughout the State of Texas, are hereby directed to observe the following regulations:

1. No arrest will be made unless based upon two respectable citizens; except in cases when the suspected party is liable to escape before such basis for action can be obtained.

2. When parties have been arrested, whether upon affidavits or otherwise, the Provost Marshal by whose order the arrest was made, shall cause the accused to be brought before him for examination with the least possible delay, together with such witnesses as can be procured to establish any charge alleged.

3. The examination shall be conducted as far as, in accordance with the statute law of the State for Justices Courts. No *unnecessary* delays however for a strict and technical compliance with the details of said statute must be permitted; and only such will be extended as the Provost Marshals shall deem conducive to the ends of justice.

4. If the facts adduced upon the examination are such as will establish the guilt of the accused, they will be sent before the nearest Military Commission with the accused. The testimony of each witness must be subscribed on said transcript; and the names & residence of all parties connected with the transaction, with the time and place, as definitely as possible, must be set forth and the whole certified by Provost Marshal.

VI. Prisoners will be securely confined, but no harsh measures must be resorted to, unless rendered imperatively necessary for his safe custody.

## VII. PASSPORTS

Provost Marshals may issue passports to loyal citizens, who have taken the oath of allegiance, to pass and repass within the limits of the State, at discretion. They are not authorized under any circumstances to grant passports to persons liable to military duty under the Conscript Law.

No charge will be made for Passports.

Offices of the Confederate army travelling under orders, and showing them, will not require other passports.

### Form of Passport

THE CONFEDERATE STATES OF AMERICA.

Jurisdiction of _____ County, Texas.
No _____

These are to request all persons in authority and all others whom it may concern. To let _____ a citizen of _____ and a resident of _____ going by _____ To _____, about _____ affairs pass safety and freely on said route without give him any hindrance, but, on the contrary, affording him all manner of protection, so far as necessary.

Witness my hand, at my office in _____ this ___ day of _____ 186_.

_____ Provost Marshal

Signature of bearer:

_____

DESCRIPTION:

Age _____    Eyes _____    Face _____
Height _____    Nose _____    Complexion _____
Weight _____    Mouth _____    Peculiarities _____
Hair _____    Chin _____

8.  A Monthly return of the disbursements, all accounts for expenses and all requisitions for funds to defray them, but be sent to these Head Quarters for approval by Brig Gen H. P. Bee.

There is neither rank nor pay attached to the office of Provost Marshal but the actual expenses will be paid.

9.  The Governor of the State having placed the State troops at the disposition of the Confederate authorities, Provost Marshals are directed to call on them to assist in the discharge of their duties, when no Confederate troops are in the immediate vicinity.

10. Provost Marshals are to exercise a wholesome and efficient service over all travelers – to see that they are provided with proper passports, and to hold all persons without such evidence of their loyalty, to a strict accountability.

They will regulate the sale of all intoxicating liquors whenever the latter becomes necessary.

They will regulate and establish a tariff of prices on all articles of prime necessity, whenever the disloyal and avaricious render this course necessary in exorbitant charges.

11. When travelers present themselves before a Provost Marshal within this state, it is not necessary for a new passport to be issued. The Provost Marshal will simply endorse the old passport.

Should it, however appear that the first passport was issued without the oath of allegiance having been administered, Provost Marshal will administer the oath, register the party, and issue a new passport.

12. A register of all persons who have taken the oath, and all to whom passports have been issued, must be kept by the Provost Marshal. Said register shall show place of birth, place of residence, age, occupation, general description, and State or Country, of which a citizen.

12. By General Order No. 45, Department of Texas, all officers commanding troops are required to comply with requisitions made upon them for aid or assistance by the Provost Marshal. This does not confer authority upon the Marshals to order any officer. The officer is himself

responsible for the mode and manner of complying with and executing the requisitions.

14. Provost Marshals will exercise their authority with judgment and discretion, and with the least annoyance possible to good and loyal citizens. No arbitrary or tyrannical acts will be tolerated, and upon proofs being furnished of the same, the Provost Marshal so offending will the summarily dismissed and otherwise punished under the law.

By order of Brig. Gen. H. P. BEE
E. F. Gray,
Major & A. A. Gen'l

# 24. Captain Duff's Report – June 23, 1862

HEADQUARTERS CAMP BEE
Near San Antonio, Tex., June 23, 1862

Maj. E. F. Gray
Acting Assistant Adjutant-General
Headquarters Sub-Military Dist. Of the Rio Grande
San Antonio, Texas

Major:

I have the honor to report for the information of the brigadier-general commanding the district that agreeably to Special Orders, No. 242, I broke up my camp at this place on the morning of the 28th of May ultimo and took up the line of march for Gillespie County. I reached Fredericksburg, the county seat on the morning of the 30th, and immediately proclaimed martial law as existing within the limits of the county, and in Precinct No. 5 of Kerr County, giving six days to enable the citizens to report to the provost-marshal and take the oath of allegiance. I found the people shy and timid. I visited with a part of my company several of the settlements and explained to the people the object of our visit to their county. In a few days they displayed much more confidence in us, and in a corresponding ratio more desire to serve the Government.

At first I found in impossible to obtain forage for the horses of my company from the fact that the people who were favorable to the Confederate States Government had sold, whilst those who still had corn would not sell for paper money. I therefore directed Lieutenant Lilly[1] to wait on Mr. F.

Lochte[2], a wealthy merchant of the place who had bought largely the produce of the country, and who would not sell for paper currency, and inform him that I required fifty bushels of corn. After some little hesitation he agreed to furnish it. After this I had no difficulty in getting forage and all other necessary supplies.

On the night of the 3d instant I received an order from the adjutant-general's office to cause the arrest of certain citizens of Medina County, and to endeavor to break up a chain of communication between the disaffected by private express.[3] As to my action under this order I refer to my report dated the – instant.[4]

On my return to Fredericksburg I found beyond doubt that the few citizens of the place who were friendly to this Government did not posses moral courage enough to give information to the provost-marshal of the sayings and doings of those who were unfriendly, and upon consultation with Lieutenant Sweet[5] I determined to summon them to meet him and myself – They obeyed the order and made affidavits in regard to certain citizens of the county, viz: Sheriff Braubach[6], Captain Kuechler[7] (State troops), F. W. Doebbler[8], a grocery keeper, and Mr. F. Lochte, merchant. The affidavits made were sufficient basis on which to warrant the arrest of these men. I detached parties for this purpose and succeeded in arresting Mr. Doebbler. The others had all left the town. Braubach was afterwards arrested in Austin by Corporal Newton[9], of my company, and Mr. Lochte at Fredericksburg by Lieutenant Lilly, when he thought my company sufficiently distant to insure his safety. Captain Kuechler I did not succeed in arresting. He was the only one of the four who had not taken the oath of allegiance. These men are all inimical to our country and posses a vast amount of influence among the laboring and agricultural classes. Lochte, Doebbler and Braubach are now in the guard house at San Antonio and their absence from Gillespie County will tend more to make the people of that county united in favor our Government than anything else.

In connection with this subject I may be allowed to suggest that steps should be taken to arrest Captain Kuechler. He is a man of great influence; a German enthusiast in politics and a dangerous man in the community.

In Kerr County there are a few men who are bitterly opposed to our Government. These men are headed by an old man by the name of Nelson.[10] I took care that he and his party should be notified in good time to report to the provost-marshal. This they failed to do and Nelson sent me a defiant message. I then sent a detachment of State troops kindly placed at my disposal to arrest him, but he had taken to the cedar brakes and escaped.

Most of the inhabitants of that county are frontiersmen. Some of them, if not all, renegades from justice from other States, and men who will not fail to injure a political or personal enemy whenever an opportunity offers. A party of them burned the entire fences of an old man because his sons had gone to the war and because he was a good Southerner.[11]

On the 11th instant I moved my company from Gillespie County to Blanco County and declared martial law in existence there. Here I found the great majority of the people friendly, enthusiastically so, to the Confederate States Government. I ascertained, however, that there exists a small clique who are bitterly opposed to our cause in the eastern part of the county bordering on Travis. The names of the leaders of this party are Prescott[12], King[13], Howell[14], and two brothers, or father and son, by the name of Snow[15]. Information reached me which led to the conviction that these men, or a majority of them, with some of the rabble, had gone to Fredericksburg armed and equipped to endeavor to raise a party to fight my command, but on arriving at Fredericksburg they found that they could nothing so returned home, and through one of their understrappers, a man by the name of Eaton[16], endeavored to create a feeling in the community against my company by manufacturing and circulating the basest falsehoods in regard to it.[17] This Eaton acknowledged to me to have done, but the fellow was evidently so worthless that I took no steps in the matter. On the return of their party from Fredericksburg, Mr. King, one of their number, immediately started for Austin, where it is generally supposed by the citizens of Blanco the headquarters of the traitorous clique exists. A few days afterwards General Jack Hamilton[18] was in that section of country, and although I have no positive evidence to that effect I have every reason to believe that King was dispatched by his party to report to Hamilton the state of affairs in the upper country, and that in consequence of the information thus conveyed he repaired to the disaffected settlements to attempt in them the creation of a military organization.[19] I have undoubted information that strangers in large numbers have been gathering within the last few weeks at Guy Hamilton's ranch in Travis, near the Blanco County line. As many as twelve have passed Captain Cleveland's[20] house in two or three days, all inquiring the way to Hamilton's.[21]

I am assured by the best citizens of Blanco that the disaffected of Kerr, Gillespie, Llano, Travis, Blanco and neighboring counties are organizing and that the rendezvous of the party is at or near Hamilton's ranch.

On the 18th instant I broke up camp at Blanco City and moved my command to Kendall County. On the evening of the 19th I made camp near Boerne. Here I caused the arrest of Julius Schlickum[22], a merchant, who has been bitterly opposed to us and who I have reason to believe took an active part in forwarding expresses and information to Federal prisoners at Camp Verde and the disaffected citizens of his own and adjoining counties. He has been almost always in possession of news from the seat of war at least two days in advance of the mail. He controls from 100 to 150 votes in Kendall County. Mr. Schlickum is now a prisoner in the guard-house at San Antonio.

On the morning of the 20th instant I received Special Orders, No. 299, directing me to repair with my company without delay to San Antonio. On the same day I took up the line of march for this place where I arrived on the 21st instant at noon.

I have the honor to be, major, your obedient servant,


James Duff
Captain, Commanding
Company of Texas Partisan Dragoons.

ENDNOTES
Captain Duff's Report

01. Edwin F. Lilly is something of a mystery man. The only U. S. Census that was located showing him is the 1860 Bexar Census. There he is listed as being born about 1840 in Georgia, a law student and single. From San Antonio newspapers accounts it can be established that he was practicing law by 1861 and 1862. When the 30th Brigade District was organized in early 1862 Lilly was elected captain of the Wilson County Precincts 1 & 2 Company of the Fifth Independent Battalion. He enrolled in Duff's company on May 7, 1862, and was either elected or appointed junior second lieutenant. Lilly was in command of the detachment from Duff's company in the pursuit force. After the battle he was in charge of the detail that executed the wounded insurgents. When the unit was increased to battalion size he was appointed battalion quartermaster and later the regiment quartermaster with the rank of captain. Lilly is last shown as present in the regiment in August, 1864. After the war Lilly fled to Mexico. No further data has been located.

02. Heinrich Frederick Lochte, Sr. was born on October 17, 1809, in Peine, Hanover. He married Dorothy Moellering about 1835, likely in Hanover. They were the parents of at least five children. The family arrived in Texas on the *Herkules* in November 1845 and settled in Fredericksburg. He was in the mercantile business. He was tried by the Confederate Military Commission for failure to accept Confederate money and fined $100.00 and 35 days in jail. Heinrich Frederick Lochte, Sr. died on July 19, 1867, at Fredericksburg in Gillespie County.

03. This comment establishes that there was a courier service between Hill Country Unionists and the U. S. Consuls in Mexico.

04. This report has not been located.

05. James Robert Sweet was born about 1818 in Nova Scotia. He married Charlotte Annie James on May 23, 1840, at St. John's Church in New Brunswick, Nova Scotia, Canada. They were the parents of at least six children. The family arrived in Newport, Rhode Island on January 1, 1849. By 1850, they were living in San Antonio and Sweet had opened a mercantile business on Soledad Street. Sweet was an alderman and elected mayor, serving from January 1, 1854, until January 1, 1856. In 1859, he was again elected mayor and served from January 1, 1859, until May 2, 1862, when he resigned and enrolled in James Duff's Partisan Ranger Company where he was elected first lieutenant. He previously served in a local militia company

and in September, 1861, he was elected first lieutenant in the Alamo Rifles. He was elected the president of the Texas Power on January 7, 1862. When General Bee declared martial law in Bexar County he was appointed provost marshal. He accompanied Duff's company to Fredericksburg in May, 1862. Sweet was an original member of the Confederate Military Commission from June 28th until October 28, 1862. When Duff's unit was increased to battalion size he was elected captain of the original company which became Company A, 14th Battalion Texas Cavalry. Sweet was promoted to major on February 7, 1863, and to lieutenant colonel in May, 1863, when the battalion was increased to regimental size and named the 33rd Regiment Texas Cavalry. He remained with the regiment until the end of the war when he fled to Mexico and helped form the Cordova Colony. He returned to the U. S. in 1866 and received a presidential pardon at New Orleans on February 2, 1866. He returned to San Antonio in 1867 and purchased an interest in the *San Antonio Herald* which he operated until ill health forced his retirement. James Robert Sweet died on December 12, 1880, in San Antonio.

06.   See Document 8, Endnote 2, p. 33 for a bio on Philip Braubach. He was one of the Unionists condemned by the Nimitz's Gillespie Rifles.

07.   See Document 1, Endnote 4, p.19 for a bio of Jacob Kuechler. Capture Duff stated Kuechler was a captain of state troops. Many histories have concluded this rank was based on the fact that Kuechler was trying to organize a company for the Frontier Regiment or because he was captain of the Gillespie Company of the League's military battalion. These are incorrect. The reason Duff identified Kuechler as a captain was because he was the captain of a militia company of the 31st Brigade District. His company was Company E, Second Battalion of the 31st Brigade District. Kuechler was one of the Unionists condemned by the Nimitz's Gillespie Rifles.

08.   See Document 12, Endnote 30, p. 68 for a bio of F. W. Doebbler

09.   Henry Martin Newton was born on December 22, 1834, in the Cherokee Nation [Oklahoma]. By 1850, the family was living in Bexar County and by 1860, he was a merchant at Camp Verde in southern Kerr County. Newton enrolled in Duff's Company in May, 1862. He was very likely in the pursuit force. Newton remained in the company until the end of the war. He married Lucinda E. Smith on June 26, 1867, in Bexar County. They were the parents of at least five children. The family set up housekeeping in Bexar County. Henry Martin Newton died on January 31, 1918, in Bexar County.

10.   This "old man" was Hiram Nelson who was born about 1800 in Orange County, North Carolina. He married Mary Ann [Polly] Roundtree about 1832 in either Missouri or Illinois. They were the parents of at least eight children.

The family arrived in the Texas Hill Country about 1854 and settled west of Fredericksburg and Kerrsville. The Confederates tried to capture Nelson several times but failed. Finally he was captured about August 4, 1862, near Spring Creek by Captain Henry Davis, who ordered Nelson hanged on August 22, 1862.

11. This "old man" was Robert Alexander Gibson. See Document 17 Endnote 1, p.33.

12. This is likely Aaron P. Prescot. In 1860, he was living in Lampasas County. He was born about 1830 in Maryland. The date he arrived in Texas is not known. Prescot married Sarah Jane Mackey on July 10, 1850, in Rusk County. They were the parents of at least four children. Prescot was a private in D. H. Moseley's Company, Second Frontier District in February, 1864. The last record of Prescot is the August 17, 1867, Brown County Voter Registration List.

13. It is unclear who exactly this man King was. The 1856-1859 Gillespie tax rolls show an Edward A. King as owning land in the newly-created Blanco County. King's name next appears on the 1861 Blanco tax rolls showing he owned 160 acres on the Pedernales River. He enrolled in Freeman's Blanco County Pedernales Cavalry Company on August 24, 1861, as a bugler. King is shown on the roster for the September 7, 1861, re-organization and on the roster for November 14, 1861. This is enough data to shown that an Edward A. King was in Blanco at the time of Duff's arrival in June, 1862. Edward A. King was very likely a member of the Kerr [American] Company of the League's military battalion. King's name last appears on the 1863 Blanco tax rolls. The only Edward A. King located on the 1860 Census is an individual that was born about 1829 in North Carolina. It is not known when this King arrived in Texas, but the 1850 Harrison Census shows him as single and twenty-one years old. The 1860 Harrison Census shows him as as 30 years old, a farmer, born in North Carolina, and living in his father's household. It is not clear if he is married. Edward A. King married Francis Ann [maiden name not known] about 1860, in Harrison County. They were the parents of at least five children. King is back in Harrison County by 1870 and 1880. It appears that Edward A. King died about 1890, likely in Harrison County.

14. Like King, it is not clear who Howell was. The 1856 Gillespie tax tolls show that John T. Howell owned 160 acres of land in the area ceded to Blanco County. The 1857 Blanco tax rolls show that he owned 320 acres on Walnut and North Grape Creek. The 1860 Blanco Agriculture Census shows he was living near Round Mountain in northern Blanco County. The 1862 and 1863 Blanco tax rolls continue to show he still owned 320 areas on Walnut and North Grape Creek. Howell was very likely a member of the Kerr [American] Company of the League's military battalion. Captain John

Donelson, commander of Confederate forces in the Gillespie, Blanco, Kerr, and Kendall County area hanged Howell on August 5, 1862.

15. There is a great deal more information about the two men named Snow: the first is Moses Moran Snow who was born about 1831, in Newton County, Georgia. He was an uncle to William F. Snow, below. Moses M. Snow arrived in Texas about 1853. He married Allay Jayne Pruitt on October 10, 1855, in Hopkins County, Texas. They were the parents of four children. The family arrived in Blanco County by 1858, where Snow served as an early sheriff. Snow enrolled in the Pedernales Cavalry Company on August 24, 1861. His name appears on the November, 1861, company roster and on its March 1862 payroll. Moses M. Snow was a member of the Kerr [American] Company of the League's military battalion. He was a pro-Union bushwhacker, who operated in eastern Gillespie and western Blanco Counties in 1862-1864. Captain Dorbandt's Burnet County militia company killed Moses Moran Snow on January 16, 1864. The second is William F. Snow who was born about 1840 in Georgia. He was a nephew of Moses Moran Snow, above. The exact date that Snow arrived in Texas is not known, but it was by 1860, as his name appears on the 1860 census for Kaufman County. Snow married Sarah [Sallie] E. Burton on September 13, 1860, in Kaufman County. They were the parents of at least one daughter. William Snow enrolled in the Pedernales Cavalry Company on August 24, 1861, and remained with the company until at least November of 1861.He was a member of the Kerr [American] Company of the League's military battalion. He was also a pro-Union bushwhacker who operated in eastern Gillespie and western Blanco Counties during 1862-1864. Lieutenant James Waldrip's Gillespie County militia detachment killed William F. Snow in early 1864 on Williams Creek in western Blanco County.

16. Archibald B. Edon was born about 1835 in New York. Edon arrived in Texas on February 13, 1854, and settled on North Creek. In 1856-1858 he paid taxes on 160 acres. His post office was Westbrook in northern Blanco County. He married Jane [maiden name not known] about 1857, likely in Blanco County. They were the parents of at least two children. Edon enrolled in the Pedernales Cavalry Company on August 24, 1861, and served until at least March, 1862. He was a member of the Kerr [American] Company of the League's military battalion. His name last appears on the 1863 Blanco tax rolls. He was likely executed in late 1863 or 1864, as his widow married Alexander King about 1866, again likely in Blanco County.

17. These falsehoods were that an older woman, among others, had been mistreated by Duff.

18. Andrew Jackson Hamilton was born on January 28, 1815, in Huntsville, Madison County, Alabama. About 1843, he married Mary Jane Bowen, in

Alabama. They were the parents of six children. In 1846, the family settled in Fayette County, before moving to Travis County in 1849. In 1850, Governor P. H. Bell appointed Hamilton as acting attorney general. He served as a member of the Fourth Texas Legislature from Travis County in 1851. In 1859, Hamilton was elected to the U. S. Congress. He returned to Texas in 1861, elected as a state senator by a special election. In 1862, Hamilton fled Travis County into the mountains to a location now known as Hamilton's Pool on a ranch owned by his brother, Morgan Hamilton. In July, 1862, he fled Texas entirely. With a group of about fifteen other Unionists, he reached Matamoras and went on to Washington D. C. On November 14, 1862, President Lincoln commissioned Hamilton as brigadier general of volunteers and as military governor of Texas. He was in Brownsville briefly in 1863 and 1864 when the Union invaded. After the invasion failed he returned to New Orleans. When the war ended he returned to Texas and served for two years as a Reconstruction governor. Andrew Jackson Hamilton died of tuberculosis on April 11, 1875, in Travis County.

19. This was the first indication the Confederates had of Unionist plans for some type of military organization. The Confederate authorities did not realize initially that a potentially much stronger military organization had been created by the Hill Country Unionists, which they would have to use force to destroy.

20. John Treadwell Cleveland was born on October 1, 1798, in Salem, Barnstable County, Massachusetts. By 1823 the family had moved to Howard County, Missouri, where on October 30, 1823, he married Louisiana Hughes. They were the parents of eleven children. The date the family arrived in Texas is not known. They first settled in Travis County but by March 4, 1856, the family was living on Cypress Creek in northern Blanco and he received mail at Westbrook. In retaliation for his secessionist views Unionists burned his home to the ground on November 18, 1863. John Treadwell Cleveland died on January 14, 1875, at Cypress Creek, Blanco County.

21. Morgan Calvin Hamilton was born on February 25, 1809, in Madison County, Alabama. He was a brother to Andrew Jackson Hamilton, above. He arrived in Texas in 1837, and owned a mercantile business in Austin. He was a clerk in the Republic of Texas War Department from 1839 to 1844. Hamilton acted as interim Secretary of War of the Republic of Texas from 1844 to 1845 and statehood. His name appears on the Travis Voter Registration List in 1867-1869. Morgan Calvin Hamilton died on November 21, 1893, in San Diego, California, where he was visiting. He was interred in Oakwood Cemetery at Austin, Texas.

22. Julius Schlickum was born about 1825 in Prussia. He was a Forty-Eighter and Freethinker. Schlickum arrived in Texas on the *Franziska* from Munster in 1846. He returned to Prussia and on September 27, 1849, married Caroline Therese Klier. They were the parents of three children. The 1850 Gillespie Census shows Schlickum living in Gillespie County with his brother-in-law, William Klier. Schlickum was a major participant in the 1854 San Antonio German Convention in San Antonio that attempted to unite the various German settlements into a political union. However, he urged the convention to be careful and not go too far in opposing the Texans. Schlickum moved to Boerne and opened a mercantile store. He was a Kendall Justice of the Peace in early 1862 and elected captain of Company B, [Kendall Company] 3$^{rd}$ Regiment, 31$^{st}$ Brigade in the spring of 1861. He was not an insurgent, but a Unionist. After being arrested by Captain Duff he was tried by the Confederate Military Commission and found guilty of Unionist activities. Schlickum was sentenced to prison for the remainder of the war. Along with h Philip Braubach and Friedrich William Doebbler, he escaped on July 19, 1862, and fled to Piedras Negras, Monterrey, and finally Matamoras where he made arrangements for his family to join him. Shortly before they arrived, Schlickum died of yellow fever.

## 25. Captain de Montel's Report – July 7, 1862

Camp McCord
July the 7th 1862

Colonel James M. Norris
Colonel, Commanding
Frontier Regiment Texas Rangers

Col;

The following report for the month of June 1862 is hereby respectfully presented to Colonel James M. Norris, Commander Frontier Regiment.

Up to June 15th no signs of Indians being discovered, the _____ force at Camp McCord was employed preparing quarters for men and animals in procuring shelter for commissary stores and forage in the near camp.

On the morning of the 16th I started for Camp Montel on Seco Creek. On the 16th evening word reached Camp McCord reporting Indians on the upper Medina. 2nd Lieut A. Gates ordered Sergeant Hill[1] out with 10 men to examine into the report. On the 17th which at Camp Montel, preparing to go on a scout to the westwards through the mountains [an] express reached me [at] Camp McCord, reported that 20 Indians had passed near the West Frio, and were last seen as reported by express from San Antonio between San Geronimo and Medina River, some 25 miles below Camp McCord; that express also informed that 2nd Lieut Gates had started two hours after report reached Camp McCord with 16 men in pursuit. The former report that the Indians had gone down the West Frio

some 20 miles west of here and were next seen some 25 miles
south of their, near the foot of the mountain caused me to
believe they were aiming to go through their former grounds
of depredation, Blanco & Kendall Counties. I therefore
changed my destination and instead started west. I took the 15
men who were prepared and returned the same night east, to
Camp McCord intending to increase my force at the later
camp by 10 men, cross the mountains and get ahead of $2^{nd}$
Lieut. Gates and the Indians somewhere near the Cibolo or
Guadalupe River. On arriving at Camp McCord however I
found Lieut Gates and party returned and received the
following report from the later to wit:

> *I followed the express send to the camp to the place
> where the Indians had been seen last and found 9
> men, well-mounted and armed to the teeth who
> informed me that they belonged to the German
> settlement on the Medina above Castroville and
> they were cattle hunting, that is was them the
> express had taken for Indians they had seen him
> and the other man mentioned by the express–Lieut
> Gates returned to the camp.*

> *I will state for the information of the Col that this party is a
> part of the so-called "Independent Battalion" of Medina
> County and a part of Capt Haby's Company (Militia)
> ordered out by said officers to keep the conscription
> officer off of them and getting hold of them and to join
> Lincoln's forces in opportunity should offer and that they
> besides a number of others parties of Medina County still
> remain in the mountains for the above reason.* [Emphasis
> added]

Next day, I took a part of the men from Camp Montel & Camp McCord on a scout to the head of the Medina River and after examining all the head of the streams as far westward as the Nueces. I returned by the way of the main Frio by Camp Dix on Rio Frio, Camp Montel to Camp McCord after an absence of 8 days and passing over a distance of about 200 miles.

The party of Sergt Hill returned after an absence of 4 days and reported no signs found.

*Second Lieut B. F. Patton[2] in command at Camp Montel on hearing rumors of Indians, started out with 12 men to westward and after remaining absent some 7 days returned and reported plenty of union men in the mountains, but no Indian signs.* [Emphasis added]

On the 29the instant I received communication from General H. Bee, Commanding Department of Rio Grande. I ordered 2nd Lieut Gates with 12 men to scout the country along the heads of the streams.

On the 30th I departed for San Antonio according to request of the military Commander of the Department of Texas.

Very respectfully your most obedient servant,
Charles de Montel
Capt D Company
F. R. T. R.

ENDNOTES
Captain de Montel's Report July 7, 1862

01. No additional data has been located on G. W. Hill.

02. Benjamin Franklin Patton was born about 1837 in Bastrop County, Texas. His name first appears in Blanco County's 1859 tax rolls as owning four town lots in Pittsburg (Blanco City). He served with his brother-in-law John W. Sansom in several ranger companies prior to the war. In 1860, he was living near Curry's Creek. Patton enrolled in de Montel's Company, Frontier Regiment in March, 1862, and was elected second lieutenant. He reenlisted in Lawhon's Company, Frontier Regiment on December 29, 1862, and was either elected or appointed second corporal. Patton deserted in March of 1864 and on April 1, 1864, enlisted in Company I, First Regiment [Union] Texas Cavalry. He was transferred to Company C on July 14, 1864. Patton deserted on August 7, 1864, at White Rancho, Texas. He was a member of the group that recovered the insurgent's bodies in August, 1865. Patton married Augusta Loenger on June 23, 1866, in Kendall County. They were the parents of five children. Benjamin Franklin Patton died about 1890, in either Blanco or Kerr County.

# 26. List of Luckenbach Rangers

*List of Luckenbach Rangers contained in notebook of Sylvester Kleck*

Sylvester Kleck[1]
August Duecker[2]
Jacob Kusenberger[3]
August Schoenewolf[4]
August Hoffmann[5]
Joseph Petsch [Poetsch][6]
Moritz Weiss[7]
Adolf Ruebsam
[Ruebsamen][8]

August Luckenbach[9]
Adolf Vater[10]
Christian Schaefer[11]
Louis Ruebsamen[12]
Philip Beck[13]
Heinrich Weiershausen
[Weyerhaeuser][14]
Christian Petsch [Poetsch][15]
Conrad Bock[16]

*List of Luckenbach 'Buschwachers' located in the billfold of Sylvester Kleck*

Sylvester Kleck
August Duecker
Jacob Kusenberger
August Schoenewolf
Herman Hoffmann
*[Herr Hoffmann. This is August Hoffmann]*
Joseph Petsch [Poetsch]
Moritz Weiss
Franz Weiss[17]

Adolf Ruebsam [Ruebsamen]
August Luckenbach
Adolf Vater
Christian Schaefer
Louis Ruebsam [Ruebsamen]
Philip Beck
Heinrich Weiershausen
[Weyerhaeuser]
Christian Petsch [Poetsch]
Conrad Bock

ENDNOTES
List of Luckenbach Bushwhackers

01.   Sylvester Kleck was born on December 31, 1844, in Hohenzoeller, Prussia.
      The family arrived in Texas on the *Andacia* from Harthausen in 1846; by
      1850, they were living in Gillespie County. Kleck was very likely a member
      of the Gillespie Company of the League's military battalion. He was also
      likely to have been a member of the August insurgent group, returning to
      Gillespie County after the Nueces battle. Kleck was in the October insurgent
      group and wounded in a skirmish at the Rio Grande crossing. He spent several
      months in Mexico recovering from his wounds. Juanita Sanches was one of
      the women who nursed him back to health. They were married about 1862 in
      Mexico and were the parents of six children. After the war Kleck and his
      family returned to Gillespie County. He served as Gillespie County sheriff in
      1869, 1870, and 1874. Kleck served several terms as constable of Precinct
      Number 1. Sylvester Kleck died on August 21, 1914, in Gillespie County
      from a fall from a ladder.

02.   August Duecker was born in 1828 in Prussia. He was likely a Forty-Eighter.
      Duecker arrived in Texas on the *Texas* in 1853. He married Louise Feuge on
      June 11, 1854, in Gillespie County. They were the parents of at least four
      children. Duecker was a member of Braubach's home guard company from
      February, 1861, until February, 1862. He was the second sergeant in
      Kuechler's company of December, 1861. He was a member of the Gillespie
      Company of the League's military battalion, and a member of the insurgent
      group who survived the Nueces battle. He returned to Gillespie County and
      hid in the attic of the family home. Louise Feuge Duecker died on January 1,
      1863, while August Duecker was in hiding. He agreed to serve as a teamster
      for the Confederates, but Captain Van der Stucken arrested him and held him
      in the Austin jail. Family oral traditions say he escaped. Duecker married
      Wilhelmine Knetsch Lindemann, the widow of John A. Lindemann, on
      February 22, 1866, in Comal County. They were the parents of seven children.
      August Duecker died on April 19, 1894, in Gillespie County.

03.   Jacob Kusenberger was born about 1834 in Nassau. He arrived in Texas on
      the *Washington* in 1845, at which time he claimed he was fifteen years old.
      Kusenberger married Auguste Molzberger on January 4, 1857, in Gillespie
      County. They were the parents of at least four children. He was a member of
      the Gillespie Company of the League's military battalion and fled with them
      in August. He survived the Nueces battle and with Henry Schwethelm and
      Carl Graff went on the Mexico afterwards. He enlisted in Company A, First
      Regiment [Union] Texas Cavalry on October 27, 1862, at New Orleans. He
      was promoted to corporal on July 6, 1863, and to sergeant on January 1, 1864.
      He was mustered out of service on October 31, 1865, at San Antonio. Jacob
      Kusenberger died on November 30, 1927, in Gillespie County.

04. August Schoenewolf, Jr. was born on December 20, 1834, in Saxony. The family arrived in Texas on the *Johann Detthard* in January, 1846, and settled in Gillespie County. Schoenewolf married Sophie Beckmann on March 2, 1857, in Gillespie County. They were the parents of at least six children. He was likely a member of the Gillespie Company of the League's military battalion, and may have been in the fleeing insurgent group in August, 1862. If so, he returned to Gillespie County. In October, 1863, he enrolled in Menges' squad. Many members of this group were pro-Union bushwhackers. Schoenewolf next enrolled in Krauskopf's Company, Third Frontier District and served until the end of the war. August Schoenewolf, Jr. died on September 11, 1905, in Gillespie County.

05. August Hoffmann was born on December 9, 1842, in Prussia. He arrived in New Orleans on the *Friedrich der Grosse* in 1854. He boarded a ship for Indianola and settled on South Grape Creek. Hoffmann was a member of the Gillespie Company of the League's military battalion. He was among the group who fled Texas in August, 1862. Hoffmann survived the Nueces battle and returned to Gillespie County where he hid for the next three years. He married Sabine Stalp on April 5, 1865, in Gillespie County. They were the parents of nine children. August Hoffmann was the last surviving member of the League when he died on March 4, 1935, on South Grape Creek.

06. Joseph Poetsch [Petsch] was born on November 4, 1838, in Nassau. The family arrived in Texas on the *Washington* in 1845 from Frickhofen and settled in Gillespie County. He was very likely a member of the Gillespie Company of the League's military battalion. He was very likely in the August insurgent group. If so he returned to Gillespie County. Joseph Petsch married Anna Maria Weinheimer on November 21, 1865, in Gillespie County. They were the parents of at least seven children. Joseph Poetsch died on December 24, 1917, in Gillespie County.

07. See Document 13 Endnote 21, p.85 for a bio of Moritz Weiss.

08. Adolph Ruebsamen was bon about 1840 in the Duchy of Nassau. He was a brother Louis Ruebsamen, below. The family arrived in Texas on the *Harriet* from Reh in 1845 and settled in Gillespie County. He was a member of the Gillespie Company of the League's military battalion and fled with the August insurgent group. Ruebsamen survived the Nueces battle, but Confederates captured and executed him in late August, 1862.

09. August Luckenbach was born about 1833 in Nassau. He, along with two brothers and three sisters, arrived in Texas on the *Johann Detthard* in December 1845. Luckenbach married Henriette Berth Goebel on September 26, 1858, in Gillespie County. They were the parents of at least two children. Luckenbach was a member of the Gillespie Company of the League's military battalion. He was also a member of the August fleeing insurgent group and

wounded, but escaped from the battle. Confederates captured and hanged him on August 14, 1862, just north of San Antonio.

10.   Adolf Vater was born about 1839 in Prussia. The family arrived in New Orleans on the *Falcon* from Hamburg on November 22, 1853, and arrived at Indianola in 1857. He was a member of the Gillespie Company of the League's military battalion. He was in the killed at the battle site.

11.   Christian Schaefer was born about 1844 in Nassau. The family arrived in Texas about 1855, and in Gillespie County shortly thereafter. Schaefer was a member of the Gillespie Company of the League's military battalion. He was engaged to twenty-one-year-old Minna Kutscher. Schaefer fled with the August insurgent group and was killed at the battle site. On February 16, 1863, Minna Kutscher gave birth to a son who was named Christian Schaefer.

12.   Louis Ruebsamen was born about 1843 in the Duchy of Nassau. He was a brother to Adolph above. The family arrived in Texas on the *Harriet* from Reh in 1845, and settled in Gillespie County. Ruebsamen was a member of the Gillespie Company of the League's military battalion and fled with the August insurgent group. He was very likely wounded, but he escaped the battle. Confederates later captured and executed him on August 24th.

13.   Phillip Beck, Jr. was born about 1837 in Wuerttemberg. The family arrived in Texas on the *Andacia* from Winterlingen, Wuerttemberg in 1846, and settled in Gillespie County. Beck was a member of the Gillespie Company of the League's military battalion and likely a member of August fleeing insurgent group. He survived the battle and returned home. Beck fled Texas and on March 30, 1863, he enlisted in Company C, First Regiment [Union] Texas Cavalry at Carrollton, Louisiana. Confederate forces captured him after the Battle at Los Rucias on June 25, 1864. His Union service records show he took the oath of allegiance to the CSA on August 7, 1864. No record of him serving in the Confederate forces has been located. It is not known what happen to him.

14.   Heinrich Weyershausen [Weiershausen] was born about 1829 in Nassau. The family arrived in Texas on the *Auguste Meline* in 1845, and settled in Gillespie County. Weyershausen married Henrietta Flick on August 6, 1851, in Gillespie County. They were the parents of three children. He was a member of the Gillespie Company of the League's military battalion and fled with the August insurgent group. Weyershausen was killed at the battle site.

15.   Christian Poetsch [Petsch] was born about 1843 in Nassau, a brother to Joseph Petsch, listed above. The family arrived in Texas on the *Washington* in 1845, and settled in Gillespie County. He was a member of the Gillespie Company of the League's military battalion and was in the August insurgent group. He

survived the battle, but no further nformation has been located regarding him in the aftermath.

16. Conrad Bock was born in 1840 in Prussia. The family arrived in Gillespie County about 1854. Bock married Pauline Flick on May 5, 1860, in Gillespie County. They were the parents of one child. He was a member of the Gillespie Company of the League's military battle and fled with the August insurgent group. He survived the battle, but was captured and executed on August 24, 1862, just north of Boerne.

17. See Document 13, Endnote 21, p.85 for a bio of Franz Weiss.

## 27. Captain Davis's Request for Confederate Troops

Camp Davis
July 25, 1862

Colonel James M. Norris
Colonel, Commanding Texas Frontier Regiment

Col;

Our country is getting in a deplorable condition, or specially this portion of the line. I am satisfied unless something is done soon our companies will have to concentrate. Our camps are threatened by the Union men in the mountains. They say they must have provisions and by Mr. King[1] an attack on the weak camps along this portion of the line they can supply themselves. I am confident beyond a doubt that they are concentrating in larger bodies with what aim nobody is able to tell. There are no Indians in this portion of country, the patrol scouts have become worthless, the generally meet the Union men in larger numbers than themselves, consequently they can do nothing. I am really afraid sometime they will get the scouts' horses. The patrols that I send out cannot compete with from twenty-five to forty well armed men, unless there are Confederate troops sent to this frontier to aid the sections, Regiment companies will have to be concentrated. The opposes (sic) of our government are getting so numerous on this line, that I think we will have to abandon Indian hunting and turn our attention to Yankee hunting, for it is apparent that no Indians are coming into a country where so many signs of white men is found. I hope our Col will look into the matter immediately, and place us in a condition to not only defend ourselves, but arrest those men and being them to _____.

I mainly make these suggestions to show the Col. the condition of affairs on this side of the line, for which purpose I suppose our Major visits headquarters in person.

Every thing as far as I can learn is getting along smoothly in the western division of this line, both the officers and men move _____ together. I have the honor in to _____ myself.

Respectfully Your Obedient servant,
H. T. Davis[2], Capt.

ENDNOTES
Captain Davis' Request for Confederate Troops

01. Mr. King is the same Edward A. King that Captain Duff spoke of in his June 23<sup>rd</sup> report. See Document 24, Endnote 13, p.139.

02. Henry T. Davis was born on June 13, 1834, in North Carolina and settled in Hays County, Texas. He married Susan T. Brownrigg on February 3, 1859, in Bexar County. The 1860 Hays County Census shows Davis as twenty-six years old, and a merchant by profession. His wife is listed as Susan, described as eighteen years old, and born in Texas. No children are listed. After the year-long enlistment ended, Davis and about half of his company joined Duff's battalion as Company F. He remained with Duff's command until the end of the war, reaching the rank of lieutenant colonel. After the war, Davis and his family moved to Orange County, Texas, where he died on October 4, 1888.

# 28. Letter–Colonel James M. Norris – August 1, 1862

Head Quarters
Texas Frontier Regiment
Camp Collins,
August 1st, 1862

Colonel J. Y. Dashiell[1]
Adjt & Insp Genl.
Austin, Texas

Col:

I have this evening received a very extra ordinary (sic) communication from Capt H. T. Davis, Company F, a copy of which I herewith send.

I now write to ask you to represent the facts to the Confederate States authorities and endeavor to influence them to send a force into the section of country indicated by Capt. Davis to effectually rout and disperse the forces of Lincoln and rid the country of them. I do not wish to go after them for the following reasons.

We are just now getting fairly to work on the line; we anticipate a plentiful harvest of scalps, within the next month or two. I have the pleasure to announce even now that we have within the first four months of our service killed more Indians that any two regiments have for two years – if we except Col Ford's fight. (I speak of Frontier protection Regiments.) We have killed ten, of which I have sufficient proof to have no doubt beside the one that Capt Salmon's men shot from his horses which I have no doubt was killed; but as they did not get the scalp and I have no positive proof. I shall wait for further developments before I report as killed.

Having just received ammunition to enable us to work properly, I am exceedingly both to break up my present plans. I am perfectly willing to engage Mr. Lincoln's friend if I can do so without losing too much time from my regular work and to _____ [missing words – *Editor*]

If I have to go after them to protect the men and property belonging to this Regiment and fortune shall favor me. I hope that I shall not be required to administer oaths as they will neither make good citizens nor soldiers. Please instruct me fully.

I have the honor to be your obedient servant,

James M. Norris
Colonel Commanding
Texas Frontier Regiment

ENDNOTE
Letter Colonel Norris, August 1, 1862

01. Jeremiah Yellott Dashiell was born on September 23, 1804, in Maryland. He received his medical degree from the University of Baltimore at the age of nineteen. He was the founder of and professor of medicine at Louisville Medical College in Louisville, Kentucky. He married a woman with the surname of Cottman about 1832, likely in Kentucky. They were the parents of one child. The family moved to New Orleans. His wife died about 1842, and about 1844, he married Mildred Walker Hornsby in Louisiana. They were the parents of five children. In 1846, at the outbreak of the Mexican War, he was appointed an army paymaster. He was appointed colonel and assistant adjutant general, and inspector general of Texas State Troops. After the war he was the editor of the San Antonio *Herald* until his death on March 14, 1888, at San Antonio in Bexar County.

## 29. Lieutenant Colonel Benton's[1] Report
## August 20, 1862

Camp Clark (San Marcos)
August 20, 1862

Editor of the Herald:

From information received at the military headquarters, San Antonio, a few weeks back, it was believed that a portion of the citizens of the frontier counties were in a state of rebellion against the Confederate States, and that an absolute necessity existed for an armed force to be sent to certain counties for the purpose of suppressing the same. I was ordered to proceed with a detachment consisting of Capt. J. K. Stevens'[2] and Lewis Mavericks'[3] companies, with permission to take additional forces to expedite the business. Capt. E.B. Millett[4] with 40 men was added to my force. The counties assigned me consisted of Burnett, Llano, San Saba, Mason, and Kimball.

On arrived in Burnett I was gratified to find every thing quiet, being warmly and hospitably received by the citizens, who, after an explanation of my mission, assured me that there would no opposition to the requirements of the government. I feel it my duty to our State and the Confederacy, as well as an act of justice to the citizens of the counties composing my district, to give these facts. And I now take occasion to say, that I have not met any people who came forward more cheerfully and promptly to take the prescribed oath than the people of the counties above mentioned; and no one to my knowledge failed to do so, or absented himself to avoid any requirement made upon him. I called upon various persons to name any who was absent on that account, or to make the proof required by my instruction before I could make an arrest, and failed to find any one who could or would make oaths to any fact that would justify my making arrest. To the first person I met with I made known my mission, produced my authority, and stated I held in one hand the olive branch, and in the other the sword. I was answered that I would have no difficulty in the discharge of my duty, and satisfaction expressed that they had an opportunity in common with other sections to do their duty, which all did promptly.

I could perceive no other than a feeling of satisfaction with the government through Gen. H. P. Bee, and with my course in carrying out his instruction. If this is not so, I desire that those who are dissatisfied will make a statement over their own signatures specifying wherein I have failed to do my duty under my instructions. In the discharge of my duty I took the ground that I would not become a party to any private quarrel or neighborhood difficulty, and if I have not given entire satisfaction, I am confident that but few will be found who will come forward over their signatures and make a showing. I found no one who would name or identify any man or any act, under oath, that would warrant me in making any arrest; but in every instance when I called upon them it would only be rumor, until it became a ridiculous farce. It is unnecessary to say more on this matter, but to repeat that it is my duty as commander of the expedition and Provost Marshal of the counties named, to make this statement.

I take pleasure in returning my thanks to Capt. J. K. Stevens, Lewis Maverick, and E.B. Millett, and to their officers and men for their valuable aid in all this work as Assistant Provost Marshals.

I ask you to give the above an invention with the request that the [Austin] *State Gazette* and other papers favorable to the South will copy.

Nat Benton
Lt. Col. Commanding Expedition
Provost Marshal

ENDNOTES
Lieutenant Colonel Benton's Report

01.  Nathaniel Benton was born about 1816, in Tennessee. He married Harriet Maria McCulloch about 1838, likely in Dyer County, Tennessee. They were the parents of one child. She died about 1840, likely in Dyer County, Tennessee. Benton went to the gold fields. The 1850 Census for Trinity County, California, lists him as thirty-six years old, and born in Tennessee. The date Benton arrived in Texas is not known. He married Elizabeth Jane Harrison about 1855, likely in Guadalupe County, Texas. They were the parents of three children. Elizabeth Jane Harrison Benton died in 1862, likely in Guadalupe County. On March 22, 1862, Benton raised a cavalry company from Guadalupe and was elected its captain. The company joined with others into the 36th Regiment Texas Cavalry and Benton was elected lieutenant colonel. Benton lost an arm at Blair's Landing on April 12, 1864, during the Red River Campaign. Post-war, he was elected chief justice in 1866, and served until 1867 when Federal authorities removed him from office. Nathaniel Benton died in 1872, in Guadalupe County.

02.  Joel K. Stevens was born about 1829 in Mississippi. He married Margaret C. Geir on January 27, 1848. It is not known if they were the parents of any children. The date they arrived in Texas is also not known. Stevens was a member of James Duff's Alamo Rifles in September, 1861. He enrolled in Company C, 36th Regiment Texas Cavalry on March 22, 1862, and was elected its captain. Joel K. Stevens was killed in battle on June 8, 1864, during the Red River Campaign.

03.  Lewis Antonio Maverick was born on March 23, 1839, in San Antonio in Bexar County, Texas. Mary Ann Adams and Samuel Augustus Maverick were his parents. He enrolled in Company E, 36th Regiment Texas Cavalry on May 29, 1862, and elected its captain  He was seriously wounded in the Battle of Blair's Landing during the Red River Campaign in mid-1864. He was promoted to major on General DeBray's staff in the summer of 1864. Maverick married Ada Bradley on September 20, 1865, in Bexar County. On June 18, 1866, Maverick died in San Antonio.

04.  Eugene Bartlett Millett was born on April 25, 1838, in Washington County Texas. He enrolled in Nathaniel Benton's Company B of the 36th Regiment Texas Cavalry on March 22, 1862, and was elected first lieutenant. On June 1, 1862, he was appointed captain when Benton was promoted to lieutenant colonel. He remained with the unit until the end of the war and returned to Guadalupe County. Millett married Ida Mabel Burtner on September 6, 1876, in Adams County, Illinois. They were the parents of one child. Eugene Bartlett Millett died on October 18, 1915, in Los Angeles County, California.

## 30. San Antonio Weekly Herald – August 30, 1862

Allow me through your paper to contradict certain false and slanderous reports now in circulation that this Country had men in the bush with the Lincolnites, as I can assure you as one who knows that such is not the case not one man has not left Said Country for such purpose nor none will.    In accordance with instruction from Col. Nat. Benton, Prov M., the Deputy Provost Marshal of the Country notified the people to come up to the work more readily, there was a perfect rush, everyone came the same day and at the same time. The conscript-enrolling officer enrolled and swore [illegible] 20 conscripts for the war and without even a murmur. I write this in order that the public mind may be set right as to the people of this County. We think the unfounded rumor came from the 'Bogus' inhabitants of Gillespie County, and we dislike for them to slander us until they set their own people right.

Mason, Aug 21st 1862
Respectfully yours,
G. W. Y.

## 31. General Bee's Report – October 21, 1862

HEADQUARTERS SUB-MILITARY DISTRICT OF THE
RIO GRANDE

San Antonio, October 21, 1862

Capt. S. B. Davis,
Asst, Adjt. Gen., First District of Texas, San Antonio

Sir:

Inclosed you will find a copy of the official report of Lieut.
C. D. McRae[1], Second Regiment Texas Mounted Rifles, of an
engagement between a detachment of C. S. troops under his
command and a body of unknown men in arms against the
Government.

Shortly after assuming command of this district
information was received from various sources to the effect
that the citizens of the northwestern counties of this State, or
very many of them (being chiefly foreigners by birth), were
greatly disaffected and were organizing and arming to resist
the execution of the law known as the conscript act.

In July information was received establishing the fact that
Jack Hamilton and other traitors were unquestionably in arms
against the Government and had assembled in the counties
designated, their forces being variously estimated at from 100
to 500. Numerous statements were also received that these
banded traitors were moving their goods and families, with
large supplies of provisions, into the mountain districts, and

were carrying off the property in some instances of loyal citizens, and at last, to set beyond a doubt their objects and intentions, positive intelligence was received of their having waylaid and murdered one or two well-known secession or loyal citizens. Under these circumstances I appointed Captain Duff provost-marshal for the counties composing the disaffected district, and placed under his control four mounted companies, command by Capt. John Donelson[2], Second Regiment Texas Mounted Rifles, with instructions to issue a proclamation declaring martial law, and requiring all good and loyal citizens to return quietly to their homes, and take the oath of allegiance to the Confederate and State governments, or be treated summarily as traitors in arms; also instructing him to send out scouting parties into the mountain districts with orders to find and break up any such encampment and depots as had been reported to exist there, and to send the families and provisions back to the settlements.

These instructions were fully carried out, numerous small encampments with large supplies of provisions were found, far more than could possible have been needed by those found in possession of them, chiefly women and children, who by their language and conduct removed all doubt, if any could still have existed, as to the purposes for which these supplies were intended. These were all removed to the settlements, or destroyed when the former course could not be pursued. Large numbers of young men returned to their homes, took the oath of allegiance, and enlisted in the army. From their statements it became certain that there were still many in arms who were determined to resist the Government at all hazards. Lieutenant McRae's detachment was sent after these, and having found a large trail they followed it with the result stated in Lieutenant McRae's report. Lieutenant McRae and his command behaved with admirable coolness and bravery, and did their work most effectually.

In presenting this report to the general commanding I adduce another proof of the necessity of the military authorities being clothed with more than ordinary powers to enable them to discharge their duties of the Government and people, as alluded to in my communication of the 16th instant.

I have the honor to be, captain, very respectfully you most obedient servant,

H. P. Bee
Brigadier-General, Provisional Army

ENDNOTES
General Bee's Report, October 1, 1862

01.  Colin Dickson McRae was born on September 22, 1835, in Red River County, Texas. By 1860, he was living in San Antonio. McRae enrolled in Donelson's Company K, 2$^{nd}$ Regiment Texas Mounted Rifles in February, 1861, and elected first lieutenant. In February of 1862, the company was reorganized and McRae remained first lieutenant. Company K was part of a three-company task force sent to the Texas Hill Country in late July/early August, 1862, to enforce martial law. He was the commander of the pursuit force sent after the League's insurgents. On August 10, 1862, the Battle of Nueces was fought. After the battle McRae's detachment returned to San Antonio. He was promoted to captain on October 1, 1862, after Donelson was promoted to major. McRae married Margaret D. Haw in San Antonio. They were the parents of one child who died on June 26, 1864. Colin Dickson McRae died of typhoid fever in September, 1864.

02.  John Donelson was born on April 6, 1829, in Tennessee. The date he arrived in Texas is not known but he had settled in Live Oak County by 1860. Donelson enrolled in Company K, 2$^{nd}$ Regiment Texas Mounted Rifles on September 23, 1862, and elected captain. He was the military commander of the three-company task force sent to the Texas Hill Country in late July/early August, 1862. By August 21, 1862 he replaced James Duff as the provost marshal. On until September 21, 1862, he was replaced by Captain Josiah Taylor of Company G, 36$^{th}$ Regiment, Texas Cavalry. Donelson was promoted to major on October 8, 1862. John Donelson died in San Antonio in July, 1864.

## 32. Henry Schwethelm – 1913 Letter
## to his grandson Otto*

My Dear Otto. I received your letter Several days ago. I will write to you about that Nuesses fight. And you can give it to your teacher. We Started from the head of Turtle Creek in Kerr Co. 68 to go to Mexico on the first day of August 1862.

The Governor of the State issuedt a Proclamation that all that would not take the oath of aligians to the Cofeterace had to leave the State within 30 days so we left.

But we where overtaking on the west Nuesses from about 125 or 150 Confedrate Soldiers and the[y] shot into our Camp about [h]ours before day. Then waited until day brag and the fight commenced we fought them about one [h]our and we only had 17 man left able to fight.

And then we 17 man went agross the Nuesses into the Cedar Break the[y] never followed us we left 9 or & deat and about 12 or 13 wounded. Some 25 man who had left our camp before day when the fight comenced. Me and Ernst Kramer counted our men and there was 40 left so the[y] was going back home and then I told them that I would not go home that I was going to Mexico if I had to go alone. So Jak Kusenberger and Cha Graff from Fredericksburg said if I would go they[y] would go with me. Of course we had not horses and no money but we went that was Sunday morning on the 10 day of August and we got into Mexico on the 13 without anything to eat, but after we got there we got plenty to eat. Then we went to Pedros Negros from there to Monterey and from there to Matamores and from there was sent to New Orleans by the U. S. Consul Pierce then on the 26 day of

October we got to New Orleans. And on the 27 inlisted in the U. S. Army we had a very often nothing to eat for two days in Mexico.

Now coming back to the fight after the fight Leut Lilly had all our wound man killed. He called Vollonteers to kill them and he got plenty of them. One of the Voll is living here in Kerr Co now his name is Alonzo Rees[1] he lives at Center Point he is now a great church man. I hope he will to hell some day.

Now I got all of this information from Dr. Downs[2] after the war. The[y] sent for him to forth Clark to attent to there wounded the[y] had about 45 of them. Dr. Downs had a ranch about 10 miles from Bandera at that time and I was will acquainted with him. That is about all now I suppose.

Your grandpa
Henry Schwethelm

Dear Otto two of them 14 men that went bak home two of them Henry Stieler[3] and Tho Brukish were taking Preseoner in Kerrville by Starkey and turned over to some of Capt Davis Comp. and 3 miles above Kerrville on Goat Creek the[y] them shooting tarket at them and then left them. After the war we went to the Nuesses and got the bones and buried them in Comfort.

Your Grandpa and Grandma
Schwethelm

Editorial note: All misspellings and errors of punctuation and grammar in the original document are preserved.

ENDNOTES
Henry Schwethelm, Letter in 1913

01. Daniel Adolphus [Dolph] Rees was born on December 2, 1831, in McNairy County, Tennessee. The family arrived in Texas in 1851 and in Kerr County about 1856. Rees enrolled in Harbour's company of Kerr County Minuteman organization in February, 1861, and served until February, 1862. He enrolled in Davis' Company of the Frontier Regiment in March, 1862, and was appointed/elected third sergeant. He was likely in the Confederate pursuit force and took part in the Nueces battle. He re-enlisted in Hunter's Company, Frontier Regiment on December 24, 1862. Rees married Lucy Ann Nowlin on December 3, 1863, in Kerr County. They were the parents of at least ten children. He remained with the company until the end of the war and returned to Kerr County. Daniel Adolphus [Dolph] died on March 25, 1901, in Kerr County.

02. Edmund [Edwin] M. Downs was born in August, 1816, in Caledonia County, Vermont. He married Caroline Lathrop about 1840, likely in Wisconsin. They were the parents of at least eight children. They arrived in Texas about 1858, and were living in Medina County by 1860. On January 21, 1862, Bandera and Medina Unionists burned his home. He was a contract surgeon for Texas State and Confederate troops. The family moved to California about 1875. Edmund M. Downs died in 1879 in Tustin, Los Angeles County, California.

03. Heinrich Stieler was born about 1844 in Oranienbaum in the Duchy of Anhalt. The family arrived in Texas in 1854 and in the Comfort area in 1856. He was a member of Kendall Company of the League's military battalion and fled with the August insurgent group. He survived the battle but Davis' company captured and executed him on August 22, 1862, at Goat Creek in Kerr County.

# 33. Letter–Eduard Degener – August 1,1862

August 1, 1862

To: Col. Von Bernewitz
    Brunswick
    & Government Counsel
    Ernst Bramigk
    Coethen[1]

You will receive this letter without any heading & without any signature, because I do not know whether it will ever reach you. I am in hopes that you have received my former letter through Dammeit in Hanover & by way of Mexico. The only object I have in writing, is to inform you that we are all alive & in good health. B's family[2] has been increased by the birth of a charming little daughter. The war, up to the present time has not been in our immediate neighborhood, but [its] not with[out] its inconveniences. The land is divided into Military district, the Chief in each military district having well conceived the duties of a regiment of swords. The Habeas Corpus acts suspended.[3] Summary Martial Justice. Divers Counties nearly stripped of their male population. Every one between the ages of 18 to 35 ordered to take the field, those between 35 & 50 drilled as Militia for future purposes–in exposed parts numbers volunteer for the purpose of carrying on guerilla warfare.[4] This is in consequence of young men having remained true to the Union, & having gone for months into the Mountains & ravines loafing, & followed up & chased by Confederate Troops, like Indians. It is astonishing that their efforts in taking these men prisoners have not been crowned with success. Civil war is on the eve of breaking out[5], Confederate Troops coming from all sides ascend our mountains. In order to avoid a Vendee war withdrawal across the Rio Grande – Confiscation acts, imprisonment, Martial

Law to the utmost rigor, for all those who do not adjure allegiance to the United States, swear allegiance to the Confederate States, & who do not accept Confederate money as Cash. Those who are compelled to remain here swear, receive a pass; but if he should be of opinion that on account expressions, or on account of his influence among his fellow citizens, he would be placed on the black list, he sleeps in the bushes, has tied to his plough his arms, a horse hitched in the immediate neighborhood, prepared every thing to escape or to hide. To lead such a life is at the commencement very exciting – then renders a person nervous, then annoying & ultimately becomes second nature.

The crops nearly all over the Country are a failure. Corn $2 ¾ per bushel, each bushel weighing 56 lb.; 100 lb. Flour $15.00; Powder $8.00 per lb. Each shot from a gun, after close calculation cost 7 ½ silbergroschen. No clothing procurable – Quite a common calico Dress, cost 2 months ago $8.00 – say 12 Prussian dollars. One pair of shoes like those worn by our workman, on the other side 15 Prussian dollars, in the Capital of the land, Austin. All the former germans cobblers tan beef hides & furnish shoes at $5=7 ½ Prussian & with all that. This leather is poorly tanned outside, inside it is the rawhide; the price of this so-called leather is $1.50; this is my last sheet of paper, no more to be had, no more coffee in the house, none for the last 12 month. Our sweetening, wild honey. The sale of intoxicating liquors prohibited. The last whiskey – say whiskey –which I had cost $3.00 per bottle. We all wear, even the ladies, since Christmas last Moccasins; the pantaloons & coats of men & boys made out of Deerskins tanned by ourselves. Yesterday although with a heat of 30 degrees & losing the meat I had to kill a beef for the purpose of making a lariat in order to hitch horses. For months no rain. Creek all dry, the Guadalupe River appears like a creek, further down it is said she is dry for 15 miles. Grass is brown & altogether disappears. For the last six weeks the wheat has been laying tied up in the field & is waiting for men to thrash it. The merchants having stocks on hand are amassing an enormous quantity of paper money.

The people of the south curse the once beloved United States, & prepared to fight for their rights – "Slavery, or to die in the attempt." About the events in Europe we learn nothing, nothing at all, the newspapers bring news of victories, of retreats on account of strategic purposes. We have killed more people to judge by the press, than the population of the north. What will the end to be: You who are at a distance are perhaps better enable to form an opinion of our position, than we who are in the midst of it. My opinion is as yet the same, when it will come to pass however – qui vivera, verra (who lives will see). In Arkansas they have established a tariff of prices for necessaries of life. The same thing is announced to take place here.

The Military Chiefs i.e. the Provost Marshals have by virtue of a Proclamation emanated from headquarters, the right to act at discretion with suspicious persons.[6] The troops from the South express openly the threat that they will not make any more prisoners; what this means, an American is only able to say. If the south is victorious, it may become necessary for the Germans to emigrate again. In what direction, then? The proposition was made in a San Antonio, yesterday, to make good the loss of a freed nigger to each planter, by giving him two Hessians to cultivate his land. As ridiculous as such an observation may be it shows, nevertheless, the hatred of the Southerners towards the "Dutch." They are all considered Black Republicans; that means opposed to Slavery; & the fact that Siegel with his Missouri Germans has had so many success[es] is very maddening to them, as each southern Shopkeeper lawyer is a gentleman and General at their birth.

Who every carries this letter over the Rio Grande and arrives there safe shall sign this letter. Compliments to all friends & relatives & remember us Kindly, even if you do not receive news from us for a long time. Hearty Greetings – Colonel von Bernewitz in Brunswick & Government Counsel Ernest Bramigk-Coethen. A Blockade is anyhow a ridiculous thing.

At the commencement of March a hail storm took away all my window glasses, with the exception of those on the North & west side of my house & made my shingle roof like a sive (sic); it is in the same fix this day, because San Antonio affords neither Panes of glass nor nails. Do not be astonished at the unconnectedness of my letter.

Yesterday the departure was determined upon[7], to day the horses were shod, & are saddled. One Pack Mule carries Provisions for 3 weeks for 3 persons who will be joined by 47 others, picked men.[8] One more dinner, then goodbye, who knows whether we will meet again. Not a cent of money in the Pocket, thrown amongst Indians & Mexicans robbers, where Confederate money is of no more avail then in Mexico. All this is Romance enough to satisfy a dancing tea party in Berlin.

I smoke a Pipe, covered with rawhide from top to bottom, including the sack containing fire materials, because the juice or the spit has taken possession of the whole pipe. Miserable land where a man can't even buy a pipe. Mama is baking the last bread for some time to come for her dear sons. The Mail to day announces the price of flour at /18.

ENDNOTES
Eduard Degener's Letter August 1, 1862

01.  Von Bernewitz was Degener's father-in-law and Ernst Bramigk was a very close family friend.

02.  B. is Degener's daughter, Bertha, born about 1836 in Brunswick. She married Christian Rhodius on March 15, 1854, in Comal County. The 'charming little daughter' was Mary, who was born in 1862.

03.  *Habeas corpus* had not been suspended, but it certainly may have seemed as if it had.

04.  It is interesting that Degener, who was head of the Union Loyal League, used the term guerrilla warfare to describe acts of members of the League's military arm.

05.  It is also of special interest to not that Degener described the conditions as "Civil War is on the eve of breaking out." Most writers claim that the League members that were hiding in the mountains were just trying to avoid the war and had not desire to take part in the fighting. All Unionist accounts made by members of the fleeing group stated they were going to Mexico where they would go on and join the Union Army.

06.  Martial law had been declared throughout Texas on May 31, 1962, and a provost marshal was appointed in each county. They were vested with a great deal of authority.

07.  Another very interesting comment by Degener. John W. Sansom says the decision to flee was made about July 20th.

08.  This sentence provides a great deal of information. First, it tells about how many pack animals the fleeing group had; one for every three men. Second, it confirms that not all the Unionists met at one place. There was a second group of about forty-seven men located elsewhere than the assembly area at Turtle Creek/Bushwhack Creek. This was at a base camp located on the headwaters of the South Fork of the Guadalupe River.

# 34. Camp Pedernales Post Returns – August 1862

## ENDNOTES
### Major Items shown on August 1862 Post Returns

01. "The Post Near Fredericksburg Was Established The 1st Aug 1862."

02. There were three Confederate detachments: Donelson's Company, Duff's Company, and a detachment from Taylor's battalion. There were 10 officers and 237 men. Captain Donelson was in command of the post and troops.

03. "About the 1st of Aug Capt Donelson with 100 men scouted the upper portion of Gillespie Co for 5 days in search of certain bands of traitors to the C.S. Arresting a great many he discovered that a greater portion had left the country, returning to comp he despatched Lt. McRae with 94 fresh men and horses in pursuit of them. The traitors were overtaken by Lt. McRae on 10th Aug on the Nueces River. Then a fight took place a report of which has been duly forwarded to Headquarters." *This establishes that Captain Donelson, not Captain Duff ordered the pursuit force.*

# 35. Camp Pedernales Troop Returns – September 1862

RETURN of *Camp Pedernales 10 miles west of Fredericksburg* commanded by *Captain John W.*

## ENDNOTES
## MAJOR ITEMS SHOWN ON SEPTEMBER 1862 POST RETURNS

01. "Capt Donelson was appointed Provost Marshal & Entered Upon the duties of his office the 20th Aug 1862." This established that Donelson was the Provost Marshal by August 20, 1862 and was such when the hangings on Spring Creek occurred on August 23rd.

02. "Lt McRae's detachment after the Nueces Battle proceeded to San Antonio & did not return to post."

03. "Capt Donelson was relieved at Fredericksburg on the 20th Sept 1862 by Capt. Josiah Taylor."

John Donelson

for the month of September 186 2

REMARKS

Capt Donelson
was appointed
provost Marshal &
entium upon the duties of the
office the 30th aug 1862

RECORD OF EVENTS.—[See par. XI. Circular (A. G. O.) Sept. 30, 1850.]

Lt McRaes detachments after the recent battle
proceeded to San Antonio & did not return
to post

Jno Donelson
Capt
Commanding Post.

# 36. List of Kerr County Deserters

*(Reproduced from the holdings of the Texas State Archives, from original list in the handwriting of J.M. Starkey\*)*

| # | Surname | Given Name | Age | Rank | Remarks | Type Unit |
|---|---------|------------|-----|------|---------|-----------|
| 001 | Boerner | Louis[1] | 28 | Pvt | | Militia |
| 002 | Boerner | Wilhelm[2] | 34 | Pvt | | Militia |
| 003 | Boxter | Jacob[3] | 31 | Pvt | | Militia |
| 004 | Elstner | Joseph[4] | 21 | Pvt | | Militia |
| 005 | Felsing | Ernst/Eduard[5] | 34 | Pvt | | Militia |
| 006 | Hasse | Herman[6] | | Pvt | | Militia |
| 007 | Heinen | Anton[7] | 22 | Pvt | | Militia |
| 008 | Heinen | Ferdinand[8] | 17 | Pvt | | Militia |
| 009 | Heinen | Henry[9] | 22 | Pvt | | Militia |
| 010 | Heinen | Theodore[10] | 22 | Pvt | | Militia |
| 011 | Henderson | Howard[11] | 21 | Pvt | | Militia |
| 012 | Kell | Scott,[12] | 26 | Pvt | | Confederate Army |
| 013 | Kempt | H. L.[13] | 27 | Pvt | | Militia |
| 014 | Lamb | Albert[14] | 17 | Pvt | | Militia |
| 015 | Lane | Paul[15] | | Pvt | | Confederate Army |
| 016 | Nelson | Allen[16] | 20 | Pvt | | Militia |
| 017 | Nelson | Louis[17] | 27 | Pvt | | Militia |
| 018 | Sanger | Fritz[18] | 30 | Pvt | | Militia |
| 019 | Sanger | Henry C.[19] | 24 | Pvt | | Confederate Army |
| 020 | Sauer | Gottlieb[20] | 24 | Pvt | | Militia |
| 021 | Schieholz | Louis[21] | 22 | Pvt | | Militia |
| 022 | Schreiner | Amil[22] | 22 | Pvt | | Militia |
| 023 | Schwethelm | Henry[23] | 22 | Pvt | | Militia |
| 024 | Scott | Charles Franklin[24] | 35 | Pvt | | Militia |
| 025 | Steves | Heinrich[25] | 28 | Pvt | | Militia |
| 026 | Stieler | Heinrich[26] | 17 | Pvt | | Militia |
| 027 | Strong | John[27] | 26 | Pvt | | Militia |
| 028 | Tegener | Fritz[28] | 29 | Col | | Militia |
| 029 | Tegener | Gustav[29] | 35 | Pvt | | Militia |
| 030 | Vetterlien | Charles[30] | 30 | Pvt | | Militia |
| 031 | Vetterlien | Gottlieb[31] | 32 | Pvt | | Militia |

\* Information added

ENDNOTES
List of Hill Country Men Who Deserted State or Confederate Units

01. Wilhelm F. Boerner was born abut 1830 in Hanover. The family arrived in the Comfort area in 1855, and settled on Cypress Creek near Comfort in 1856. Boerner married Laura Steves on February 14, 1861, in Kerr County. They were the parents of a son born in May, 1862. He was a member of the Kendall Company of the League's military battalion. He deserted from Company E, Second Battalion, Third Regiment of the 31st Brigade District in the summer of 1862 and was in the August fleeing insurgent group. He survived the battle but Davis' company captured and hanged him on August 22, 1862, at Spring Creek.

02. No data was located on Jacob Boxter.

03. Joseph Elstner was born about 1841 in Austria. The date the family arrived in Texas is not known, but they arrived in the Comfort area in 1854. Elstner was a member of Kuechler's company of December, 1861, and a member of the Kendall Company of the League's military battalion. He deserted from Company E, Second Battalion, Third Regiment of the 31st Brigade District and was in the August insurgent group. He survived the Nueces battle, but he was killed in Kuechler's insurgent group of October 18, 1862, in a skirmish at the Rio Grande.

04. Eduard Felsing was born about 1829 in Hessen Darmstadt. The date he arrived in Texas is not known, but he arrived in the Comfort area in 1854. Felsing married Caroline Sieckenius on January 6, 1861, in San Antonio. He was a member of the Kendall Company of the League's military Battalion. He deserted from Company E, Third Regiment of the 31st Brigade District and was in the August insurgent group. He survived the Nueces battle, but was killed in Kuechler's insurgent group of October 18, 1862, in a skirmish at the Rio Grande.

05. No further data on Herman Hasse.

06. Anton Heinen was born about 1840 in Prussia. The date he arrived in Texas is not known, but by 1854 he was living in the Comfort area. He took the oath of allegiance to the Confederacy on September 10, 1861. Heinen was a member of Kuechler's company of December, 1861. He was likely a member of the Kendall County Company of the League's military battalion. Heinen was likely one of the insurgents who turned back at Turtle Creek in late July, 1862. He fled Texas and on February 5, 1863, he enrolled in Company C, First Regiment [Union] Texas Cavalry. He was mustered out of service on October 31, 1865, in San Antonio. Heinen married Johanna Allerkamp about 1867, location not known. They were the parents of two children. Anton Heinen died about 1869.

07. Ferdinand Heinen was born on December 31, 1841, in Prussia. He was a brother of Henry Hubert and Theodore Heinen, below. The family arrived in Texas on the *Fortuna* in 1860 and settled in the Comfort area. He was likely a member of the Kendall County Company of the League's military battalion. He deserted from his militia unit; Company D, Second Battalion, 31$^{st}$ Brigade District. He was likely one of the individuals who turned back at Turtle Creek. He hid out for the remainder of the war. Heinen was a Texas Ranger from 1874 until 1877. He married Pauline Meckel on December 31, 1876, in Kerr County. They were the parents of twelve children. Ferdinand Heinen died on April 12, 1923, in Kendall County.

08. Henry Hubert Heinen was born in October, 1838, in Prussia. He was a brother of Ferdinand Heinen, above and Theodore Heinen, below. The family arrived in Texas on the *Fortuna* in 1860 and settled in the Comfort area. He was likely a member of the Kendall Company of the Leagues military battalion. He deserted from his militia unit; Company D, Second Battalion, 31$^{st}$ Brigade District. Heinen was likely one of the individuals who turned back at Turtle Creek. He hid out the remainder of the war. Heinen married Wilhelmina Stieler in Kerr County on August 14, 1864. They were the parents of at least seven children. Henry Hubert Heinen died in 1914 in Kendall County.

09. Theodore Heinen was born about 1840 in Prussia. He was a brother of Ferdinand and Henry H. Heinen, above. He was a member of the Comfort Home Guard in February 1982 as well as a member of the Kendall County Company of the League's military battalion. He deserted from his militia unit; Company D, Second Battalion, 31$^{st}$ Brigade District. He was also likely one of the men who turned back at Turtle Creek and hid out for the remainder of the war. Theodore Heinen died on November 15, 1914, in Kerr County.

10. Howard Henderson was born in 1842 in Tennessee. His parents died when he was young and Henderson came to Texas in 1857, with two uncles. They settled west of Kerrville just north of the present town of Ingram. He was very likely a member of the Kerr [American] Company of the League's military battalion. He deserted his militia unit – the John Henderson squad – and fled toward Mexico. Along with three other individuals, Henderson joined the insurgents on the trail. He survived the battle, went directly to Mexico and, enrolled in Company A, First Regiment [Union] Texas Cavalry in New Orleans on October 27, 1862. He remained with unit until the end of the war and was mustered out of service on October 31, 1865, at San Antonio. Henderson married Narcissa Turknett on May 20, 1866, in Kerr County. They were the parents of at least ten children. Howard Henderson died on November 18, 1908, in Kerr County.

11. Scot Kell was born about 1835, in Indiana. He deserted his Confederate unit; Hunter's Company, Frontier Regiment on August, 1863. See Document 11, Endnote 25, p.55 for a bio of Scott Kell.

12. H. L. Kemp was born about 1837 in Tennessee. The date he arrived in Texas is not known, but by 1860, he was living in Fayette County. By early 1862, he was living in Kerr County. He was likely a member of the Kerr [American] Company of the League's military battalion. Kemp deserted from Company E, Second Battalion, Third Regiment, 31st Brigade District and fled Texas. On January 31, 1863, he enlisted in Company A, First Regiment [Union] Texas Cavalry in New Orleans. He was captured at the Battle of Las Rucias on June 24, 1864, and died as a POW at Hempstead, Texas, on October 15, 1864.

13. Albert Lamb was born on October 23, 1844, in Michigan. The family arrived in Texas about 1855, and settled in Burnet County. By early 1862, he was living in Kerr County. Lamb was likely a member of the Kerr [American] Company of the League's military battalion. Lamb deserted his Kerr County militia unit; Company E, Second Battlion, Third Regiment, 31st Brigade District. Albert fled back to Michigan where about he married Josephine Stout. They were the parents of at least seven children. Lamb died on January 17, 1916, at Otsego in Allegan County, Michigan.

14. No data was located on Paul Lane

15. Allen Nelson was born about 1842 in Johnson County, Illinois. He was a brother of Hiram Louis Nelson, below. The family arrived in Gillespie County about 1854, and settled in the vicinity of Johnson Creek. Nelson was a member of Harbour's Company of Kerr Minutemen of February, 1861, and served until February, 1862. He was very likely a member of the Kerr [American] Company of the League's military battalion. Nelson deserted from Kerr Militia Company D, Second Battalion, Third Regiment, 31st Brigade District. Family stories say that the Confederates captured him about August, 1862, but he escaped and fled to Mexico. On October 27, 1862, he enrolled in Company A, First Regiment [Union] Texas Cavalry in New Orleans. Nelson was promoted to corporal on July 6, 1863; to sergeant on November 1, 1863; and to first sergeant on February 25, 1865. Allen died of pneumonia on June 14, 1865, in Fort Adams, Mississippi.

16. Hiram Louis Nelson was born on November 9, 1835, in Washington County, Illinois. He was a brother of Allen Nelson, above. The family arrived in Gillespie County about 1854, settled in the vicinity of Johnson Creek, and in 1857, moved to where the current Texas Boys Camp is now located. Nelson married Olive McDonald on August 9, 1855, in Gillespie County. They were the parents of ten children. Nelson served in the William Banta's Ranger Company in 1860. Nelson deserted from Company D, Second Battalion, Third Regiment, 31st Brigade Distinct in June, 1862. According to Nelson family stories Hiram Louis Nelson went to Matamoros to manage an import-export business about 1862. After the war the family returned to Kerr County. Hiram Louis Nelson died on May 8, 1922, in Kerr County.

17.  Fritz Sanger [Saenger] was born about 1828, the location of birth is not known. He was likely a brother of Henry C. Sanger, below. The date the family arrived in Texas is not known. By June, 1862, Sanger was living in Kerr County. Sanger was likely a member of the Kendall Company of the League's military battalion. He deserted his militia unit; Company E. Second Battalion, Third Regiment, 31$^{st}$ Brigade District in June, 1862. No further data.

18.  Henry C. Sanger [Saenger] was born about 1836, the location of birth is not known. He was likely a brother of Fritz Sanger, above. The date the family arrived in Texas is not known. By June, 1862, Henry C. Sanger was living in Kerr County. He was likely a member of the Kendall Company of the League's military battalion. Sanger deserted his militia unit; Company E, Second Battalion, Third Regiment, 31$^{st}$ Brigade District in June, 1862. No further data.

19.  Gottlieb Sauer was born about 1838 in Bavaria. The date he arrived in Texas is not known. By 1860, he was living near Comfort in Kerr County. Sauer was the second corporal in Kuechler's company of December, 1861. He was likely a member of the Kendall Company of the League's military battalion. He deserted his militia unit; Company E, Second Battalion, Third Regiment, 31$^{st}$ Brigade District in June, 1862, and fled Texas. On February 6, 1863, he enlisted in Company C, First Regiment [Union] Texas Cavalry, but deserted on August 3, 1864, at Rancho Martinez near Brownsville, Texas. No further data.

20.  Louis Schieholz was born about 1833 in Hanover. He arrived in Texas and the Comfort area in 1855. He was a member of Kuechler's company of December, 1861. He was likely a member of the Kendall Company of the League's military battalion. He deserted from his militia unit; Company D, Second Battalion, Third Regiment, 31$^{st}$ Brigade District about June, 1862 and fled with the August insurgent group. Louis Schieholz was killed at the battle site.

21.  Amil Schreiner was born about 1839 in Riguewihr, France. The date the family arrived in Texas is not known. Amil and his brother Charles moved to Lower Turtle Creek about 1857. Schreiner was a member of Harbour's Kerr County Minuteman Company from February, 1861, until February, 1862. He was a member of the Kendall Company of the League's military battalion. He deserted from his Kerr militia unit; Company E, Second Battalion, Third Regiment, 31$^{st}$ Brigade about June, 1862, and fled with the August insurgent group. Amil Schreiner died leading a counter-charge during the Nueces battle.

22.  Henry Joseph Schwethelm was born on September 4, 1840, in Langst, a village just outside of Dusseldorf, Prussia. The family arrived in Texas about 1850, and in the Comfort area in 1854. Prior to the war, he was a member of several Ranger companies: G. H. Nelson's company, E. A. McFadier's company, and

John W. Samson's company. Schwethelm was the second corporal in Harbour's Kerr Minuteman Company from February, 1861, until February, 1862. He married Emelia Stieler on March 19, 1862, at D'Hanis. They were the parents of three sons. Schwethelm was a member of the Kendall Company of the League's military battalion. He deserted from his Kendall militia unit; Company D, Second Battalion, Third Regiment, 31$^{st}$ Brigade District. Schwethelm fled with the August insurgent group and survived the battle. He and two other individuals went from the battle to Mexico and on to New Orleans where in October he enlisted in Company A, First Regiment [Union] Texas Cavalry. Schwethelm was in the Las Rucias battle on June 24,1864, and instead of returning to his unit he fled to Mexico. In 1867, Governor E. J. Davis appointed him a Ranger captain. Henry Joseph Schwethelm died on August 16, 1924, in Kerr County.

23.  Charles Franklin Scott was born about 1836 in Texas. He married Mary Ann McDonald on September 15, 1855, in Gillespie County. They were the parents of three children. They lived in western Kerr County. Scott was a member of the Kerr [American] Company of the League's military battalion. He deserted his Kerr militia unit; John Henderson's squad in the summer of 1862. He accidentally shot off a toe and could not flee Texas. Confederates arrested him on August 4, 1862, while he was at home. Davis' company hanged him on August 22, 1862, at Spring Creek in western Gillespie County.

24.  Heinrich Steves, Jr. was born about 1834 in Prussia. The family arrived in Texas on the *Neptune* in 1849 and settled in the Comfort area in 1855. Steves was a member of Kuechler's company of December, 1861. He was a member of the Kendall Company of the League's military battalion. He deserted his Kendall militia unit; Company D, Second Battalion, Third Regiment, 31$^{st}$ Brigade District in the summer of 1862, fled with the August insurgent group, and was killed at the battle site.

25.  Heinrich Stieler was born about 1844, in Oranienbaum, Duchy of Anhalt. The family arrived in Texas about 1854, and in the Comfort area in 1856. He was a member of the Kendall Company of the League's military battalion. He deserted his Kendall militia unit; Company D, Second Battalion, Third Regiment, 31$^{st}$ Brigade District and fled with the August insurgent group. He survived the Nueces battle, but was captured and executed on August 22, 1862, on Goat Creek in Kerr County.

26.  John Strong was born about 1835 in France. The date he arrived in Texas is not known, but by 1862, he was living in Kerr County. Strong deserted his Kerr militia unit; Company E, Second Battalion, Third Regiment, 31$^{st}$ Brigade District in the early summer of 1862. He fled Texas and on October 27, 1862, enlisted in Company A, First Regiment [Union] Texas Cavalry at New Orleans. Strong was appointed to sergeant on July 6, 1862, and to first

sergeant on November 12, 1863, and to second lieutenant on March 9, 1864. He was dishonorably discharged on June 29, 1864. Strong married May Ann Elizabeth McDonald on January 11, 1866, in Kerr County. They were the parents of two children. John Strong died in November, 1870, as a result of an accidental gun shot.

27.  Fritz Tegener was born in February 1833, in Graeben, Prussia. He was a brother of Gustave Tegener, below. Tegener was both a Forty-Eighter and Freethinker. He and two brothers arrived in New Orleans in November, 1851, and made their way to Texas shortly thereafter and by 1856 were living in Kerr County. Tegener married Susan Evelyn Benson on December 21, 1858, in Kerr County. They were the parents of three children. Tegener was elected the Kerr County treasurer in August, 1860. He was very likely a founding member of the Union Loyal League and was the commander [major] of its military element. He was elected commander with the rank of colonel of the Third Regiment, 31$^{st}$ Brigade District in early 1862. He deserted his Kerr militia unit in the later summer of 1862 and was the leader of the insurgent group who fled in August, 1862. Tegener was seriously wounded in the opening shots of the Nueces battle. He escaped and returned to Kerr County until he recovered from his wounds. He was wounded again in October, 1862, in a skirmish on the banks of the Rio Grande, but escaped to Mexico. He remained in Mexico until the end of the war, at which time he returned to Kerr County. Tegener and Susan Benson were divorced in early 1866. Tegener was elected a member of the 11the Texas legislature in August, 1866, and served until November 13, 1866. He married Augusta Strunk on October 16, 1866, in Travis County. They were the parents of five children. Fritz Tegener died in 1901, in Travis County.

28.  Gustave Tegener was born about 1830 in Graeben, Prussia. He was a brother of Fritz Tegener, above. Tegener was both a Forty-Eighter and Freethinker. He and two brothers arrived in New Orleans in November 1851, made their way to Texas shortly thereafter, and by 1856 were living in Kerr County. He was a member of the League's Kendall Company of the military battalion. Tegener married Mary Jane Payton on May 6, 1862, in Kerr County. By early June he had fled to the mountains. Tegener deserted his Kerr militia unit; Company E, Second Battalion, Third Regiment, 31$^{st}$ Brigade District. The Confederates arrested him about August 4, 1862, and on August 22$^{nd}$ he was hanged near Spring Creek.

29.  Charles Franklin Vetterlien was born in January, 1832, in the Duchy of Altenburg. He was a brother of Gottlieb Vetterlien, below. Vetterlien was both a Forty-Eight and Freethinker. It is believed the Vetterlien brothers arrived in Texas on the *Gaston* in 1857. He was a member of the Kendall Company of the League's military battalion and fled with the August insurgent group. He survived the Nueces battle and with his brother made

their way to El Paso where they served as teamsters for the Union army.
Vetterlien returned to Comfort after the war, and died there in 1914.

30. Gottlieb Vetterlien was born about 1831 in the Duchy of Altenburg. He was a
brother of Charles Vetterlien, above. Vetterlien was both a Forty-Eight and
Freethinker. It is believed the Vetterlien brothers arrived in Texas on the
*Gaston* in 1857. He was a member of the Kendall Company of the league's
military battalion and fled with the August insurgent group. He was likely
wounded but survived the Nueces battle. He and his brother made their way to
El Paso where they served as teamsters for the Union army. He may have
died in El Paso from complications of wounds sustained in the Nueces fight.

## 37. From *Die Deutsche Pioniere Zur Geschichte des Deutschthums in Texas* 1894

By Paul Weber

At the far end of the main street in today's town (Comfort of about 1400 inhabitants [1894]), on a knoll that dominates the town and countryside, stands an unadorned white obelisk, a monument, on the front side of which are the words

### TREUE DER UNION

The side walls list the day of death and the names of the 35 young German men who fell, victims to the Confederation. The cause of their deaths is related as follows:

About one year after the outbreak of the Civil War there existed within the circle of settlements of Fredericksburg, Sisterdale, Comfort and Boerne a secret bank of Germans who had vowed to remain true to the Union and, if it became necessary, to flee to Mexico. It is not to be forgotten that the Confederation at the outbreak of the war granted each citizen who did not want to stay under the Confederate flag, 90 days to leave.

In the month of July, 1862 there were some 60 young Germans who, upon the advice of older Germans such as Edward Degener, Simon and others were ready to get out of the way of the Confederation and to flee to Mexico. As their leader, they picked Jacob Kuechler[1].

In the meantime, a young Scot named Stuart[2], who had been taken into the secret society, announced his intention of withdrawing from the society and from the flight to Mexico. He was judged to be a traitor to the cause and his death was decided upon. It fell to the lot of Ernest Beseler to carry out the execution. The well-aimed shot of Beseler's and the death of the Scot were the signal to make a hasty start for Mexico.

On the way to Mexico their youthful spirits and carefree fun took precedence over caution and the real purpose of the trip. They took advantage of the time in joyous hunting and other amusement.

Colonel Duff in the meantime had orders to pursue the fleeing band and to deliver them living or dead. On August 9th, the fleeing band became aware of their pursuers and some 30 of them abandoned the group and avoided a confrontation by hastily taking off in a different direction.

There is a circumstance to mention that would play a role in the fate of the fleeing band. A few days after they had started their march, they met a German by the name of Bergmann[3] who had fallen upon a store of provisions in an open field. Perhaps as joke or out of hunger, they took the food away from him, for which, Bergmann, out of anger, put the pursuers on the trail of his countrymen.

The morning of August 10, 1862, found the remnants of the fleeing band approximately 30, surrounded by Duff's horde. In the ensuing battle which took place on the Nueces, and which was described in the first part of the book in the biography of Jacob Kuechler, the following Germans fell:

| | |
|---|---|
| L. Baucr | Ernst Beseler |
| F. Behrens | H. Weyershausen |
| L. Boerner | A. Bruns |
| Ha. Degener | F. Vater |
| Hr. Degener | A. Schdreiner |

| | |
|---|---|
| J. G. Kalenberg | H. Mardwart |
| C. Schaefer | L. Schierholz |
| H. Steves | E. Telgmann |
| M. Weirich | A. Vater |

The deplorable remainder of the survivors drew back under threat of inevitable death and eventually returned to their home settlements.

The terrible anger of the Confederate band which subsequently raided the settlements also murdered those who had been captured at the Nueces.[4] There were:

| | |
|---|---|
| A. Boerner | A. Luckenbach, |
| T. Bruchkish | L. Ruebsamen[5] |
| C. Bock | H. Stieler, |
| H. Flick | F. Toys[6] |

In constant danger of being captured and murdered, 17 of the survivors turned and made a second attempt to reach Mexico. They took the same route previously taken and reached the Rio Grande but were captured before they could cross into Mexico. On the 18 October 1862, the following men fell there:

| | |
|---|---|
| J. Elstner | F. Felsing |
| Hermann[7] | V. Hohmann |
| Peter [8] | Bonnet |
| M. Weisz | F. Weisz[9] |

ENDNOTES
Weber's Book

01.  Jacob Kuechler was not the leader of the August insurgent group.  Fritz Tegener was the leader.

02.  Basil Stewart was born about 1835, in Scotland.  He arrived in Texas County by 1862.  He was a member of the Kerr [American] Company of the League's military battalion.  Ernst Beseler shot and killed him on July 5, 1862, just north of Comfort.

03.  Charles Bergmann [Burgmann] is also something of a mystery man.  He is often called a Confederate spy, but this is not correct.  The first time he can be positively identified is the 1862 Kerr County listing the names of males not in the military.  This shows him as thirty-six years old, which would mean he was born about 1826.  There is an individual listed on the 1860 Bexar Census that also is likely to be him.  The census shows him as twenty-nine years old, born in Germany, working as a teamster for the U. S. Army.  This would mean he was born about 1831.  He was very likely a member of the Kendall Company of the league's military battalion.  The Kerr provost marshal issued him a travel permit on August 2nd to travel within the military jurisdiction.  This indicates that he may have been one of the men who took supplies to the fleeing insurgents.  McRae's casualty list shows Burgmann as a 'volunteer guide.'  How he became a Confederate guide is not known.  One explanation is that he may have been captured by the Confederates and agreed to lead them, as an alternative to being hanged.  The other explanation is as Weber says; the insurgents took supplies from him, without paying for them and out of anger he reported them to the Confederates.  He was wounded in three places during the Nueces battle.  After he recovered from his wounds, he enlisted in Company B, Duff's 14th Battalion Texas Cavalry.  On November 22, 1862, he was placed on detached service to the Confederate Quartermaster Department.  After the war Burgmann fled to Mexico.  Don Biggers in his book *German Pioneers in Texas* says Negro Seminole Indian killed him after the war, throwing his body into the Rio Grande, but there is no confirmation of this account.

04.  The belief Weber expresses here is a myth that just will not go away.  These men were **NOT** captured at the Nueces battle.  They survived the battle and were **LATER** captured and executed.  There were nine, not eight insurgents executed following the battle, as Weber states.  Two were killed near Boerne, two more killed on Goat Creek in Kerr County, and the remainder killed in the San Antonio area.  The reason for this myth is the way the inscription reads on the *Treue Der Union* Monument.  It reads: *Gefangen genommend und ermordet* [captured and murdered].  Almost all who have written about the events assumes this means they were captured and murdered at the Nueces.  Not so.

05.  Louis Ruebsamen was born about 1843 in the Duchy of Nassau. The family
     arrived in Texas on the *Harriet* from in 1845 and settled in Gillespie County.
     Ruebsamen was a member of the Gillespie Company of the League's military
     battalion and also a member of the Luckenbach Bushwhackers. He fled with
     the, insurgent group of August, 1862, and was likely wounded early in the
     battle. He survived the battle, but was captured and executed about August
     24, 1862, near San Antonio. The ninth insurgent captured and murdered after
     the battle was Adolph Ruebsamen, a brother of Louis. Adolph Ruebsamen was
     born about 1840 in the Duchy of Nassau. Adolph Ruebsamen was a member
     of the Gillespie Company of the League's military battalion and also a
     member of the Luckenbach Bushwhackers. He fled with the August, 1862,
     insurgent group. He survived the battle, but was captured and executed about
     August 24, 1862, near San Antonio.

06.  Heinrich Friedrich [Fritz] Tays [Taps] was born about 1842 in Hanover. The
     family arrived in Texas on November 28, 1845. He was very likely a
     Freethinker and a member of the Kendall Company of the league's military
     battalion. He fled with the August insurgent group and survived the battle.
     Tays and Conrad Bock were captured near Boerne on August 23, 1862, and
     hanged on August 24, 1862, just north of Boerne on Cibolo Creek.

07.  Henry Hermann was born about 1833 in Brunswick. He married Sophie
     [maiden name not known] about 1853, likely in Brunswick. They were the
     parents of at least two children. The family arrived in Texas about 1854 and
     settled in northern Bexar County. Hermann was likely a member of the
     Kendall Company of the league's military battalion. He likely also to have
     been a member of the August insurgent group: if so, he survived the battle and
     returned home. Hermann was in the Kuechler's party who fled in October,
     1862. He was killed on the Rio Grande on October 18, 1862.

08.  There are actually only seven names (not eight) on the *Treue Der Union*
     Monument, listed as having been killed on October 18, 1862, at the Rio
     Grande. 'Peter' and 'Bonnet' are the same individual; John Peter Bonnet was
     born on February 9, 1833, in Charlottenberg, Prussia. The family arrived in
     Texas in 1846 on the *Harriet* and settled in northern Bexar County. Bonnet
     married Sophie Katharine Dorothea Tays, a sister of Fritz Tays, above on
     March 22, 1855, in Bexar County. They were the parents of four children.
     Bonnet and his family settled in north Comal County by 1860. In mid-October
     1862, Peter Bonnet and his four brothers decided to flee Texas with Jacob
     Kuechler leading the seventeen-man group. They were overtaken at the Rio
     Grande in October, 1862. Peter Bonnet was seriously wounded but made it to
     Piedras Negras, Mexico, with help from his brothers. He died on January 12,
     1863, from his wounds.

09. There was an eighth man who also died from his wounds of October 18, 1862; Fritz Lange. Johannes Christian Frederick Lange was born on June 20, 1832, in Hanover. The family arrived in Texas in 1851 and settled between Camp Verde and Zanensburg, now Center Point. Fritz Lange married Auguste Hasser on December 7, 1853, in Bexar County. They were the parents of three children. He was a member of the Kendall Company of the league's military battalion. Lange was in the Kuechler's party of October, 1862, and wounded at the Rio Grande on October 18, 1862. He recovered somewhat in Mexico and returned to his home, but died about 1866.

## 38. Letter–Julius Schlickum – December 21, 1862

Gulf of Mexico
On Board British Frigate *HMS Hope*
December 21, 1862

Dear Father!

You are most likely very surprised, to receive a letter from me, written on high sea, after so many years of silence. I'm on the way to New York and from there, I'll mail the same and send it on its way. I begin to write now, while there is time and quiet and I can write more detailed about everything.

First, the comforting news that Therese and the children are well in Boerne, under the protection of Holzapfel.[1] The Ranslebens are also doing fine. Wilhelm is a soldier in the Eastern Army (Union) and stationed on the Rio Grande and only has to swim across the river to freedom.

We are a long time without any news from you. We, ourselves, lived through eventful times. On the following pages, I'll tell you what we have experienced.

We opened our business in Boerne at a most unfavorable time; it was the beginning of the political turmoil, but nevertheless, we were successful. We had many customers and made money. This fateful revolution didn't find many supporters among the West-Texas Germans. The division of the Union in the interest of the slaveholders, was not in the interest of the free working Germans in West-Texas. They couldn't and wouldn't enter into the arguments over secession with the South. They were not inclined to help, to destroy the best form of government the world has ever experienced for the sole purpose of establishing a requiem whose only purpose was the extension of human enslavement.

However, the Union Party was in the minority and we had to submit. Meanwhile, I was elected to the office of 'Justice of Peace' in our District. Later when they organized the Militia, I was elected to Captain, and later I was Lieutenant Colonel. Our business continued to thrive. The cost of goods was steadily rising; gold and silver was no longer in circulation, instead, the Confederate Banknotes were the currency of the day. Soon we were able to pay off all our outstanding loans and started to establish our own business building.

In January 1862, Therese blessed me with a "HEDA II [second son], a healthy, sturdy rascal (Hugo), not as strong as Julius was at birth but looks very much like him and is not as sedate. He was crying a lot the first few months. Our Julius grew into a fine boy. He is still chubby, speaks very well, is very healthy and commands the whole household; Holzapfel is extremely fond of him and spoils him rotten. Katherine is still the same, a small but tireless talker, she has forgotten nothing about her long journey from Germany. She is vain like a peacock, loves to dress herself and carries herself very proper. She listens to every spoken word. She is a lovely, trusting child and shares all she has with Julius.

In Spring came the conscription laws of the Confederate States that applied to all males from 17-50 years of age. At the same time the movement of the Northern Army, like dispatching the fleet, made it apparent, that Texas would become the arena of the war.

The fear of being drafted and the hope that the Union Army would soon raise the flag of the reigning government in it's honor, prompted the Germans and Americans near Fredericksburg to form and organize a sort of secret of brotherhood. This was to be mainly for protection against surprise attacks, burning of the settlements and hangings from the southern oriented parties. I was approached to join and take command. With fearful worry did I watch the unfolding of this association because I was too familiar with the circumstances not to see the danger and futility of this undertaking. I knew too well that a few backwoodsmen could not lead war against the State of Texas; a State who had about 15,000 men in service with weapons. What did we have? Hunting guns, little powder, and if we were to battle, no line of retreat. In spite of all rumors, I could not believe in an early arrival of the Union Army. The Government of the U. S. could not send troops to Texas, as long as the situation in Virginia and Tennessee was so uncertain. Therefore I refused emphatically to be part of this undertaking and tried with all my power to reason and convince the leaders of this group to reconsider this foolish attempt. I repeatedly depicted to them the ruin of the settlement in the end. In vain!

Simultaneously I was offered a commission as Captain from the South; when I refused, they offered me profitable army supply deliveries. I did not want to be involved with either one. By refusing, I became more suspect. In March and April, Northwest Texas (this encloses all German Settlements) was declared under siege, occupied with troops and all citizens over 16 years of age were required to swear allegiance to the Confederacy. Many who didn't feel secure, left house and home and retreated into the hills. A time of fear and terror ensued. I saw it coming. Many were arrested and brought to San Antonio. I too had warnings from dependable sources about my imminent arrest. However, I felt free of any quilt and believed I had noting to fear. I was not a supporter of the South, but I had broken no law and was not involved in anything that would speak against me.

Therese became ill; she had a terrible infection in the abdomen and suffered great pain. Fearful and worried I awaited the arrival of the doctor, who lived 12 miles away. Unfortunately our maid had left several days earlier and we were without help. I stayed awake all night and early in the morning I went outside. Our living quarters are about 500 feet from the store, situated on a hill. I looked out, two horsemen stopped at the gate, carbine in hand, farther out, another one, and then another; in short, about 30 men had encircled our house. I knew why. Quietly I went back into the house, to prepare my deadly ill wife for that, what was about to come; I did it as tenderly as possible. I then returned to the gate, where at this time the commander had arrived. I knew him. He extended his hand; "Mr Schlickum, I'm sorry, but I have orders for your arrest." I replied: "I was waiting for you already yesterday." When he became aware that my wife was sick, he allowed me back into the house, until his Captain with more troops would arrived to dispense further detail. He then had the house occupied by his men. Around noon the captain arrived. Through the help of rich friends I offered the captain $25,000 – for bail, if he would leave me in the house until the doctor arrives and gives me the result of Therese illness. He denied the request and I was arrested. Spare me the words about my feelings when I had to leave my sick wife and crying children behind.

> Continued in the home of his brother Ferdinand.
> New Orleans, February 20, 1863.

I, with other prisoners was transported to San Antonio. I had permission to ride my own horse. In San Antonio, we were put in prison, it was a converted house. Already 17 of my fellow sufferers, all Germans were already here; most of them well to do and well educated. One of my friends, Mr. Braubach, sheriff of Gillespie County, was bound in chains with attached cannon balls. There were among others, Mr.

Richarz from Duesseldorf, the Judge of Medina County, my friend Radeleff from Fredericksburg and many more. We were strictly guarded and harshly treated. We ordered our food from the hotel, for $20.00 a month, because we did not want the food from the soldier's canteen. After 2 days, I received a letter from Holzapfel, that Therese was better and recuperating, but no longer could she nurse the little one. In spite of our daily reclamation, it took almost 6 weeks before we would get a hearing. The charges against me; "General disloyalty." Witnesses attested that I had more loyalty to the North than to the South and I quoted with satisfaction from the News Paper, about all defeats of the South and more dumb things of the sort. I defended myself to the Military Commission that the witnesses only expressed suppositions and had no facts to represent, that I had the right to my own opinion, that a Military Court is not [a] Revolutionary Tribunal to sit in judgment about beliefs. Nevertheless, I was charged with disloyalty and antipathy against the South, (Disaffection of the Confederate Government, was the verdict.) and sentenced to prison for the duration of the war. Two of my friends had the same sentence. Others were banned and some had to pay high monetary fees. A saber-rattling regime of the most distasteful sort, governed in the State of Texas. All civil laws were nonexistent. The smallest provocation was sufficient for this lot, to arrest honest men and jail them and let them wait for months until they saw fit to inform them about the reason for their arrest. (To be imprisoned for the duration of the war meant as much as being hanged from the next tree. Many had it happen to them literally.)

Before I was arrested, I already had made arrangements "for change of air" and now I let my friend know that the time had come. I set the time for the night of July 18/19th. Braubach and Doebbler had the same sentence as I and wanted to come along. I was supplied with weapons and sleep tonic (laced whiskey for the solders) and a note, that horses would wait for us outside the city at 1 A. M. Our friends were very busy.

On the 18th in the afternoon, to my great shock, came Therese. I couldn't believe my eyes! She knew of our plan and her concern, unrest and love, prompted her to see me one more time. I was terrible worried and told her, that she put herself in great danger and that now, I would have to give up my plan, so that she won't be compromised. She implored me, that under no circumstances must we forego our plan and not to take any consideration for her. She only stayed a short time. I have not seen her since.

Our prison had 4 windows and 6 posted guards, door #2 leads to the firehouse, door #1 leads to a free area, facing the main guard-house. Door #2 was locked and barred, but for sometime already, we had an opportunity to open it.

Night approached, we retired early, but no one could sleep. It was 1 a.m. – the changing of the guard. Outside was a clear moonlit sky, as light as in daytime. One of the sentries sat by the widow and looked in. We had no choice. We were contemplating if we should offer him a drink with the sedative-laced whiskey. We always had alcohol and the soldiers never refused a drink. Suddenly a comrade called out "Let me have . . . your . . ." He turned around and in the shadow we glide through the half open door – the door creaked – in the Firehouse, door #1 was opened quickly. A few people passed by. In the shadowed side of the courthouse, across from us, stand two figures with hats in hand, our friends. With cocked pistols, we creep out. The guard didn't see us he walked back and forth, having his back in view, we dared to jump, if he would have seen us, he never would have opened his eyes again.

In the nearby doorways, our friends were positioned with their guns to secure our escape should we have been detected. Soundless we proceed forward. Finally, outside the city, we hear a whistle from a nearby Mesquite bush, we give the counter-sign. Six horsemen, holding their saddled horses, came toward us. A short greeting, a deep breath and a deep drink from our Cognac bottle, which made the round and away we ride. In stretched gallop we chased into the night over the prairie, avoiding all roads and paths and in less than two hours we put 22 miles behind us. At dawn we found refuge in a narrow, _____ laying and densely wooded valley. "These, in the middle of the dry river bed, in the dry river bed, in the midst of the brush in a cave, you find refuge there and hid. You also will find food. So long." And our friends ride on to get rid of our horses. They easily could betray out hideout, were they around. We were free! In this forest, maybe about 100 acres and 2 miles from water, we spent about six weeks, until the hottest pursuit was over.

Soon we learned that the troops searched day and night for us; along the frontier and the Rio Grande, the river between Texas and Mexico, was particularly sharply watched. They had orders to shoot or hang us wherever we were found. The homes of our friends were often searched.

Of course nobody suspected and would believe that we were so close to the city. They searched for us for away as we had presumed. We kept sharp outlook, never made fire and fetched our water 6 miles from the spring, near the farm of our friend, Wilhelm Huster, who also supplied us daily with groceries, bread and salted meat. Huster helped in our escape and also helped many others. The result was his death sentence, mainly because he helped in our escape. Pray for him.

In the morning after our escape and just as I had feared, they interrogated my wife before the Military Commission. She was accused of aiding in my escape. She was intimidated by threats to reveal my whereabouts. She stood firm and unafraid. She was held in the city under penalty of a $5,000 bond, if she were to leave. She rented an apartment and sent for the children. To me, she sent a message, telling me not to worry, she is in good spirits. After continued hearings and inquiries she had to ____, it became clear, that she would stay firm, and reveal nothing. Through friendly mediators and the absence of several days of the General, who was very bitter towards her, they obtained the permission for her to return to Boerne and they lifted her bond. From several sides I was told that Therese behaved very admirable throughout this ordeal, she showed great dignity and strong will. She was admired by her friends and respected by the foe.

During the time of my imprisonment, my friend Jakob Kuechler and 200 men, relocated to the hills, since the invasion of the Northeast Troops didn't happen, and they decided to go to Mexico instead. 68 of his companions were willing to follow him, among them Wilhelm Klier, the rest returned home and swore allegiance to the Confederate States and were promptly drafted into their service. Kuechler is a courageous man who knows the woods and in spite of Cooper's Leather stocking (Cooper's series of fiction Leather stocking) a very good hunter and also academically well learned. However, he is the personified *Phlegma* "don't hurry–don't push" [*Nur Nicht Draengeln*]. He is a true *Urwald-Bummler* [stroller through primate forest and wilderness] and in unhurried "*Gemutlichkeit*" he and his men roamed through the hills. There was no hurry! They hunted deer, harvested wild honey, cooked and roasted their meals in leisure and in the evening they sang songs. The end of July, the train reached the West bank of the Nueces Springs. From here to the Rio Grande was only a day's trip of 40 miles. They put up camp, bound the horses to graze and cooked their evening meal. Two men stood guard, while they rested under a few cedar trees on the edge of a thicket. Across the campsite was a mighty steep cliff. It was one of those soft, Southern nights. Bright stars set against a clear dark blue sky. At 3 A. M. in the morning the guard called out: "Wake up! We are betrayed!" The very same moment came a cracking RATT TATT TATT and lightening flashes all around, from all sides came a hail of bullets and whistled around their ears into the camp. All this was enforced by a terrible hollering and screaming, as if 1,000 Indians were possessed by the devil. "Don't expose yourself, hold your weapons at hand! Don't shoot! Calm Blood!" Kuechler called to his men. It was the plan of the attackers to chase the men out of the camp and then capture them. Since nobody moved, their plan was foiled. The enemy instead, in all quietness during the night, surrounded the cedar grove, the springs and cut off the road. The enemy had 175 men.

After the fire ceased and quiet ensured, eight Americans of the Union loyalists stole away from the camp, others followed and as dawn broke, Kuechler had only 35 men left. This small group was determined to fight and die if necessary. They used the few trees for cover. Each only had a six-shooter and a hunting gun. All of them Germans; many had a wife and children at home. They were the elite of the German youth in West Texas, all of them excellent hunters, sure shooters, raised at the frontier in the wild hills and woods, at home on the pathless prairie. Stouthearted young men and all of great intelligence. Most of them I knew and saw them growing up under my eyes.

It was barely dawn when the movement of the troops could be heard and soon followed the command: "Forward! Charge! To hell with them! Kill them all!"

Kuechler encouraged his men: "Don't use your powder carelessly. When you shoot, have a sure target."

The Rangers send a hail of bullets into the camp of the Union loyalists and stormed the camp with howling like that of Indians. Without giving any sound, our men let them approach to about 50 feet and with deathly aim they shot into their ranks. Surprised and with great loss they did retreat. In the course of two hours they enemy attempted three more attacks and always could approach to about 25 – 30 feet and were thrown back each time with great losses.

The Rangers, besides their overwhelming manpower, also had the advantage of the terrain. They had the thicket of cedar bushes for cover, they had better guns, they already had the newest Sharps rifles, which could be loaded from the back with shells, while our men had only muzzle guns. Brave Wilhelm took his place next to Kuechler, and Kuechler told me, Wilhelm stood like a man, fought fearless to the end. He brought you honor, death father. He was one of the few not wounded. After the 3rd and last attack, they decided to throw back, there were only seven men not wounded and eight wounded men who still could walk. 19 young men lay dead or deathly wounded on the *Walstatt* [symbolic of a holy sacrifice ground]. There lay the two sons of my old friend Degener of Sisterdale on the ground, the pride and joy of their parents. Both were will liked and known as bear hunters and welcome by everyone. There lay Karl Beseler, the very close friend of both, equally fearless and brave as they. He was killed during the night while standing sentry. There also was Paul, a Mexican who was purchased from the Indians as a child and raised as a German. My friend Tellgmann from Brounscluocig (sic) his body pierced from three bullets and still fighting.

The other side also had losses, 44 Rangers killed, 18 deathly wounded, and died soon thereafter. The Germans were aiming with deadly precision, so that the Rangers had very few slightly wounded men.

The Germans knew their firepower was too weak to withstand another attack. The decision was made to retreat. The cover was provided by the dying men. Tellgmann started a lively opening fire with his pistol and the others joined and under this diversion the survivors found a passable passage to climb the cliff under the protection of dense underbrush and lost themselves into the night.

Here ends my specific report about Wilhelm, your dear oldest son. Sometime later I was told, that he got lost from the others and found his way alone and on foot hundreds of miles through the wilderness, no food, no clothing but for shirt and pants. Half-starved and sick he arrived one evening at his brother-in-law's home. Ransleben, without thought and in his shock and confusion, went to town the following morning to seek council and advice. He went from one to the other, haunted by fear, does not know what to do.The result was, that the news about Wilhelm's return had spread like wildfire. The same day, in the evening, he was arrested, even though the poor fellow lay sick in bed. He was imprisoned until morning and then transported to San Antonio. Ransleben went with him and transported him in his own wagon. This was lucky for Wilhelm, because near Boerne the solders hanged the other three prisoners during [the] night. Ransleben watched over

Wilhelm during the night and so saved his life. In San Antonio, Wilhelm was under strict security. A clever lawyer defended his case, for intersession from friends, there was no lack, since he always was loved and respected. Finally he was set free. After he swore allegiance, they stuck him into uniform. He no longer is in personal danger.

Kuechler managed to escape with his men under the most difficult circumstances; they healed the wounded and finally reached the settlement. They had lost everything, horses, clothing, food.

The Rangers plundered the camp and killed anyone and anything alive in cold blood. A great number of those who had left the camp earlier, were captured and hanged without trial. How this band later harassed the folks in Fredericksburg, many tell you in the enclosed letter, it is from a woman whose husband was a victim of this band. She asked me about information concerning him (oh me) and in spite of her hope full outlook, she'll never see him again, his corpse is the prey of vultures and wolves.

In September, we prepared to leave our hideout and Texas. Two acquaintances who were in the battle of the Nueces were brought to us by friends and a third one joined us later. One fine evening, after we were supplied with horses, food, water and weapons, we rode off.

This story of our flight, how we were betrayed, how we detoured long miles around settlements and military post to avoid being seen, how, like Indians, we always had to cover our tracks, what methods we used to escape the searching eye of roving hunters, would fill page upon page and is too intricate to detail.

Finally we reached the border. The Rio Grande was too high and swift to cross. Three times we came to the river in different places a days ride apart. One time, in the middle of the day, we found ourselves in the midst of a Ranger camp, but we could retreat unnoticed. In the end we were without food, our gunpowder was wet and useless and we had to return to a settlement. On this tour we were factually out of food for three days, not one bite to eat. These were hard days, but not as agonizing as one day in the burning sun, without a drop of water to quench the consuming thirst.

Fortunately, we were not recognized as we purchased food, rested and tended to our horses. I purchased powder and then we started on our journey again. Our friends from Mexico had sent a small boat and we set out to cross the river by night. The river was still swift and on the rise, but we dared, right under the Stockade of Fort Duncan, the Rangers.

In the morning at 1 A. M. we greeted Mexican soil. For the first time, after a long time of danger, we could breathe free without fear! And could show our face without threat. Our adventure was not over yet! We had to leave our horses across the river on the Texas side and as soon as we arrived in Piedras Negras engaged a Mexican national, to swim across the same night to retrieve our horses. He found our horses at the designated spot and brought them at dawn to the river. He was just about to drive them into the water, when he was spotted by the Americans, stopped, arrested and naked, as he was, brought to the town of Eagle Pass to the Provost Marshal. But already before then, in town, he found an opportunity to escape by horse. The bullets, that were sent after him, didn't find it's mark. Piedras Negras is across from Eagle Pass and Ft. Duncan, divided by the river. Soon we learned that our horses were held by the same man, who had stopped the

Mexican. We also heard that the Farm, only 9 miles away, had only 3 men living there. We decided to recapture our horses. Four of us went undetected to the river across to the Farm's location. We built a raft from dry wood and at dusk we launched the same. We bundled our weapons, clothing and blankets on top of the raft and pushed and pulled, with the help of the Mexican, swimming, the raft thru the swift and forceful current across the river. The river is about 750 feet wide–we crossed with luck. We dressed, brought our weapons in order and then approached the farm with caution. Wow! There were no horses to be found. The moon vanished, but it was a clear, starry night. In the end, we approached the building. Braubach and I crawled on hand and feet closer, carefully taking care that the dogs won't catch wind of us. Soon we discovered that our horses were tied between the house and the barn. We returned to our companions, who were waiting behind bushes, about 50 feet away. The dogs became restless and started to bark. While we were debating what to do, the door of the house suddenly opened and in the bright light we saw a number of armed men coming out. I almost believed in magic, as people suddenly came from all sides – we were almost surrounded, there was no time to loose, too close were the men. We aimed our guns and before we could think, a barrage of fire came from all sides; a platoon firing party. We pressed against the ground, wedged behind sheltering, low growing shrubs. They couldn't see us and the bullets flew harmless over our heads. Our answer to the attackers was swift. Lamenting and cussing they returned to the house, carrying a wounded soldier with them who died during the night. As soon as the shooting started, the Mexican had run away. After the attackers retreated, I looked for my companions and to my surprise, I found myself alone. I was not inclined to chase after them and I didn't want to leave

without the horses. Carefully I crawled in a big circle around
the building, I heard the hoof of horses walking and at the
same time I saw a man, leading two horses. Before he could
spot me, I grabbed him from behind with one hand and
holding the pistol to his head with the other. "Don't move, or
I'll shoot," I said to him in English. "Oh, Don Julio don't kill
me, it's me," he said in Spanish. It was our loyal Mexican,
who, in the confusion of the shooting, took advantage of the
situation and cut the horses lose and brought them out. "Where
are the missing horses," I asked. "There were only three and I
brought them to the fence and since one horse didn't want to
be led, I'm glad I got two." I thought for a few moments, went
back to the fence, found the horse and put the rope around his
nose, swung onto its back and followed the Mexican thru the
bushes. No one followed. They were afraid. On the bank of
the Rio Grande, we met up with our group; they were
surprised and didn't believe their eyes when they saw the
horses. We drove the horses into the water, launched our raft
and soon we were on the other side. It seemed we fell into a
trap. The horses were brought to the farm to taunt us to come
back and during the night they had brought in about 30
soldiers. Why they didn't put up a better fight, remains a
puzzle to us. After landing, we discovered to our surprise, that
we rescued strange horse. Well! It's not our fault and in the
same night I sent the horses with three of our men to
Monterrey. Braubach and I remained in Piedras Negras, where
after a few days we were joined by Kuechler and Wilhelm
Huster. They and 15 others crossed the river about 15 miles
above and were detected by the Rangers and shot at. They lost
their horses and only 11 of them reached the free shore,
among them were two friends of Wilhelm's, the brothers
Weiss and Mr. Felsing, the husband of the lady, who in
company of Mrs. Oswald and Therese, came from Germany.

Now we traveled inward for 280 miles to Monterrey. Here I found many acquaintances who greeted me jovially. Regretfully, I soon found out that I could not establish an income here and didn't want to live from the support of my friends. Just as I was thinking about going farther into the interior, Gustav Schmidt, from Harper, arrived via Houston here in Monterrey. He made me an offer to travel for him to New York. Of course I accepted with both hands. Three weeks later we traveled together to Matamoras and from there I went by boat to Havana. After a stormy voyage of 17 days, I arrived here on the first Christmas Day. On this voyager, I started my letter to you. Meanwhile I wrote to you and my sisters thru Mr. Leye. I remained in Havana until January 2 and met here Mr. Jenny from Chur, Switzerland. He is the Pasteur of G. Schmidt. I am independent and was promised a commission from the profits. I arrived in New York and for 15 days I visited many business establishments and came back thru New Orleans, to visit my brother Ferdinand, from where I'm now visiting.

Here I purchased with my own money a small schooner that is flat enough to negotiate the shallow sandbanks by Matamoras. I'll load the schooner with grain and other goods for use and then with set sail. As soon as my arrival is secure, I immediately will make arrangements for wife and children to join me here and leave the unhappy Texas behind.

From my family I hear often and know they are all right. Letters I don't receive, but I write frequently when I find a sure and trustworthy opportunity.

About the local politics I don't want to express myself. I was very disappointed when I saw the North. It seems almost so, as the reason for the war was only to make the merchants rich. Should I be successful in obtaining value, I'll return to Germany.

Ferdinand is well.  He earns $90.00 a month as Customs Inspector and is well-liked for his sincere, expressive talk, his loyalty, and punctuality at work. His wife and children are healthy and satisfied. With longing I'm looking for mail and news from you. My family was secured for one year. When I left Texas, I had 700 lb. flour in storage. My holdings I secured against confiscation by transferring them to our loyal friend Holzapfel.  The circumstances in Texas you can measure by the fact that on Jan. 1, 1863 100 lb. of flour cost $40.00.

Continued March 2, 1863

Yesterday, Ferdinand received your letters. Thanks be to God, you are all well. Yes, dear Father, we will be with you soon, as you would have it.  However, I don't want to return with empty hands and I'll try with great diligence and fervor to earn money while Holzapfel in Texas, will put our properties for sale.  To become a burden to you I can't and don't want to.  You must also not forget and understand that I'm not well suited for the present circumstances there. It would be difficult for me to take a dependent or submissive position. If you are willing to do a favor for me, please, intercede by Excellency the Swiss President, to assign me a large Consulate in this Region.  This would be of great value to me.

1,000 greetings to dear Mother and brothers and sisters. I am and remain you loyal and devoted son.

Julius Schlickum

Endnotes
Letter Julius Schlickum, December 21, 1862

1. Holzapfel referred to is Johannes Holzapfel who was born about 1802 in 'Germany'. His wife was Martha Schmidt. They arrived in Texas on the *Herschel* from Münchhausen, Hessen, on October 16, 1845, at Galveston. They were original members of the German Protestant Congregation of New Braunfels. Johannes Holzapfel is shown on the 1850 Comal Census as age 48, a laborer, born in Germany. His wife is shown as Martha, age 47, also born in Germany.

## 39. John W. Sansom's Account of Nueces Battle.[1]

I was not called by the guard at two o'clock, but I awoke just about three o'clock, and a few minutes later was called. I had not undressed when I lay down, but had slept as soldiers it, "on my arms," so rising at once I followed the guard, Mr. L. Bauer.[2] When we had gone about sixty yards, he in front and I about twenty feet behind him, he entered a dense cedar-brake, and as he entered, was, without being hailed, shot dead by a Confederate[3] lying in ambush at that point, I replied to the shot by firing instantly at sixty or more Confederate who at the sound of the first gun rose from their blankets and rushed pell-mell over a space of open ground to a part of their command which lay under the cedars some sixty yards south[4] of the place where Bauer was killed. The shot that killed Bauer alarmed the camp, and fast and furious firing began between the contending parties. At its very beginning, Ernest Bosler[5], a Unionist guard, who unluckily stood between the two fires, was killed, but whether by friend or foe will never be known. I saw him fall and know that he fell fighting. A moment later the Confederates made a charge upon the Unionists which gallantly repulsed, and a counter-charge made upon the Confederates.[6] While repulsing the advance of the Confederates, or during the counter-charge, Major Tegener[7] was seriously wounded in three places, and two members of his command also received wounds. I think there was up to this time a hundred shots exchanged, then came a lull of an hour during which there was but an occasional shot fired.

The camp of the Unionists had been approached by the Confederates from the East and South.[8] According to my watch the battle began a few minutes after three o'clock A. M., two hours sooner, I have reason to think, than the Confederates intended it should begin.

As will appear from what I have already said, I was not in the Unionist camp at the time the firing commenced, but about sixty yards away from it. When I sought to join my friends there, they very naturally took me for an enemy, and firing on me, came very near to killing me, one passing through my clothing and grazing the skin above my stomach, and another cutting the flesh from a finger of my right hand.

I crawled to a place out of sight of both parties and began to think what I could and should next do. It occurred to me at once, that I could do the greatest good for myself and Unionist comrades by making a careful reconnaissance of the Confederate forces, and this I did effectually by creeping around to their rear, so near to them, as to fully satisfy myself concerning their numbers and their location. [9]

\* \* \*

I went quickly to a point northwest of the camp, and thence crawled on my stomach into its friendly precincts. But careful as I was, I narrowly missed being fired at. When about twenty feet from the camp, I heard the click of the locks of guns about to aimed at me, and called out, "Don't shoot, Sansom." No reply being made, I repeated the call, and was then answered by Captain Cramer[10], who said: "Come on, come on, Captain, I came near shooting you."

Knowing what I did, I at once advised Captain Cramer and Lieutenant Simon[11] (they were brothers-in-law) that if they wished to continue the fight, the Unionists should abandon their present position and select one where they would not only be less exposed to the fire of the enemy, but have a better chance to damage the enemy. I then went to Major Tegener, who although bleeding profusely had not relinquished command . . . and advising a prompt withdrawal of our forces. He seemed to favor the move . . . During a conversation I had with Lieut. Degener,[12] he asked if I knew what the plans and intentions of our officers were, I told him that I believed they had determined to withdraw to a better position. "Withdraw!" he exclaimed; "Never! Our two guards have been killed, Major Tegener and two others of our comrades wounded, and if we leave here, they will get our horses, our rations, and all our equipage. I would rather fight here until every man of us is killed than to go anywhere else." . . . [Sansom stated] "I am in favor or retirement for our present position, so am going to carry my saddle with me and look out the safest route for our withdrawal." The Scott boys, Henderson, and Hester, who had heard all that was said, immediately proposed to accompany me and the five of us; I carrying my saddle, made our way cautiously to the spot where young Bauer lay dead, face downward.

* * *

By this time he had tied a number of the horses to the trees; day began to dawn, and the firing commenced . . . The Confederates made a determined charge upon the Unionist camp. All of them, however, were driver back except one man, presumably an officer. He did not retreat, but shouted in a commanding voice, "They are giving way boys, come on, charge." Encouraged by that information the Confederates faced about and again charged, and won the fight.

## ENDNOTES
### John W. Sansom's Account of the Nueces Battle

01. *Battle of Nueces River In Kinney County, Texas, August 10, 1862* by John W. Sansom, Privately published by John Sansom, 1905.

02. Leopold/Ludwig Bauer was born about 1839 in Prussia. Wilhelmina [maiden name not known] and Gottlieb Bauer were his parents. He was a brother-in-law of Ernest Cramer and Ferdinand Simon, both members of the fleeing insurgent group. Bauer and his family arrived in Texas about 1853 and the Comfort area in 1854. The 1860 Kerr County Census shows him as 21 years old, a farmer, single, born in Prussia, and living in his father's household. Bauer was a member of the Kendall Company of the League's Military Battalion and fled with the insurgent group. He was killed at the battle site and likely his body was not recovered.

03. Bauer was shot and killed by 2nd Lieutenant Harbour of Davis' Company.

04. The actual direction the Confederates fled was to the east, not south.

05. Ernst Beseler was born about 1842 in Wesel, Prussia. Augusta Strube and Charles A. Beseler were his parents. His father was a Forty-Eighter. The family arrived in Texas on the *Fransiska* from Prussia in 1848. Ship records show Ernst as being 6 years old. Ernst was a second lieutenant in Company C, 3rd Regiment, 31st Brigade District. He was a member of Kuechler's company of December, 1861. Beseler was a member of the Kendall Company of the Union loyal League's Military Battalion. He was the insurgent who killed Basil Steward, the first person killed in the insurgency. He was a member of the fleeing insurgent group and was the second insurgent killed.

06. This counter-charge was led by Amil Schreiner crying out *"Laszt uns unser Leben so teuer wie moeglich verkaufen!"* [Let us sell our lives as dearly as we can!] Schreiner was killed leading the charge.

07. Frederick [Fritz] Tegener was the commander of the League's Military Battalion. He was born in February 1833 in Graeben, Prussia. Fritz Tegener was a brother of Gustav and William Tegener who were killed during the insurgency. They arrived in Kerr County in 1856. Fritz Tegener married Susan Evelyn Benson on December 21, 1858, in Kerr County. Tegener eventually made his way to Mexico where he waited out the war. He divorced Susan Benson and was elected to the 11th Legislature in August, 1866, and served until November, 1866. He married Augusta Stunk on October 16, 1866, and served in the 12th Texas Legislature from August 18, 1869, until December 2nd 1871. He died in 1901 in Travis County.

08. This wing of the Confederate force approached from the North and East.

09. In this edited portion of Sansom's account, he tells about circling behind the north and south wings of the Confederate force.

10. Ernest Cramer was born on May 23, 1836, in Schweinfurt, Bavaria. He first arrived in Texas in 1853 and worked as a merchant. Cramer was a first lieutenant in Captain John Sansom's 1859 Ranger company. He returned to Bavaria in late 1859 and arrived back in Texas on the *Iris* from Schweinfurt in 1860. By 1861 he was living in Kerr County. On September 12, 1861, Cramer married Charlotte A. Bauer in Kerr County. He was an early member of the Union Loyal League. He was major of the 3$^{rd}$ Regiment, 31$^{st}$ Brigade District and elected captain of the Kendall Company of the League's Military Battalion. He fled to Mexico later in the war where he remained until the end of the war. Cramer left Texas in the mid-1870 and moved to Idaho where he died on July 10, 1916.

11. Ferdinand Simon was born about 1826 in Hesse-Darmstadt. He was a Freethinker and likely a Forty-Eighter. He likely arrived in Texas on the *Strabo* in 1845. Simon married Caroline Bauer, the sister of Leopold Bauer on May 14, 1855 in Bexar County. Simon took the oath of allegiance on May 27, 1861. He was a member of the Kendall Company of the League's Military Battalion. He was wounded at the Nueces battle and later captured. He was initially sentenced to be hanged, but when martial law was annulled he was transported to Austin for trial. The result of the case is not known. Ferdinand Simon died in July, 1878, near Boerne.

12. Hugo Degener was born about 1842, very likely in Brunswick. Maria [maiden name not known] and Eduard Degener, the leader of the Union Loyal League, were his parents. His father was both a Freethinker and Forty-Eighter. The family arrived in Texas in 1852 and settled at Sisterdale. Hugo Degener was a second lieutenant in Kuechler's company of December, 1861. He was also a lieutenant in the Kendall Company of the League's Military Battalion and fled with the insurgent group. Hugo was seriously wounded in the Nueces battle, unable to withdraw and therefore covered the withdrawal of the others. He was executed by order of Lieutenant Lilly.

## 40. R. H. Williams's Account of Nueces Battle[1]

Our detachment led up the stony slope that would land us on the little prairie where was the camp; and our orders were to wheel to the right on the top, creep through cedar-brakes, and line up on the far side of the camp. The rest of the party, marching straight to the enemy pickets were to be captured without noise and, the camp not being disturbed, the whole force was to wait till daybreak came, and at the sound of a signal shot from McCree's [McRae's] pistol, charge right in.

\* \* \*

We halted in dead silence. Hardly had we done so when a rifle shot, coming from the far side, rang out in the stillness of the night. Some idiot, over-excited, had loosed off at a sentry, and instantly the camp was in a buzz like a swarm of bees. Men rather ran hither and thither in great confusion . . . Presently the Germans, having recovered from their surprise and got their arms, fired a volley at our comrades on the far side, but without much execution in the darkness of the night. This was replied to by our people, and the firing became general on their side.

So far we hadn't fired a shot, and our presence was unsuspected; but now two of their picket-guards came running in a few yards in front of our position, driving some horses before them. One shot was fired without effect; three more followed, and a heavy thud told that one at any rate was killed. One of our party ran out and brought in the dead man's arms, a Colt's six-shooter and a Jaeger rifle.

From where we lay to the cedar-brakes round the mott, or clump of timber, was about fifty yards of open ground, and we were now ordered to double across this independently, and then find what cover we could.  In the darkness, made more intense by the shadows of the great trees, all got across safely, and taking cover at varying distances from the camp, opened fire on its defenders.  Some of the men blazed away in great excitement, and foolishly exposing themselves; one of our party getting a bullet through his arm and one through each thigh.

The defenders still showed a bold front, and dared us to come on.  They even threatened to charge out on McCree's [McRae's] party, some of who were inclined to bold, but were promptly rallied by Harbour.[2]

On our side the bullets were whistling pretty thickly over the heads of six or seven of us who were fighting together, and from our then position it was difficult to return the fire with much effect.  Very cautiously then, now crawling, now dodging behind trees, I worked my way up the edge of the mott in which the camp stood, followed by my comrades.  There for a brief space we kept up a galling fire on the defenders, but when four or our party had dropped, one with a bullet through his head, and the others severely wounded, we, the three survivors, had to retire the way we came.

The defenders by this time had lost very heavily, and began to make off in small parties through the thick brush.  From our side a few of us pursued one of these, but soon lost them, and when we got back the camp had been taken.

otle*

NDNOTES
R. H. Williams' Account of the Battle.

01. *With the Border Ruffians* by R. H. Williams, University of Nebraska Press, Lincoln, Nebraska, 1982, Page 246-248.

02. William Talon Harbour was born on October 28, 1833, in Perry County, Alabama. Permelia Jane Callaway and Abner Harbour were his parents. He arrived in Kerr County by 1857. Harbour organized a forty-man minuteman company in Kerr County in February, 1862, and served for a year. He enrolled in Davis' company in March, 1862, and was elected the senior second lieutenant. Harbour led the Davis detachment in the pursuit force. He married Mary Elizabeth O'Brien on September 30, 1863, in Kerr County. After the war the family moved to Kemper County, Mississippi, about 1866. Harbour died on January 21, 1891, in Kemper County, Mississippi.

## 41. Edited Journal of Fritz Schellhase

I, Fritz Schellhase[1], my brother Gottfried, Jr., and sisters Friedricke, Sophie and Minna and parents, Gottfried and Sophia, we were five of us children, arrived in Texas on December 20, 1853[2], and came to Comfort in 1854. We were the first settlers, or some of the first. All of them, except my parents, are living yet.[3] My father bought a lot in Comfort and improved it, and built a house. We lived in Comfort for two years when my father got 160 acres of government land. Then we moved five miles from Comfort on Hesenwinkel creek. Our neighbors were four brothers, Gus, Edward, Robert and Heinrich, Jr., (Henry) and two sisters, Laura and Emilie, and their widower father, Heinrich Steves. On day Ed Steves came to my father and asked him if he could get me to work for him. I was 10 or 11 years old at the time. My father agreed for me to work for him, and my wages were one bushel of corn meal a week so that my parents had something to live on. Times were hard. Ed Steves was a bachelor so I and he batched together for about a year and got a long fine. Finally Ed got disheartened with batching, and decided to do so no longer. One day he asked me, "Fritz, can you tend to things here at the home?" I told him I could, "But what do you want to do?" His reply was, "I want to go to New Braunfels and get me a wife." The next morning he hooked two yoke of oxen to his wagon and drove to Braunfels. And he stayed 12 days before he came back with his new wife. Late in the evening I heard the whip in the distance announcing that he was coming so I opened the gate for him to drive in. He got off his wagon and said to me, "Fritz, here is my wife. Her name is Johanna Kloepper.[4] Now we don't have to batch any more. She will wash and cook for us." She was very nice to me. She would come to the field where I was working and bring me cool water and lunch that I enjoyed very much. She would say, "Boy, now eat. If a person is young he wants to eat. It always taste good."

Laura Steves was the last one at home. She married Wilhelm Boerner[5], but Boerner did not live with his dear wife but one year. He was killed by the Confederate Home Guard at the Nueces Massacre on August 10, 1862. A few weeks later she gave birth to their son, but she died of childbed fever shortly afterward. The child lived and was baptized Henry (Heinrich). Henry was brought to Laura's sister Emile, who had married Rudolf Voigt[6], to be raised. Henry went to high school and grew up to be a good man.[7] Ed Steves and Johanna had three boys, the oldest Albert, then Ed (Edward Jr.,) and Ernst was the youngest one. I have played with them many times. Just before the Civil War started, Ed Stevens went to his father and asked for a loan. His father asked him what he wanted the money for. Ed said he wanted to buy a machine to thrash wheat. So his father loaned him the money, and Ed sent for the machine. The machine arrived just before transportation was closed in anticipation of the war, but it was here.

Then the war started. In 1861 was a hard time. The Northern soldiers in the area were arrested and taken as prisoners to San Antonio[8], and what they had was sold at auction. So Ed Steves went to San Antonio and bought six mules to work the thrasher. So the work began, but the mules were not trained for that kind of work. We finally got them to go. Gottlieb Saur[9] was the mule-driver then. One day Mr. Saur came to my father's and called me out. He said Ed Steves had sent him to get me to drive the mules. I went to see Ed and he said, "Fritz Schellhase, I want you to drive the mules." I asked him, "What are you going to do?" He said he was going to escape and go to Mexico with the bushwhackers. So I took his place and drove the mules. We worked up the Guadalupe Valley to Wilvirn [sic] [Boerne?]. At that time there was only wheat and the crop was good that year. Then the news came that the Confederate Home Guard soldiers under Col Duff[10] had overrun and massacred the bushwhackers on the 10th August 1862. The bushwhackers were 74 men[11] from Comfort and nearby who were intending to go to Mexico, but they had the misfortune of staying too long in their camp to go hunting. The Confederate soldiers found out where they were but did not know how strong they were. So they sent ten men to get a 150 more from Fort Clark.[12]

On August 9th Franz Weiss[13] and Henry Stieler[14] went hunting after dinner, and came to a place where they saw three men sitting on a hill. They knew that they were soldiers so they returned to the camp and told their comrades, "We saw three soldiers on a hill." But their words were in vain. One them later said, "They laughed at us. Our commanders did not believe us."[15] Someone who was there told me: "The next morning before daylight, about 3:00, they fired on us so we fired on them, but we were too weak for good fire. So we disappeared in the brush, one here the other yonder. Louis Boerner[16] was on guard. He was one [of] the first ones that fell."[17]

Then the Confederates went into the Unionist camp, murdered the wounded by shooting them in the head as they lay on the ground.[18] Then they put ropes around the necks of the dead ones and drug them into the chaparral bushes to a pile about 150 yards from the camp. The soldiers stayed in the camp for they had good shade from cedar trees. The next day, two bushwhackers, Henry Stieler, who was 16 years old, and

Wilhelm Boerner (Boerner was captured elsewhere after the battle and executed, the man captured shortly after Steves was captured was 18-year-old Theodor Bruckisch) were hiding, but got lost and stumbled into the Confederates' and were asked what they were doing. They said they were hunting oxen, but could not talk English. The soldiers put a ropes [sic] around their necks and hung them. When they were dead the soldiers took them down and drug them to others and piled them on the same pile.[19]

Two other bushwhackers who survived the massacre, Henry Stueler [Stieler] and Brokes [Bruckisch] came together and went to a fork in the river.[20] There they fell out with each other. One said, "We have to go right." The other said, "We have to go left. But [Stieler] knew that he was right so he went along the North Fork[21] of the Guadalupe. He went down the river until he got to the Kerrville Road. One mile west of Kerrville he went to a man by the name of Ries (Rees). He wanted to get a furlough.[22] He was too young, he was not 18 years old yet, but Ries knew him well so he gave him the furlough.[23] Then [Stieler] went to Kerrville and stopped at Mrs. [Tegener].[24] As he came into the house, Mrs. [Tegener] said, "That is my Fritz's gun, how did you get it?" [Stieler] said, "I traded with your Fritz." So she asked, "Where is Fritz, did he come through?" He said, "I don't known, me and Fritz were separated and were not together for some time."

At that time a man named Lowrance[25] along with [Bruckisch] came in, and at the same time some Confederate soldiers came in, too. Lowrance turned [Bruckisch] over to them. The soldiers asked [Bruckisch] if Henry [Stieler] was in the war, too. He said he was. The soldier took [Stieler] and [Bruckisch] prisoners. At that time the soldiers had their camp on the waters of the Pedernales River. They took their prisoners with them, but ten miles from Kerrville they shot and killed them.[26] Then they sent word to [Stieler's] parents and told them they had killed their son. [Stieler's] mother and sister[27] hitched two horses to a wagon and went to Kerrville and inquired where the dead men were. When they found them, they loaded them on the wagon and took them to Comfort for burial.

When the war was ended, the people here were notified to get together and go to Mason Creek at a large watering place. There we met; we 24 men.[28] The next day we went to Bandera, from there we went over the Sabinal River. We went down the river until we struck the San Antonio Road. We followed that until on the other side of the Frio River. Then we went right toward Fort Clark to cross the Nueces River. On the other side of the Frio we broke our wagon axle so we had to cut a tree to make a replacement. On our wagon Professor Brinkman[29] and Mr. Serger (Emil)[30] were good carpenters. When the axle was ready we started again. In the evening we came to Fort Clark, close to Fort Clark Springs, the water being very nice. The old buildings were about all gone. Only one post still remained there. And Mr. Serger climbed up on and tied our Union Flag on top. We stayed until the next morning, then we went to an old shoemaker and asked him to give us information about the road. He told us to go to a man who lived two miles from Fort Clark. That man was acquainted with the area for he had lived there for some time. He went with us to the place on this side of the river near where the battle had been. We had to leave our wagon and two mules there. Gottlieb Saur, the mule driver, and Mr. Ed Steves, the owner of the team and wagon, could not get through the brush. The next morning we saddled our horses and rode through the brush up to the Nueces River and arrived

at the old camp site where the massacre took place. Five or six
big Cedars stood there, and being very nice shade, we stayed
there. Mr. Serger climbed up on a high cedar and tied our
Union Flag on the top of it. Then we went through the brush to
find the bones. At last we found them on a pile surrounded by
rocks.[31] The bones were all there, there being 18 skulls.[32]
They were all on top. Each of us had sack and so we filled our
sacks with the bones. Then we went back to our wagon. We
had a big box on the wagon where we put the bones in the box
and put a lid on it. Then we started back.

Someone remarked that we had better cut another tree so if
we should break another axle we would have a replacement.
So we cut a tree and tied it under the wagon because there was
no room for it on the wagon. The next morning we hooked up
but did not get far. The road was rough, and about three miles
on our way back we broke the second axle. We had a young
mare that we tied to a cedar limb. She got frightened, and
rearing backward she broke the limb. And away she ran
dragging the limb behind her which made matters worse. We
though she spied Indians. She ran toward home. Five of our
men followed the runaway mare. We told them that as soon as
we got the axle done, we would travel toward Fort Clark, but
we decided to wait for them. But they were not back at
sundown, and not back at 11 that night. So we decided that 10
more of us should go and see what happened that they did not
come back. I and nine others were going to look for them, and
as we were saddling our horses they rode into camp. We sure
were glad to see them. We thought they had trouble with
Indians and got killed. They told us that when they found the
mare she was rundown and still had the limb on the rope. But
she was so tender-footed that she could hardly walk. So the
men went in the bottoms and gathered some old rawhide. They

made shoes and tied them under her feet so that she could walk, but it was slow. Since we now were all together we traveled homewards.

We came through Bandera, and four miles above Comfort we crossed the Guadalupe. Then we were on the Kerrville and Comfort Road where we met a company [of] Union soldiers. The first company we met swung their hats and bid us good day. Two miles from Comfort we met a second troop. They gave us the road and as we drove by they joined us back to Comfort to Serger's home. Mr. Serger, known to be an excellent cabinet maker, made a special box to bury the bones that we brought. When they were buried the soldiers fired a three-shot salute over the grave.[33] [Of the] men who gathered these bones; I was the youngest one and the only one still living. The others are all dead and gone.

I was a freighter for the soldiers for two years after the war. My home was around Comfort then. I took my oxen and hooked them to my wagon and hauled wood planks to San Antonio and brought back provisions for the government soldiers so they had something to eat. Camp Verde was their camp then. The soldier invited me to come to Camp Verde where they were going to have a ball. That was my favorite entertainment in those days. They had a large platform and a big crowd was there. There were three couples that were engaged to marry. Mr. Otto Brinkman and Miss Ochse, Mr. Anton Heinen and Miss Allerkamp, Mr. Meyer and Miss Perner were the three couples, and I went together to the ball. It was a happy time and I enjoyed it fine until midnight when a crowd of Irish soldiers got drunk and got into a fuss that broke up the pleasure. Anton Heinen came to me and asked me to leave with him. I said I would so we went together until we crossed the Guadalupe toward Comfort. When we got on the Kerrville Road, Anton held up and asked me to take his bride home. I said yes, but asked him what he was going to do? He said he was going to Kerrville. He was going to marry tomorrow, so I guess he wanted to have a little fling. Anton left and the crowd whooped and hollered hurrah. Miss Allerkamp was a close neighbor to me so I carried her home just at sunrise. We had a happy time.

ENDNOTES
Fritz Schellhase's Journal

01. Frederick Schellhase was born in 1846 in Kleinen Brandenburg, Prussia. He married Margaret Garrison on July 26, 1871, in Kendall County. Fritz Schellhase died in 1928, in Kendall County.

02. It is believed the Schellhase family arrived in Texas on the *John Ed. Grosse* in 1853 and settled in Kerr County.

03. The first settlers arrived in Comfort in 1852.

04. Julius Bose, a Comal justice of the peace married Edward Steves and Johanna Kloepper on December 20, 1857, in Comal County.

05. William F. Boerner was born about 1830, in Hanover. The date he arrived in Texas is not known. He arrived in the Comfort area with his parents in 1855. The 1860 Kerr County Census shows him as thirty, single, a farmer. Boerner married Laura Steves on February 14, 1861, in Kerr County. Boerner was in the fleeing Unionist group and survived the Nueces battle. He was later captured and hanged at Spring Creek on August 24, 1862.

06. Emile Steves and Rudolph Voigt were married on February 8, 1852, in Comal County.

07. Henry Boerner was born in September, 1862.

08. These were the federal soldiers that had been guarding the Texas frontier prior to the Civil War. After the firing on Fort Sumter in April, 1861, the Confederate government ordered all remaining Union soldiers in Texas to be captured as prisoners of war. They were captured at the 'Battle of Adams Hill' in May, 1861, and kept at Camp Verde and later at San Antonio.

09. Gottlieb Saur was born about 1838, in Bavaria. The date he arrived in Texas is not known. He arrived in the Comfort area in 1853. The 1860 Kerr Census shows him as twenty-two years old, single, a farm laborer. Saur was the second corporal in Kuechler's company of February, 1862. He fled Texas and on February 3, 1863, he enlisted in Company C, First Regiment [Union] Texas Cavalry. He deserted on August 3, 1864, at Rancho Martinez near Brownsville.

10. James Duff was born May 17, 1827, in Scotland. He arrived in the United States on November 1, 1848. Duff enlisted in Company C, 5th U. S. Infantry on January 6, 1849. He served at Fort Gibson and on the Texas frontier and

received his discharge on January 5, 1854.  Duff was the post sutler at Fort Belknap where on December 18, 1856, he married Harriett Paul, the daughter of Major Gabriel Rene, the post commander and a future Union brigadier general.  He moved to San Antonio in 1858 and received several large contracts to furnish the U. S. Army with supplies.  At the beginning of the war he organized a militia company and he was later promoted to lieutenant colonel.  On January 27, 1862, Governor Lubbock appointed Duff a state brigadier general in command of the 30th Brigade District.  In May he resigned and he was commissioned a Confederate captain.  He made two expeditions to the Hill Country, one in May and the second in August, 1862.  Duff returned to San Antonio by August 24th and received authority to increase his command to a battalion.  He was promoted to major on January 3, 1863, to lieutenant colonel on February 7, 1863, and to full colonel on May 2, 1863.  He fled to Mexico and went back to Great Britain after the war.  Duff returned to the United States in 1877 to manage the Denver office of the Colorado Mortgage and Investment Company of London, England.  He returned to England in 1885.  James Duff died on April 16, 1900, in London.

11. Sixty-four insurgents left for Mexico in early August.  Another four Anglos joined them on the trail making the total number of insurgents at the Nueces battle as sixty-nine.

12. Schellhase is incorrect about getting men from Fort Clark.  What happened was Charles Burgmann, who had been in the insurgent assembly area, and was either captured by a Confederate scout or the insurgents refused to pay him for goods and supplies.  Burgmann told the Confederates about the departure of the insurgents.  Captain John Donelson, the Confederate troop commander, dispatched a ninety-six-man pursuit force.

13. Franz Weiss was born about 1843 in Prussia.  He was a younger brother of Moritz Weiss, who was also in the fleeing group.  Franz was wounded in the Nueces battle, but survived and returned to the Comfort.  In October he joined another insurgent group attempting to reach Mexico.  A Confederate force overtook them at the Rio Grande and in the ensuring fight both the Weiss brothers were killed.

14. Henry Stieler was born in 1844 in the Duchy of Anhalt.  The family arrived in the Comfort area in 1856.  The Kerr County Census for 1860 shows Stieler was sixteen years old, single, and living in his parent's household.  Stieler survived the Nueces battle but was captured about ten days later near Comfort.  He was executed on August 22, 1862.

15. Several other accounts tell of seeing "strangers" on a nearby hill the afternoon of August 9th.  When the group seeing the strangers returned to camp and told their story, another group said they were the group seen and as a joke they hid.  This is why Weiss and Stieler's account was not taken seriously.

16. Louis Boerner was born about 1833 in Hanover. The date he arrived in Texas is not known. He and his parents arrived in the Comfort area in 1855. The 1860 Kerr Census shows Boerner as twenty-seven years old, single, and a wagoner by profession. Boerner was killed at or near the battle site.

17. Two of the guards on duty when the Confederates opened fire at three a.m. were Leopold Bauer and Ernst Beseler. Both were on the north side of the camp and were killed in the opening exchange of gunfire. The other two came running into the camp at the start of the firing. This is the only account that says Louis Boerner was on guard and *was one of the first to fall*. If Boerner was *one of the first to fall* it may be he was killed on the afternoon of August 9th as there are rumors of an insurgent captured prior to the battle.

18. The wounded insurgents were executed by Lieutenant Lilly, William G. Wharton, William Rees, and perhaps Oskar Splittgerber.

19. Schellhase is incorrect about any incident such as this. He has confused the Stieler and Bruckisch story with this account. This incident did not take place.

20. Bruckisch and Stieler must have reached the Guadalupe River. It forks near the current community of Hunt. The south fork heads southwest and this was the route the insurgents took on their way to Mexico. The north fork heads north and ends just north of the current MO Ranch and Conference Camp.

21. Stieler could not have gone along the north fork as it turns away from Kerrville and Comfort. It is likely he went to the right at the fork and traveled up the Guadalupe River toward Kerrville.

22. Sidney Benner Rees was the Kerr county clerk. He was born in 1829 in Tennessee. He arrived in Kerr County with his mother, brothers, and sisters about 1855. He was the Kerr district clerk in 1856. On March 15, 1860, Rees married Emily Tedford. They were the parents of thirteen children. In early August, 1862, Rees was elected the Kerr county clerk. Sidney B. Rees died in 1909, near Center Point in Kerr County.

23. What Stieler likely attempted to get was a travel permit. The Kerr provost marshal is known to have issued travel permits and it may be that Rees was also authorized to issue some type of pass.

24. Mrs. Tegener was Susan Benson Tegener. She was born about 1844, in Illinois. She arrived in Kerr County with her parents in 1854. She and Fritz Tegener were married on December 21, 1858, in Kerr County. Susan had two brothers, John Washington and William Thomas Benson in Davis' Company, Frontier Regiment. She was likely one of the sources of information that the insurgent group had fled. She and Tegener were divorced in May, 1866. She married Charles Curren on December 6, 1869, and they left Kerr County.

25. Daniel Boone Lowrance was born April 1, 1829, in Tennessee. He married Leah Ann Thompson on February 24, 1855, in Alabama. He and his family arrived in Texas in 1859. The 1860 Kerr Census shows him as thirty-one years old, with a wife and two children, living between Kerrville and Camp Verde. He signed the Kerr County petition requesting Kuechler's company be disbanded. Family stories say he was wounded during the Civil War and died of his wounds on August 21, 1875, the thirteenth anniversary of the date he turned Stieler and Bruckisch into the authorities. Another account says he "died from gunshot wounds of supposedly friendly companions."

26. Where and how Stieler and Bruckisch were killed has been the subject of much speculation. Some accounts claim they were killed at the battle site. Others say they were shot near Kerrville, as in this account.

27. Stieler's mother was Wilhelmine Urban Stieler. His sister was Wilhelmine (Minna) Stieler. His mother was born in 1823 in the Duchy of Anhalt. She married Gottlieb Stieler about 1845, in the Duchy of Anhalt. They were the parents of five children. The date they arrived in Texas is not known, but they arrived in the Comfort area in She developed "mental illness" after finding her son's body and because of the many visits by Confederate scouts looking for other insurgents at her home. Wilhelmine died in 1897, near Comfort. Minna Stieler was born May 22, 1845, in the Duchy of Anhalt. She arrived in Texas with her parents. She married Heinrich Hubert Heinen on August 14, 1864, in Kerr County. Minna Stieler Heinen died on June 4, 1919, near Comfort. The Stieler ranch property still exists, along the road between Comfort and Fredericksburg.

28. The men who recovered the bodies were: Henry Schwethelm, Emil Serger, Ferdinand Schultz, Edward Steves, Fritz Schellhase, William Boerner, Peter Ingenhuett, Robert Schaefer, Edward Degener, Wilhelm Heuermann, Benjamin F. Patton, Fritz Saur, Carl Tellgmann, Christian Rhodius, Gottlieb Stieler, Otto Brinkmann, and Ulrich Rische.

29. Professor Brinkman was Otto Brinkmann who was born August 15, 1832, in Westphalia. He arrived with his brothers Alexander and Carl, on the *Mississippi* in 1855. They settled near Comfort in 1858. The 1860 Kerr County census lists Otto as twenty-seven years old, and a carpenter by trade. He married Johanne Carolina Ochse on June 23, 1867, in Kerr County. Otto Brinkman died in 1915 at Comfort.

30. Emil Serger was born on March 27, 1831, in Prussia. The date he arrived in Texas is not known. He arrived in the Comfort area in 1856. The 1860 Kerr Census shows him as twenty-nine years old, single, a carpenter by trade. Emil Serger died in 1900, in Comfort, Texas

31. This description supports the Siemering account, which says that in the second attempt to reach Mexico the insurgent group spent a night at the battle site. They collected the bones of their fallen comrades and placed them in a pile with the skulls on top. The *San Antonio Freir Presse fuer Texas* accounts says, "It is useless to attempt to describe the feeling with which they observed the pyramid of skulls . . . A simple stone barricade, in the manner of gravestones, encircled the pyramid. The other bones, with few exceptions lay piled together in two other locations."

32. The number of skulls recovered from the battle site is somewhat of a mystery. Here Schellhase says there were eighteen. The *Treue Der Union* monument list nineteen names of men killed at the battle site. The September 1, 1865, newspaper account says there were sixteen skulls. It is known that not all nineteen bodies were recovered. One insurgent crawled across the Nueces River and died in a small canyon north of the camp. Ten years after the battle, John Sansom led a ranger company to the battle site. As they were resting, Sansom revisited the site and located a skull near the location of where Leopold Bauer was killed.

33. In the second attempt to reach Mexico the insurgent group spent a night at the battle site. They collected the bones of their fallen comrades and place them in a pile with the skulls on top. There was a detachment of federal troops from the 4th United State Cavalry Regiment sent to escort the returning party and the bodies. They remained and escorted the bodies to the burial site on August 20, 1865. Edward Degener gave a very emotional and patriotic oration, followed by the firing of a salute of three salvos over the grave.

## 42. The Usener Brothers' Story
### As Related by Raymond Usener
### March 22, 1997

I'm Raymond Usener and think that I quality as a descendent of the Nueces Massacre. Michael Weirich[1] whose name is on the *Treue Der Union* monument in Comfort, Texas, was a brother to Elizabeth Weirich who later married Jacob Usener[2], and consequently my grandparents. This does not mean that Jacob Usener was in the battle itself but leads to another important aspect of the difficult times during the Civil War.

The Usener family had settled east of the Live Oak Creek, about a mile north of where Lady Bird Johnson Park is now, and were close neighbors to the Weirichs, who made their home on the east side of the Live Oak Creek. Both log houses still standing. Also still standing across the road from the Weirich house is the Live Oak school building, the first rural school in the county.

Since Michael Weirich, and Jacob Usener, and his brother Ludwig[3] were such close neighbors I'm sure they were close friends and [in] true accord as to the loyalty of their newly-adopted country. They did not believe in slavery so when martial law was declared in 1862 the Confederate troops were conscripting age-eligible men into the Confederate military. By this time many of the eligible men had become citizens and others about to, and they did not want to be disloyal to the allegiance they had pledged. One can only imagine the tension that was building, especially among parents with eligible sons.

When word came that a group was organizing to join the Union forces, or flee into Mexico, Michael Weirich, Jacob, and Ludwig Usener were among some 68 men. The plan was to travel west to cross into Mexico and then to New Orleans[4]. On the way something must have prevailed that caused some to disband from the group and return home.[5] Of those that headed homeward some split up into smaller groups. Why, is unclear but stories were that difference in opinion as how to elude the Confederates. Sadly as it came about some were overcome and murdered. The story is that Jacob and Ludwig Usener were in a group of twelve. There were also several other groups. These groups came to be known as the *"Busch Wachers." Busch Wacher* translated to English would say brush watcher, observers, vigilant or simply Robin Hoods. These groups were loyal to the Union and only in the defiance of the Confederates.

When they came home they found the situation intolerable. The Confederates were beginning their siege of adjuration, harassment, plundering, murdering, and burning homes.[6] In addition there was a marauding gang and Indians to contend with. One can understand that these *Busch Wachers* as they were called, became protectors over their homes and neighbors, but at the same time became the hunted. Stories have it that families would display signals to alert if there was danger, or if clear to pick up provisions; signals like certain laundry on the line, horse saddled or unsaddled, horse or ox tied to a certain tree, what team used on the plow, or how the lantern was displayed at night so it could be seen from an observation point. One observation point was *Der Spitze Berg*, meaning the pointed hill west of Fredericksburg, which overlooks the Live Oak area. Other settlements had signaling codes that were picked up from observation points.

My grandfather passed away at the age of fifty-five and at the time when my father was only two. The stories that I'm relating came from an old bachelor uncle[7], who was the second oldest of nine children. He was proud to show his father's cap-and-ball pistol, still in the family, which he carried during those years. He told us that his father was an expert shot with that pistol, an expert horseman, and had to turn sly and cunning like an Indian in order to survive. Of the twelve that started off, he and his brother Ludwig and one other were the only three to survive. I say here only three survives. There was mention that the Confederates overtook several of this group – three or four – and they were hanged in the western part of the county.[8] How many more were killed by the Confederates remains a question. Some of this group claimed amnesty; one in particular had medical experience, who treated the sick and wounded.

The Civil War has left a deep scar on the families and descendents of the Germans that settled the Hill Country of central Texas. To this date there [are] older descendents that are hesitant to relate some of these stories; until they do, these will go unpublished.

Just recently I heard a sermon and the topic was, 'Give us this day our daily bread,' and by this I am relieved and feel that grandfather Jacob Usener and his comrades were guided in making a decision to be protectors over their families and their neighbors otherwise I might not have all the privileges that we have today.

ENDNOTES
Usener Brothers' Story

01. Michael Weyrich [Weirich] was born about 1839 in Coblenz, Rhineland-Palatinate. The family arrived in Texas in 1853, and settled in the Live Oak Creek community in Gillespie County. Weyrich was a member of the Gillespie Company of the League's military battalion and fled with August insurgent group. He was killed at the battle site.

02. Jacob August Usener was born on September 6, 1834, in Nassau. He was a brother of Ludwig, below. The family arrived in Texas on the *Semiramus* on August 10, 1845, and settled in the Live Oak community in Gillespie County. Usener was a member of the Gillespie Company of the League's military battalion and fled with the August fleeing insurgent group. He survived the battle and returned to his home where he hid for the remainder of the war. Jacob Usener married Elizabeth Weyrich on February 27, 1866, in Gillespie County. They were the parents of at least nine children. Jacob August Usener died at his home on June 5, 1889, in Gillespie County.

03. F. Ludwig Wilhelm Usener was born on January 20, 1841, in Prussia. He was a brother of Jacob, above. The family arrived in Texas on the *Semiramus* on August 10, 1845, and settled in the Live Oak community in Gillespie County. Usener was a member of Kuechler's company of December, 1861, and a member of the Gillespie Company of the League's military battalion and fled with the August fleeing insurgent group. He survived the battle and returned to him home where he hid for the remainder of the war. Ludwig Usener married Elisa Schild on June 24, 1874, in Gillespie County. They were the parents of fifteen children. F. Ludwig Wilhelm died on June 28, 1930, in Gillespie County.

04. One of the Nueces battle myths is that the insurgents did not want to fight for either side and were leaving to avoid all military service. This statement by Usener makes it clear they were planning to go on the New Orleans, which means they were going to join the Union Army.

05. At this point in the narrative become confusing. Usener seems to be combining two stories into one statement. There were two occasions the insurgents turned back. The first was at the assembly area. In the first part of Usener's narrative he seems to be talking about those that turned back at Turtle Creek. However, the second part of the narrative seems to be referring to those who left the battle site after the opening shots.

06. Here Usener is referring to Captain Donelson sending out scouting parties, and forcing the suspected insurgent families into the settlements. This began shortly after the insurgent party left Turtle Creek about August 2. The roundup of insurgent families began about August 4th.

07. This was likely Adolph Usener who was born on August 4, 1856, in Gillespie County. He died on February 19, 1925, in Gillespie County.

08. Some of those were hanged on August 22, 1862, in the Spring Creek area.

## 43. Albert Schutze Interview
*San Antonio Express*, August 31, 1924
Was a Survivor of the Nueces Battle[1]

Out of Kerrville, in the heart of the "hill country," came the news the other day of the death of Capt. Henry Schwethelm. To the average reader the item conveyed possibly nothing more than the passing of another of the early pioneers, who apparently thrived on the hardships that are a part of the blazing of the trail through which civilization shall flow.

Schwethelm, however, was different. He weathered the anxiety and toil of pioneering, and more than that he got thrills that come with the baptism of fire when a country is at war with itself. He was one of the two men escaping the Nueces River Massacre, of which a monument now stands at Comfort as the mute reminder. Others who survived that grim onslaught of men, under the Confederate banner, have passed on.

Last year the story of that early-day tragedy was related by Capt. Schwethelm to Albert Schutze of this city, who induced to visit this hardy pioneer by Alex Brinkmann of Comfort, who has been collecting much of the historical data of the early settlers in the hill country. Capt. Schwethelm's biography as written Mr. Schutze, and in which the Nueces River tragedy is fully set forth is given below:

Heinrich Joseph Schwethelm was born in Duesseldorf, on the Rhine, Germany, on the 4th Day of September, 1840. When he reached the age of 10 years, his parents emigrated to America, and it was the particular birthday he remembers so well, as he celebrated it on board of the emigrant vessel, and that he suffered all day with a terrible case of seasickness. They landed at New Orleans. Coming by boat to Indianola, Texas, they made their way to New Braunfels, where they arrived in November, 1850.

After his parents had settled in New Braunfels, young Schwethelm was sent to the English school at that place which he entered January 1, 1854. Mr. Schwethelm spoke with fondness of his teacher at this time, a Mr. Paul, an Englishman by birth, and a fine scholarly man. The most of his schoolmates were boys that had attended the school prior to his arrival and were a great help to him in assisting him to acquire the new language of which he was entirely ignorant. After six months attendance he became quite handy and in 12 months efficient in its use, speaking the language better than in after years. The rules of the school were very strict in one point, which was that they converse in English only during school. They had full liberty to speak their mother tongue at home and elsewhere. He attended this school one year and then attended the German-English school at Comal Town, just across the Comal, which was taught by Mr. Harms, who was also a good teacher, which he attended for two years.

As his home was somewhat distant from this school he remained overnight at the teacher's home during bad weather, and Mr. Schwethelm in reminiscent mood, recalled the pleasant comradeship he had form with little Anna Harms, the teacher's only daughter at the time. In 1853 his father moved to the Martinez, where his father had bought a place. This new home was about 12 miles from San Antonio on the Seguin road. His father had become a farmer and stock-raiser. In 1854 his father was struck by the gold fever, and with about two dozen San Antonians left for Sacramento, Cal., leaving his wife and son, the only child, on the farm. After the first year of his absence the Martinez creek had dried up entirely on account of a severe drouth Mrs. Schwethelm wrote her husband that she thought it advisable to sell out and she would join him in California as they had to haul water for stock and home use, and it had become quite a burden. But her husband answered her letter and advised them to hold out another year as he was making money at the time, and would then return, which he did, and he then sold out and bought a farm a Comfort, Texas, to which place they moved in March, 1857.

Up to this time the boy had helped his mother and spent most of the latter years as cowboy and farm help, not having acquired any trade. Having a most indulgent father his life was free and easy in those days. In the fall of 1857 he joined the Ranger force of Capt. H. L. Nelson at San Antonio, his age being 17 years. The main incentive to join the Rangers was the salary, which at that time amounted to the munificent sum of $35 per month, provisions and horse feed thrown in. Quite an inducement at that time. Arms and horse were furnished by the recruit. Although his enlistment lasted only four months, when the company was mustered out again at San Antonio, Schwethelm experienced some thrilling adventures under this command. The neighborhood of Goliad and Helena, where his company operated with a lot of rowdies and Mexican cut-throats and it was quite a job to handle this class of desperadoes. In a fight with an outlaw band 15 Mexicans were killed, the Ranger company not suffering any loss.

After being mustered out, he remained with his parents for a short while and then enlisted in the range force commanded by Capt. John W. Sansom, from Curry's Creek, below Sisterdale in 1858. The company had its camp at a location known as Ingram. The company consisted of 35 men. A great deal of lawlessness existed in this part of the State at the time in the way of cattle stealing, rustling, and even murder, by individuals and bands. An atrocious crime was committed during this time, when a gang of bandits hung three inoffensive Germans on Johnson's Creek above Ingram. The bodies were then thrown from the bluff into the creek below, about 50 or 75 feet. William Tegener, a brother of Judge Fritz Tegener, whose name will appear later in this narrative was one of the victims. The rangers could do nothing towards the capture of the perpetrators, as they were unknown and had fled.Schwethelm was in Sansom's command six or seven months when he was mustered out in 1859 at Kerrville. He then remained at home more or less until the Civil War began.

On the 19th of March, 1862, he married Miss Emilia Stieler in D'Hanis, who has ever been his faithful helpmate and consort. They celebrated their golden wedding in 1912 on their ranch, eight miles from Kerrville, on the Fredericksburg road. Three stalwart sons were the issue of this of this marriage, all live and doing well.

The German element in the counties of Gillespie, Kendall, Comal, and Kerr were not in sympathy with secession and opposed to slavery, and there were instances where several Americans were of the same mind and thought: consequently when the Governor of the State issued a proclamation that all persons who would not take the oath of allegiance to the Confederate States would have to leave the State within thirty days, a group of the younger men at a certain place and after a conference agreed to leave the state for Mexico[2].

They arranged a final meeting to assembly at Turtle Creek, about 15 miles west of Kerrville, on August first. At the appointed time, 68 young men, the oldest not more than 35 years of age, fully equipped with rifles and six-shooters[3], the rifles mostly of German make, and mounted on good horses with pack animals, met at the designated place. Fritz Tegener was elected commander of the troop, and on the following morning they broke camp early and leisurely wended their way to the Rio Grande. Feeling secure from being followed or intercepted, they were in no particular hurry and passed away a good deal of valuable time. Instead of making to the place of security in four days, they jogged along at the rate of only five to ten miles a day, spending a great deal of their time in hunting for game, which was plentiful enough. Some of them, being fond of wild honey, searched for wild hives of bees, and took things easy in a general way[4]. Mr. Schwethelm was opposed, as well as several others, to this unpardonable delay, and openly expressed themselves about the matter.[5] Tegener laughed at their fears, being over-confident that they were not being followed nor their where about known. Some of his followers were not pleased at Tegener's optimism, but, realizing their duty was obey their commander, reluctantly submitted to the situation. Had Tegener heeded their warning, this narrative would not have been written.

On the first night of the meeting the horse of one of the troop members had become unhobbled and make his way back to Tegener's Creek, where Tegener had a sawmill, and being followed by the owner until caught, was the cause of the trouble that occurred later. As the owner reached the mill he got his horse but had involuntarily run into a gang of Duff's company, who halted him, and questioned him as to where he came from, where he intended to go, and finally exacting the truth from about the Germans. They then compelled him to go back where they had assembled, and the direction they had then taken.[6] His captors had received some inkling of the departure of the German, and accidently stumbling on the

German, who, by the way, was somewhat "green", having recently arrived from Germany, took him along, following the trail of Tegener's troop.[7] This was easily done as the Germans had some 80 horses and traveled in regular formation. Duff's company[8] consisted of 125 men, who were in pursuit, and contrary to the leisurely traveling of their prey, were doubling their time and on August 9 came close enough to use precaution in proceeding with the attack they had in contemplation.

The Germans under Tegener arrived close to Nueces River and had gone into camp at a nice place, where there was find water and grass, and the commander had joyously exclaimed that this was an ideal place to stay the day, that day being a Sunday. Several among his troops and Mr. Schwethelm in particular, vigorously protested against this stating that they had been dallying along too easily and furthermore some of the members of his command had observed two horsemen on a distant hill apparently on a reconnaissance of some kind. Mr. Schwethelm and two of his messmates threatened to abandon the troop and make their way to the Rio Grande[9].

That night 28 of the German troops gave up the trip and returned to Fredericksburg and vicinity, by taking a new route from that by which they came, and managed to evade anyone in pursuit, but some of them were shot or hung later during the war[10].

Answering the remonstrances of Schwethelm and others, Tegener agreed to start the next morning, and promised they would not unsaddle their horses until they were over the Rio Grande. In the meantime their pursuers had spotted their camp and made arrangements for attack. The Germans had placed on guard four of their number during the night. About

3 o'clock in the morning the Germans were aroused by the shooting in the proximity of the camp, which proved to be the death knell of two of their guards, Ernst Beseler and Leopold Bauer of Comfort. The other guards thereupon came rushing into camp. Every man was then ready to repulse the expected attack. But not until daybreak and after the killing of the guards had there been any movement made by Duff's men. The latter, in the meantime, hidden by the cedar brush, had encircled the camp and all at one a volley of shots poured in the trapped Germans.

Duff's voice was heard to exclaim, "Charge them, boys, charged them! Give them hell!"[11]

The space the Germans occupied was partly open, whilst that of the attackers was hidden by cedar bushes which were quite thick where they were concealed.

The firing on both sides lasted for about an hour. Duff's men, meeting with a larger loss than expected, owning to the excellent marksmanship of the Germans, had withdrawn to where they had left their horses. The unfortunate German who had unwillingly betrayed his comrades was killed in the melee whether by the Confederates or his friends is not known[12]. Out of the 40 members of the German contingent, 23 had been killed or wounded. The 17 remaining, after a hasty consultation, scattered in various directions and finally made their way home in the neighborhood of Fredericksburg, with a few exceptions. Among the latter were Messrs. Schwethelm, Kusenberger and Graf. These three agreed to proceed to the Rio Grande, arguing with their comrades that by going back the were likely to be killed anyway, and as they only had about 40-50 miles to reach their goal, started across the Nueces tramping on foot, without food, and afterwards without water, hiding during the daytime and making as much headway as the could at night.

As the trio left the battlefield and were about ten miles from same, they crossed the road leading from Fort Concho to Fort Clark, and as Mr. Schwethelm was somewhat acquainted along this road, he knew that a Major Riordan owned a ranch in the neighborhood and told his comrades that he would reconnoiter and see if he could get some provisions.

His comrades wanted to go along, but he explained to them that if they were to approach the place by that number, suspicions might be aroused. It was only about one-half mile when Schwethelm reached the place, and asked for something to eat, which was given him and being questioned, invented a story that he had come upon one of Joe Ney's hay[12] wagons who was furnishing Fort Clark with hay from D'Hanis, and having gotten off to find a deer to kill, had become lost. As he sat down to eat the meal placed before him at the dining table, two men rode up, tied their horses and entered the house. One was Dr. Downs from Fort Clark and Captain Duff[13], the leader of the Confederate company.

Major Riordan[14] asked them where they came from, and Duff answered they had just come from a fight on the Nueces, and that Dr. Downs had been called by courier from Fort Clark to dress the wounded. When Major Riordan had asked if the fight had been with Indians, Duff answered;

"No! – with a bunch of d–d Abolitionists."

Mr. Schwethelm hearing this, as he was in full view of all present asked the question; "Well, did you get them all?" and Duff answered: "Well, nearly all." Schwethelm's position was a dangerous one and he put this question to allay suspicion. He then learned from Dr. Downs that Duff's company had lost 10 men killed and 45 wounded[15] and afterwards learned from the same source that half of the wounded died after they reached Fort Clark. When asked about the wounded on the other side, Dr. Downs stated that when he wanted to dress the wounded Germans, Duff's men said: "Never mind, we will attend to them," and they thereupon went to the battleground and shot every wounded man in the head[16], a deed which was commented upon later "to have been remarkable good marksmanship" by Duff's men.

The dead on both sides were left to bleach in the sun and only in 1866 the friends and relatives of the slain sent three wagons to the battlefield and gathered all the human bones, and, remarkable as it may seem all the 23 skulls of the Germans were found[17]. The expedition was headed by Mr. Schwethelm after his return from the U. S. Army. The bones were taken to Comfort, Texas and buried there, and a large monument erected, having the name of all of the victims graven thereon. It has been the custom for many years to hold memorial services on each 10th of August for 50 years, when the custom was dropped.

To return to Mr. Schwethelm at the Riordan ranch: Learning from the conversation at the time, that there were eight wagons, loaded with Duff's wounded coming down on their way to Fort Clark, Mr. Schwethelm asked Duff if he could get a ride to his destination, but was refused, which was what he wanted him to do, but realizing his danger when the wagons should come up, and were supposed to be only a mile behind (of Dux [Duff] and the Doctor), so he stated that he would travel on and try and catch up with Ney's hay wagons. As soon as he was hidden from view from the house he started in a run to where his comrades were waiting, and appraise them of Duff's men being near and they hastened away as fast as their legs could carry them. Mr. Schwethelm told his friends that as he was just going to take a bite to eat, Dr. Downs and Duff came in, and his appetite had suddenly left him, and he nearly choked when he tried to take a hasty swallow of coffee. Mr. Schwethelm stated that he learned afterwards, when the war was over, that Duff had said when he told them he was going to travel on that they should have held him, as he might be one of the escaped abolitionist, but Mrs. Riordan informed him that she know him to be one of Ney's hay men. It furthermore came in evidence that Major Riordan was in sympathy with the Union cause, and his wife had come to the rescue of Mr. Schwethelm in time, by intuition that things were different than they looked.

After the first night's travel, the trio began to feel the pangs of thirst until they finally reached a waterhole with a dead cow lying at the edge. They remained at the side of this water-hole all day. Towards evening they heard the approaching tread of horsemen, and retired to a hill close by and secreted themselves there. As they had surmised, two horsemen passed within close range of them without discovering them, and after they had passed, they immediately took up their tramp during the night. On Wednesday morning, August 13, they reached the banks of the Rio Grande just at sun-up. All three of them did not have any real food from the day they fled from the battlefield up to this time, with the exception of some cactus-pears, which gave all of them a severe case of fever. They managed to swim across the Rio Grande, and after proceeding a short distance inland, they came up to a Mexican goat herder, who taking them for Indians, ran off, and notified the captain of a Mexican frontier company, similar to the Texas Ranger companies, who was stationed in the neighborhood, about 30 miles above Piedras Negras, telling him that the "Indios" were coming, whereupon the captain ordered a detachment of 25 men to accompany him and sallied forth to meet the red-skins. When coming near enough, the "capitano" ordered his men to halt, and he rode towards the supposed Indios to parley with them.

Mr. Schwethelm handed his rifle to Kusenberger and advanced towards the captain. Being conversant in the Spanish language he explained the reason from their being there, their exhausted condition, and asked for help in the way of food, of which they had not partaken since the 9th day of the month, Saturday night. The captain comprehending the circumstances, took them in charge, ordered three of his men to dismount and tendering the mounts to them, took them to his camp. Before arriving three they stopped at a Mexican hut and the capitano ordered the woman to furnish the sufferers with something to eat and a cup of coffee, which was greedily devoured by the almost famished trio. They were then escorted to the camp of the Mexicans, where they were well taken care of and remained one night. Having had a good rest, they set out on foot the next morning headed for Piedras Negras. On their way they managed to procure food at the isolated ranches, and by night camped within a mile of Piedras Negras.

Entering the place the next morning they had the good fortune to meet up with an old friend, Adolph Real[18], a brother to Casper Real[19], who lived on Turtle Creek. Mr. Real was overjoyed at meeting them and took them to the boarding-house where he was staying. Desirous of reaching Monterey, the trio, without funds, sold Carl Graf's six-shooter to Mr. Real, who was preparing to return to San Antonio, with two wagon loads of flour which he had bought about a hundred miles from Piedras Negras, and which had cost him all his ready cash, so he was only able to pay $15 to Mr. Schwethelm's father as soon as he returned to San Antonio, a promise he duly complied with.

After a two days' stay in Piedras Negras they left for Monterey, fully provisioned and with money enough to pay for provisions as soon as theirs were gone. About 150 miles from Piedras Negras, at a place called Lampazos; the first man they met was a Negro, who was much astonished to meet up with Texans as they were to meet up with a Negro in the land of the Montezumas. He had been there eight years and had run off from slavery in the United States and had come far as Lampasos and stayed there. He was called "Doctor" by the Mexican, for what reason could not be established. He directed the trio to the alcalde, but before they entered the presence of this august personage, Schwethelm had instructed his companions to act in the same manner as he did, and to keep their months shut and their eyes open, believing in the doctrine "When in Rome, do as the Romans do!"

The Mexicans in the neighborhood were devout Catholics, as evidenced by numerous Catholic pictures and statues. Mr. Schwethelm was a Catholic himself and when the three entered the room of the Alcalde he took off his hat and with bowed head made the sign of the cross, with both of companions following suit. He then mumbled something unintelligible, which should be taken for a prayer, his attendants also imitating him as directed.

Addressing the Alcalde, upon whom this performance had made a strong impression, they were cordially received by the Alcalde, a wealthy man, who invited them to stay as long as they wanted to. But they left there for Monterey at the expiration of the second day, and when within 40 miles of

Monterey met up with Carl Griesenbeck[20], on his way to San Antonio, with whom they camped that night. He informed them that friends of theirs were expecting them at Monterey, having received information that they had escaped from the Nueces fight and were somewhere in Mexico. Before meeting up with Griesenbeck, the Texans met a Mexican *caballero*, gorgeously dressed, and riding a find horse with elaborate trappings and Mr. Schwethelm hailed him and asked him in Spanish how far it was to Monterey. Looking down upon the foot passenger, he asked: *"Apied? Quin sabe! Muy lechos!"* (Afoot? I don't know! Very far.) He evidently did not know the distance himself. Leaving Mr. Griesenbeck's camp at 5 o'clock in the morning, they arrived in Monterey at 1 p.m. The three had made the trip from Piedras Negras to Monterey in 12 days, a distance of 300 miles, and remember – this was made afoot.

At Monterey they were joyously received by Dr. Dressel[21], a wealthy jeweler of the place, and taken care of in hospitable fashion. They remained in Monterey a week, and not desiring to become a burden to their friend, concluded to march to Matamoras, opposite Brownsville. Mr. Dresel had made up a collection amounting to $24, and each one of them had received a new suit of clothes. Mr. Schwethelm, who had received the money gave each of his partners $8, and they began their journey of 300 miles, the same way they had been traveling and since they had crossed the Rio Grande their wanderings had all been during the daytime. They made this tramp in nine days. Arriving at their destination, they were directed to seek out the United States consul, who received them cordially and assigned them to quarters, as well as regular meals.

In the course of two weeks, refugees from Texas began flocking into Matamoros until 76 men had been assembled. This sudden influx was caused by deserters from a company of Confederates in Brownsville under the command of Capt. Kampmann[22]. The latter had arrived in Brownsville with 110 men, and the following night, after their arrival 90 men left him with a remnant of 20 men only. The United States consul had chartered a schooner and 76 men went aboard with the intent of going to New Orleans and there enlist in the Federal Army under Gen. Ben Butler. These men arrived in New Orleans on October 26 and enlisted the next day. Before enlisting they were addressed by Gen. Butler, who told [them] they did not have to enlist unless they wanted to, and should not hesitate in saying so. Mr. Schwethelm then told him that they would enlist on certain conditions, and the first of them was that they wanted to enlist in the cavalry, as they had done enough walking to last them a long time. Furthermore, they wanted to enlist in a Texas company, and lastly, they wanted to elect their own commanding officer. Butler then asked them if they had a military man amongst them. This question had to be answered in the negative. The first two requests were granted by Butler, but as to the third he said this would be impossible, as it was against the rules of the military government. He then instructed them to elect Lieut. E. J. Noyse[23], who he had known since his boyhood, as their captain, and they then could select their subordinate officers. The men consented to this arrangement and were then mustered in as Company A, First Texas Cavalry, United States Army.

To the disgust of Schwethelm and Kusenberger, their friend did not enlist, and confided to them that he had some money and being a carpenter by trade, he expected to go to New Orleans in his line. Asked by his comrades where he got his money, he produced a $20 gold piece, which he had sewed up in his pants at the belt and which he had all the time since leaving home. That Schwethelm and Kusenberger felt outraged was natural, as he was the one who had to be helped the most in extreme trouble. He was a poor shot with a six-shooter and rifle and they therefore bartered away his six-shooter to Adolph Real. In swimming across the Rio Grande these two had to take him along between them as he could not swim; they had begged alms and received them, which they shared equally with him, and to think, when they were in direst need for a little money to improve their condition, Graf had the $20 gold piece carefully tucked away about his person and kept mum! This revelation was the straw that broke the camel's back, but it only cemented the comradeship between Schwethelm and Kusenberger. Remaining in New Orleans for about two weeks, Graf, finding no work and having spent his money, applied for enlistment in the company in which his former comrades were enrolled, but as soon as these two became aware of this they raised objections to his coming a member of their company, and succeeding in their efforts, Graf was mustered into another company which had no relationship to the First Cavalry[24].

They were encamped in New Orleans until September, 1863, until 10,000 men were sent to Brownsville, the probable object of taking Texas as a whole, but this idea was abandoned, the leaders believing it to be a move not advisable. They remained in Brownsville about six months and were then transported back to Louisiana. The trio went along in this expedition. Schwethelm and Kusenberger were sent out on scout duty occasionally but never participated in any battle or fight of any consequence. In 1865 they were sent to San Antonio overland and were mustered out in the latter place[25].

All of the Texas contingent then returned to their homes to the great relief and joy of their families.

Mr. Schwethelm then took up ranching until 1867, when he was appointed by Governor E. J. Davis to form a frontier battalion of Rangers and made captain of this. Capt. Schwethelm then organized a company of 20 men at Johnson's Creek, near Ingram. Times were still unsettled on the frontier, and the western part of Texas was mostly troubled by Mexican horse-thieves who came over from the Rio Grande. Although Indians were still roaming the country in isolated bands, they were not near as troublesome as Mexican horse-thieves, disguised as Indians. This company existed until 1877, and Capt Schwethelm commanded it during the entire time. The company consisting mostly of Germans, [and] broke up at that time; Capt. Schwethelm then returned to his ranch life. Since that time he held no official position except as County Commissioner for a time and then again as sheep inspector for quite awhile.

In concluding this short biography of Capt. Schwethelm, the writer, owing to the pressure of time, has been unable to go into details of the various exciting incidents that occurred during Captain Schwethelm's career as a Ranger, the object being to get a statement of the most memorial event, the fight of the Nueces, in which the captain was an active participant and was given in the modest and conservative way of the old gentleman. No mention is made in a braggadocio way, of how many men he has personally killed, no hairbreadth escapes from death are recorded, the only event of this that Captain Schwethelm mentioned was when he was asked if he had ever been wounded, was, that during the Nueces fight, a bullet from one of Duff's men, passed through his hat making a furrow through his long hair without touching his skin.

There is no intention sought to reopen any bad feeling among those who might yet be living on the "other side" or their descendants that existed during those stirring times, but simply an effort to keep the records straight. In this respect this particular fight, and the murdering of the Union men at the time, has been differently described, and as to the fate of the wounded denied by partisans opposed to the Germans, but in 1907, a participant and survivor of Duff's command in this particular fight, a Scotchman by birth, R. H. Williams, published an interesting book in England, whence he had returned after the Civil War, entitled *With the Border Ruffians; Memories of the Far West. 1852-1868*, which fully describes this fight and the conditions in general during those troublesome times. Mr. Williams was a rancher on the Frio River, an ardent adherent of the Confederacy, and enlisting in San Antonio soon after the beginning of hostilities, was placed in Duff's command.

ENDNOTES
Was a Survivor of the Nueces Battle.

01. This is one of a number of accounts of the Nueces battle that writers and historians claim to be a primary document because it is supposedly told by a survivor. This is not necessary true. First, it is an interview of Henry Schwethelm, who was in fact a survivor of the battle. But it was not taken until 1924, shortly before Schwethelm's death. By this time many of the myths had become accepted as facts. The author wrote from an account by Schwethelm and includes many stories that are not true, but are also myths. This book will look at other such accounts and expose the myths that have grown up regarding the battle.

02. One of the major myths regarding the Nueces battle is that the Texas Governor issued a proclamation in mid-1862, giving all who did not want to remain in the Confederacy thirty days to leave, and the August insurgent group was travelling under this proclamation. This is **not true!** No such proclamation was ever issued. There were two early proclamations that referred to those not wanting to live under Confederate governments. The first one was issued on June 8, **1861,** by Governor Clark. It gave the individuals twenty days to leave or they would be arrested as spies. President Davis issued the second on August 14, **1861,** giving those who did want to live under Confederate goverment forty days to leave or be treated as alien enemies.

03. This statement in Schwethelm's account is contradicted by Sansom's account. Samson states, "About forty of these were fairly well armed with muzzle-loading guns and six-shooters; the others were poorly armed – one man having neither gun nor pistol. Here Schwethelm clearly states they "were fully equipped with rifles and six-shooters." Since Schwethelm was an actual member of the insurgent group and not just a guide, as was Samson, his account is likely to be the most accurate.

04. The reason for the insurgent's slow rate of speed was due to the large amount of supplies and pack animals. They stopped where they did for water holes. Had they travelled further in a day, they would have had to make several dry camps.

05. There is no correlating evidence that anyone objected to the slow rate of march. Several other members of the group later gave accounts of the trip. No one says anything about the pace being unreasonable.

06. As this account says, it is likely that a horse did get away from its owner and went to Tegener's sawmill. It would have been about seven to ten miles from Bushwhacker Creek where the group met. However the account that says the Confederates forced the captured insurgent to led them to the camp on Bushwhacker Creek just doesn't ring true. Most accounts state that the

Confederates learned of the departure of the insurgent group about August 5, and immediately set out after them. R. H. Williams was in the pursuit force and gives a detailed description of the pursuit. There is no indication in his account of going to Bushwacker. Williams clearly says they went up the Guadalupe River.

07.   Here Schwethelm seems to be describing Charles Burgmann, who was likely captured by the Confederates and agreed to guide them after the insurgent group. But Burgmann was not somewhat green and just arrived from Germany. Burgmann was living in Kerr County by 1861, a year prior to this event.

08.   This is an example of the effort to demonize James Duff. The pursuit force was not from Duff's Company. It was a composite unit of ninety-four men from the several companies stationed at Camp Pedernales. It was commanded by First Lieutenant Colin McRae. There were about fifteen to twenty from Duff's Company, commanded by Second Lieutenant Edward/Edwin Lilly.

09.   Again, there is no evidence from any of the other accounts which state that Schwethelm and his messmates threatened to abandon the troop and make their way to Mexico. John Samson did warn Tegener on the night of August 9th that they had been discovered. Sansom advised him to immediately set out for the Rio Grande.

10.   Here Schwethelm's article seems to imply that some twenty-eight insurgents left the camp "that night." This is another example of either Schwethelm or the interviewer adding to the myth. Some twenty-eight insurgents did leave the camp the night of August 9-10. These left after the opening shots, leaving their comrades to battle the Confederates. Had these twenty-eight not "left early" the insurgents would have most likely defeated the Confederates. Many of these twenty-eight were in fact executed later by the Confederates.

11.   Another example to demonize James Duff. Duff was not in the pursuit force, nor was he the officer that ordered the pursuit force. Duff was back at Fort Martin Scott. The Confederate voice that was shouting encouragement to the Confederates was Second Lieutenant William T. Harbour of Davis' Company.

12.   The individual who guided the pursuit force, Charles Burgmann, was not killed. He was, however, wounded in three places, but he recovered and joined Duff's battalion in October, 1862.

13.   This is another after-the-fact attempt to demonize James Duff and show he was in the Confederate force. As stated in Endnote # 11, Duff was back at Fort Martin Scott. The Confederate who accompanied Dr. Downs was the rider which McRae had sent to Fort Clark, asking for medical assistance, and likely not even an officer.

14. Thomas Riordan was likely born in September, 1816, in Ireland. The date he arrived in America is not known. He enlisted in the U. S. Army on October 19, 1838. His unit took part in the Mexican War. After the war he was stationed at Fort Clark. His service records show he enlisted in 1860 at Fort Clark. For some reasons, he did not leave Texas with the U. S. Army. Riordan married Ellen Melefont on November 24, 1861, in Kenney County. He organized a fifty-three man home guard company on September 21, 1863, in which he served until the end of the war. When the federal army returned to Texas, he is again shown as a non-commissioned officer. Thomas Riordan died on May 21, 1867, at Fort Clark.

15. Here the Schwethelm article greatly exaggerates the Confederate casualties. Many writers and 'historians' state that the insurgents were 'just massacred' and that they never had any real chance to fight. Here an insurgent account says they inflicted a high number of causalities. The Confederate casualties were two killed and nineteen wounded; four died later of their wounds.

16. This reported statement by Dr. Downs can not be true. The wounded insurgents were executed shortly after four p. m. by Lieutenant Lilly's detail. Dr. Downs didn't arrive at the battle site until the evening of August 12th, when this alleged meeting with him took place.

17. Again, this statement about twenty-three insurgent skulls being located is not true. At least two of the skulls were not located. One was the insurgent who left the camp and went up [north] of the Nueces River and died. His body was not found until the 1870s. The second skull was that of Leonard Bauer. Samson located it in the 1870s. There were a total of nineteen insurgents killed at the battle site, which includes the wounded. There is also good evidence that two insurgents were killed prior to the battle on August 9. At the very most only seventeen skulls were located. If it is true that two were killed before the battle, their bodies were not located, which would mean that only fifteen skulls were recovered after the war.

18. Adolph Real was born on March 25, 1825, near Düsseldorf, then part of the kingdom of Prussia. The family arrived in Texas about 1847 and settled on South Turtle Creek. Real married Lina Kike [Kay] on August 13, 1856, in Bexar County. They were the parents of at least five children. It is interesting to note that the balance of the amount to purchase the six-shooter was given to Schwethelm's father and not to the Graff family. After all, the pistol belonged to Carl Graff. Adolph Real died on December 20, 1901, in Kerr County.

19. Casper Real was born on March 3, 1824, near Düsseldorf, then part of the kingdom of Prussia. The family arrived in Texas about 1847 and settled on South Turtle Creek. Real married Emilie Schreiner, the sister of Charles and Amil on November 5, 1853, in Bexar County. They were the parents of eight children. Casper Real died on August 1, 1893, in Kerr County.

20. Charles Frederick Griesenbeck was a merchant living in San Antonio. He was born in February, 1829, in Cleves, then a part of Rhenish Prussia. Griesenbeck was likely a Forty-Eighter. He arrived in Texas on the *Franziska* on December 6, 1849, and first lived on Cibolo Creek in eastern Bexar County. Charles F. Griesenbeck married Caroline Wilhelmine Kottmann on May 7, 1854, in Bexar County. They were the parents of five children. Caroline Wilhelmine Kottmann and Charles F. Griesenbeck were divorced about 1866. In September, 1867, Charles Griesenbeck married Wilhelmine Augusta H. Boeckel; in Manhattan, New York. They were the parents of at least six children. Charles Frederick Griesenbeck died on October 1911, in Bexar County.

21. The four Dresel brothers; Emil, Gustave, Julius and Rudolph, were born in Geisenheim, Hesse. All took a very active role in the German 1848 revolution and had to flee. They arrived in Texas on the *Louis* on November 20, 1848. Gustave died of yellow fever in Galveston shortly after his arrival. The other three first settled in Sisterdale, but by 1860, were all living in San Antonio. It is not clear to which brother the Schwethelm article is refers. After the war all three went to Sonoma County, California, and established the Rhineland Vineyards. All three died in California.

22. Johann Hermann Kampmann was the Captain of Company B, Third Regiment, Texas Infantry. It did suffer a great many of desertions while in Brownsville. Kampmann was born on December 25, 1819, in Prussia. He was very likely a Forty-Eighter. Kampmann arrived in Texas in 1848, and settled in San Antonio. On May 14, 1850, he married Carolina Jacobine Bonnet in San Antonio. They were the parents of five children. Kampmann died on September 6, 1885, while on a trip to Colorado. He is buried in Bexar County.

23. Edward J. Noyse was elected the captain of Company A, First Regiment [Union] Texas Cavalry. He was promoted to major later in the war.

24. Here the Schwethelm article is totally incorrect. Charles Graff enlisted in Company B, First Regiment on November 10, 1862, and served until the end of the war, being mustered out of service on October 31, 1865.

25. This account of Schwethelm's is again totally incorrect. As the Union troops were withdrawing from South Texas in the spring of 1864, Schwethelm's group was surprised by a large Confederate force. In order to save their lives several men of the unit swam the Rio Grande to Mexico. The action has been called the Las Rucias battle and it took place on June 24, 1864. Schwethelm, instead of making his way to rejoin his unit at Brownsville, deserted and likely returned to the Hill Country where he hid for the remainder of the war. He was never mustered out of service, but listed as a deserter.

## 44. *Dallas Morning News,* May 5, 1929

## THE BLACKEST CRIME IN THE HISTORY IN TEXAS WARFARE[1]

### THUS THE YEARS HAVE LABELED THE TRAGEDY OF NUECES RIVER WHERE 27 UNION SOLDIERS DIED

For Three Years the Bleaching Bones of those Young Germans, Who Left Gillespie County to Fight Against Slavery and Were Surprise and Slaughtered by a Group of Renegades, Lay Among Thorns and Underbrush at the Fork of the River – August Hoffman, Sole Survivor of the Germans Taking Part in the Fight Describes His Escape.

*By Helen Raley*

Pretty close kin are the points exclamatory and interrogatory, Proof? Well, there is the triple-engined, The Question Mark, which stayed in the air and headlines for 150 hours – thereby answering its own query in right exclamatory fashion.

And then in Texas' Palestine – that valley of Guadalupe, where climate, pasturing flocks, peaceful hills, all remind travelers of Judea – lifts a stone shaft. A memorial exclamation, undoubtedly.

But since its inscription is in German, and the '60s are now long distant, it became subject or question recently. An article appearing in *The Dallas News*, reprinted by the *National Tribune*, Washington, D. C. came to the notice of Judge C. S. Brodbent. Now resident in San Antonio, Judge Brodbent, who is 86 years of age, a past senior vice commander of the G.A.R., came to Texas in 1875, to take up sheep ranching. County Judge of Val Verde County, familiar with Kinney County history through a quarter century spent in the Big Bend, he called attention to certain facts. On request of *The News*, the present writer went on pilgrimage – first to Kendall County town of Comfort; then beyond into Gillespie County – for an interview with the only man now living who escaped from is known as the "Nueces River massacre."

Never was a place better named than Comfort. No long ago, when some enterprising "soup man" (on tour from Chicago, probably) paused in his journey along the old Spanish trail long enough to rob the local bank, press items' pointed out that this serene and law abiding village possessed nothing whatever in shape of a jail! Nor are there the usual "peace officers" – because said peace has never been liable to fracture, at least, by its own residents.

An upland hamlet, in the old Saxon sense – a place of little homes, white, green-shuttered, neat – Comfort nestles beside the main highway, thirty-eight miles northwest of San Antonio. Winding around the hilly slopes, this concrete trail follows the ancient road branching off from the Camino Real. Along the town's principal street, therefore, loom the tall poles which always march in electricity's processional, "jazzed up" by red, yellow and white striping of the Old Spanish Trail. Half a dozen substantial two-story rock buildings, dulled by age to a dingy monotint, serve for much sturdier business of mohair, wool, hides, cotton, and farm implements. There is [the] town common, bordered by a brook, and fields with grazing sheep. Standing at the western roadside, doing perpetual sentry is the monument described by a previous writer.

The inscription – *"Treue der Union"* (true to the Union) – reveals it as belonging to the Civil War era. Of the thirty-six names carved upon it, all but one are such as you find on ancient rosters of the Adelsverein and other Rhineland colonization companies. The date 1862 is just a decade later than that which saw the settlers' wagons creak into camp within this valley. At the foot of the hill an oak tree, forty inches in girth, spreads its ast (sic) top. It may remember those weary folk resolved to kindle here new hearth fires–after long periods at sea; hardships of the trek from Indianola; ravaged by hunger, cholera, scurvy; disaster in [a] store of shapes.

Meusebach and the "Founders."

A San Antonio civil leader and a Comfort business man, sons to two early immigrants, relate the tale of the "founders." Edward Steves, father of Albert Steves, came to Texas in 1848. Barely 18, he was bound for Prince Solms-Braunfels' Colony. Its sponsor the "League of Nobility," had achieved for itself a state of bankruptcy; its particular patron, Prince Solms, had fled the scene early (even as did a more famous Crown Prince much later in history!) and only be heroic exertions of that brilliant and devoted leader, Baron Meusebach, had a certain proportion of shiploads of immigrants been enable to plant homesteads at New Braunfels and Fredericksburg. Not least of his triumphs was that memorable visit to and treaty with Kotemoczy, Santana and Mopechnicope – the Comanche chiefs. This threw open the lovely valleys of the Guadalupe and Comal Rivers, with the Pedernales, to extension of settlement, even as the Colorado's stretch, near Austin had sheltered Bastrop's first colony, the quaintly named village of "Industry."

What a teammate for the latter on Texas' map is Comfort! Also it's near neighbor, Welfare! Perhaps this was in the minds of early citizens; men, who like the senior Steves and Brinkman, coming from New Braunfels, were aware of its long-manor 'Sophienberg' and other transplanted pomposities, which John Meusebach's good sense lived down.

## Alex Brinkman

At any rate, industry and comfort seems very foundation stones of the placid little town, as attested by its farms and homes. Typical is the homestead of that profound though unassuming historian, Alex Brinkman. Mr. Brinkman, whose father settled here in 1852, is an authority on the achievements of Bastrop the colonizer; Lindheimer, the "father of Texas botany;" Stern, who has been called Ben Franklin of the Texas Republic. A quaint bungalow study in the courtyard is lined with bookcases, game trophies, maps.

On one of the latter his finger traces the Nueces River's west fork, points out a spot two or three miles above Silver Lake ranch, while he reveals the true story of that monument upon the hill – the tale of a time when comfort there was more for bereaved wives and mothers. With a few minor differences facts of the battle which ended in butchery are same as related by him (after taking a survivor to this place in 1917) and by August Hoffman, sole present survivor; also is a printed account by Ranger Captain John W. Sansom's (participant in the fight); in the particularly vivid report by R. H. Williams (who took part also, on the opposite side); in Lessing's history, and in Don Biggers' interesting volume, *German Pioneers in Texas*.

## The Blackest Crime

War being war, not according to the specifications of a pillow fight, bloodshed is inevitable–as testified by Shiloh's Manassas', Chancellorsville's terrible fields. But it is shocking to learn that what one historian calls "the blackest crime of American warfare" was perpetrated on Texas soil. This slaughter of unarmed and wounded prisoners – an exact parallel for the Goliad massacre so abhorred of memory – was by command of a Scotchman name Duff (a man who had once been drummed out of the United States regular army in disgrace) and a Yankee renegade who was his lieutenant.

## Desperadoes Were Plentiful

The western frontier, resort in those days for "bad men" would naturally be the scene of violent deeds which could never be termed warfare according to the code. So it was in "Bleeding Kansas", with the offense by Freesoilers, sometimes the reverse. In Texas the year 1862 saw desperate conditions. Drained of her very best, who had sprung to defense of the Confederacy and were struggling gallantly toward the mighty Eastern campaign of '63, the Lone Star State mustered various outfits to act as home guard. The area covered was vast. The best of leaders could not exercise supervision over all the companies suddenly recruited. Bullies, bandits, cut-throats "joined up" for purpose of loot. One group, the famous Waldrip gang, many of whom had been under indictment as cattle thieves long before the war, never enlisted but ranged all over Gillespie County, committing many murders.[2] Rangers of that time testified that these fellow often put on war paint, so as to be thought raiding Indians. Then there was a certain notorious vigilante leader of Bexar County as much addicted to pious camp meeting exhortations as he was to pronouncing the sentence, "Give 'em a quick look up a tree!" Once, in the midst of pulpit fervors, he stooped to his big white hat for a bandanna to mop his heated brow. And with it, before the Faithfull's very eyes, he drew his trusty coiled lynching rope. Pity is that certain of their kind were able, through the confusion of war, to get into uniforms, whether blue or gray.

## Stanley Told Them

Chief among the latter was man Duff, who secured a captaincy to head the Texas partisan Rangers. Of course, trained men who could drill the "hay foot, straw foot" squad were needed and no one knew the circumstances of his leaving the regulars. However, following the Civil War, these were revealed right dramatically. Gen. David S. Stanley[3], veteran of the Plains service west to Denver while commanding the Southern department. Invited to lunch at a leading club, he learned that James M. Duff was a member. Thus it happened that a committee, waiting upon the absent guest of honor, was told that it would quite impossible for a ranking officer, to meet socially a man whom he had seen court-martialed for a serious offense, tied to a whipping post under the Plains![4] This revelation ended the rascal's Denver career: he betook himself to Parisian haunts, where he died.

## The "Whitewashed Yankee."

A man of like character, said to have been "whitewashed Yankee," served Duff as chief executioner. Wrote one disgusted recruit of the Partisan Rangers, "By the Captain's influence he was elected junior lieutenant in our company, but not by my vote, for I never thought him fit for even fourth corporal." He was afterward made to resign from that particular unit.⁵ Such were some of the misfits (to put it mildly!) who could glean rich pickings while brave and gallant Texans were riding to death with Hood and with Sibley. Down on the border was cotton to be sold – returns from which often failed to reach the hard-pinched Confederate treasury. Up in the Hill Country – Kerr, Kendall, Edwards, Kimble, Gillespie Counties – loot and violence were possible, with Duff as provost marshal.

## Loyal League Members

The region of the German settlements had organized the Union Loyal League, whose members were pledged not to take up arms against the Federal Government. Of course, this brought them sharply into conflict with conscription act. Martial law was proclaimed, the above countries declared in rebellion and men between 13 and 35 who were unwilling were given thirty days to leave the country.⁶ Complying with this order, sixty-five or sixty-eight men set out for the Rio Grande, intending to cross into Mexico, whence they would sail for New Orleans and join the Union Army.

## Hoffman's Story of the Fight

One of these men, August Hoffman, of Cain City, Gillespie Country, is now the sole survivor of the Germans taking part in the Nueces River fight. Mr. Hoffman, a snowy-crested, serene-looking man, reached the age of 86 Dec. 9, 1928. Yet he is not at all the sort you think of as old-timer. Rather he seems a philosopher, well preserved in mind and body. His sight and hearing are acute, his voice is strong and his sense of humor still on the job. (Chuckling, he relates how a certain cotton profiteer of the '60s used, on the Brownsville docks, to apply a smear of boot-blacking to one bale out of every lot, kicking it aside with the all-sufficient phrase,

"That's mine." Above all, he remembers "as though it was yesterday," the events of the Nueces battle.

Quietly he recounts the tale of that happy night by the flickering camp-fire. Bad enough was the dawn's awakening: but war is like that. It is the black deed perpetrated in Sunday's light, against which will always raise the protest of that stone shaft—and of honor, more enduring than stone.

## On The Way to Join The Union

"Up here in Gillespie County, we didn't notice the war much for first year, although seven-eights of us were on the Union side.  But the second year was different. Most of us who decided to go and enlist rather than be conscripted in the Southern service, were young fellows, eighteen to twenty-five. I was twenty. Among the older men were Fritz Tegener, the major in command; Captain John W. Sansom of the State ranger force and a brother of the late Captain Charles Schreiner. Meeting at Turtle Creek, eight miles south of Kerrville, we started, August 1, 1862. Our shortest route was to strike southwest, crossing the Medina, Frio, and Nueces rivers and passing the border not far from Del Rio.  We were in no hurry, sparing our horses and the few pack animals which carried our provisions, making camp in several places. We took more than a week for as much of the journey as might easily have been accomplish in three days. Then at the west fork of the Nueces, we halted at the waterhole for a day. Our horses being mostly unshod, had began to go lame on the flinty mountain trails. So it was decided to rest them, although one more day's travel would have put us safely across the Rio Grande."

## Those Who turned Back

At this point the survivor was questioned concerning some of the party who abandoned the enterprise, going back home. Captain Henry Schwethelm, who escaped after the battle, becoming an officer in the Federal army, stated before his death in 1924.[7] Mr. Hoffman agrees, thinking the number may have been higher, up to thirty-five. Soberly he picks up the narrative.[8]

"Before this, two men had visited us in camp, with the message that 'things could be arranged – it would be all right to go back.'[9] Trusting in this many went, although the time set in the Governor's proclamation had expired ten days before.[10] Some were caught and killed later on. The rest of us said we would go on. There was talk that night as to whether or not we were being followed." (A quaint bit of "human interest" attaches to this, as explained in the Sansom account – which also relates how spy Bachman,[11] betrayer of the party, afterwards fled to Mexico, where he was killed by a Seminole negro. [12])

## Woe's Omen

"We had a good time, that Saturday night. Camp had been pitched nearly 350 yards from the Nueces, on a fairly clear space of about an acre. Strategically, the camp-site was a joke – being joined to the main cederbrakes of the river bottom by a timbered strip. But we though there was no danger, so spread our blankets beside the fires after supper, and were happy.

Under jutting gray brows, the veteran's blue eyes darken. He smiles thoughtfully, makes a slight deprecatory gesture, resurrects a pioneer superstation –

"Old freighters used to say that whenever the drivers were so happy at night, next morning something would surely go wrong; if it wasn't Indians to lift their scalps, at least there would be a strayed ox team. Anyhow, we enjoyed ourselves. Everybody gave some humorous piece to entertain the outfit. I remember one was an old German poem called 'Black Crows Are still A-Flying.'"

Woe's omen? Of black dreadful-winged things circling, swooping above that place before the next night should fall?

## Selling Their Lives Dearly

"At 4 the sleeping camp was attacked. One of our guards challenged, 'Who's there?' at a slight noise. Three shots were the answer. Each was a hit, leaving one man dead and two wounded. From then until sunrise of Sunday the fight went on. Our commander being badly wounded early in the action, Emil Schreiner called us to order, leading us in a counter-charge. He was among those killed. I can remember him crying out to us, "Come on, let's sell our lives as dearly as we can!' One thing which caused much loss was the great difference between our weapons and those of the attackers. The men firing on us from cover of the cedar brakes were armed with breech-loadings guns, while we had to load from the muzzle. Of course this obliged us to stand up, exposing a perfect target.

## The Escape

"When the sun rose, a group of us who were out of ammunition watched [the] enemy shooting at our men; the latter were lying down, many of them wounded. Realizing ourselves outnumbered, we seized the chance to escape while the attackers were reloading. We succeeded in getting across the open space and up the side of a hill. It was everybody on his own hook then."

"Presently a few of us, making our way through the brush, came together we meant to wait for the rest. However, we suffered so from lack of water that finally we crept back in pairs to the river. Hiding in the bushes, we managed to evade the sentinels and get down to the brink. There we found a man lying on his back, with only his nose above the water. At first we though him one of the enemy, until someone whispered, 'My God, is it you?' Sure enough, it was a comrade, shot through the arm and breast. Carrying him to a safe distance, we made a rough bed, doctoring him as well as possible. He lived three weeks on beargrass and the fruit of prickly pear – then gave himself up and was brought to San Antonio, where he recovered. Had he surrendered to Duff's company at the time of the battle he would have been killed – as Lieutenant Lilly, understanding his superior's wish to have no prisoners, ordered every wounded German shot.[13]   When, three years later, the unburied skeletons were gathered up, in the back of each skull was found a bullet hole!"

## Williams' Account

A cowardly trick, aping (sic) the "ley fuego." In civilized warfare blood is shed, but wounded are not killed, nor prisoners. Which is the reason for calling this little-known fight of '62 the "Kinney County Massacre!" An Englishman, R. H. Williams, who with Louis Oge[14] (of loved memory in San Antonio) had ridden from their neighboring ranches eager to enlist beneath the great banner of Lee, Jackson, Beauregard and Jeb Stuart, tells of that shameful afternoon in a book published by a London firm. He says: "By 4 o'clock we had got the horses all together. Then I hurried over to where we had left the German wounded, to see how they were getting on, and was surprise to find them gone. Asked what had become of them, I was told they had been moved to better shade. Just then one of my wounded called for water. As I was giving it to him, the sound of firing was heard a little way off. I thought at first they were burying some of the dead with the honors of war, but it didn't sound like that. Possible it might be at attack on the camp; so I seized my rifle and ran in the direction of the firing. Presently I met a man who, when he saw me running said, 'You needn't be in a hurry, its all done; they've shot the poor devils.'

"Our own dead were buried in one long trench, but those of the enemy were carried to where the murdered prisoners lay and then left for a prey to the buzzards and coyotes."

Williams then goes on to relate how he, his friend Oge, and certain others who remonstrated later were detailed by the man responsible for the deed to perform a record Red Cross endurance feat. Bearing the Confederate wounded on litters, they tramped, climbed, slid along the filthy slopes all day, waterless, under an August sun, thirty miles to Fort Clark. Complete enough retaliation! According to relatives of Louis Oge, now deceased, he so deplored Duff's crimes that once, at least, he aided a hunted German to escape.[15]

### Indignation of a Gallant Confederate

Quoted in Captain Sansom's historical pamphlet is a statement from J. M. Hunter (then County Judge of Edwards County), who had been First Lieutenant of a volunteer company engaged in the fight, but was detached as quartermaster just before. Writing with the indignation of a gallant soldier of the C.S.A., he mentions by name one man (who even in old age carried a revolver, lest he suffer for that

Sunday's work), and commends the narrative as "showing the guilty parties, who will not be endorsed by innocent Confederates."

Had John Sansom's advice been heeded, there would have been no slaughter. He was on the same canny breed as Houston, Jackson, Crockett, [and] Crook. He could and did skirmish cross cacti and mesquite as [a] ranger captain, or ride as major at the head of four Indian troops. When Civil War loomed, he offered his sword to Houston – and the Union. The stern old warrior said, "My son, you are the second man to make such an offer. Ed Burleson was first." And as parting gift Sansom carried a fine revolver away from the executive mansion, whence secession was so soon to remove its master. "Use this to keep the Indians from scalping you!" had been the cryptic command.

## A Paradise by Day

Listening to his daughter's quiet recital, there came into the hearer's mind wonder whether that same revolver was in his holster as he helped pitch camp upon the Nueces. Too attractive, by far, those shady cedar brakes! In vain Sansom counseled withdrawal. Quoting from him:

"Deer, wild turkeys and other game were abundant in the country, and hunting parties were coming and going all day. It was not until about sunset that the least uneasiness was felt. About that time one of the hunting parties returned with the report that they had seen strangers whose evident desire to concealment appeared suspicious. This intelligence created considerable commotion. But at that juncture another party returned to camp, and learning of the excitement quickly allayed it by the statement that they were the strangers the first party had seen – that just to see what the others would do, they had first shown themselves and then made pretence of concealing themselves. This statement at once turned the laugh on the first party – it was too good a joke not to be enjoyed. While the supposed victims were unmercifully teased, a third party of hunters came in. Unwilling to acknowledge themselves victims of the same joke, they failed (until too late to do any good) to report that they also had seen strangers who acted so suspiciously that they had come back at one to camp to report the circumstances.

But even in the midst of all the joking and jollity, there were duties to be performed, for by the time the sun was fairly down, the horses had all be caught and tied, and a night guard detailed and instructed. Then came a feast on the game that had been killed, and after that some of the young men amused themselves by wrestling, turning somersaults, playing leapfrog and light games.  When they had tired themselves speech-making began, some of the subjects being 'America' 'Fatherland' Citizenship' 'Civil War' and 'Refugeeing in Mexico!'

## Sansom Urged Departure

"I called Major Tegener to one side and said, 'Are you entirely satisfied that our boys saw no strangers around this evening?' I added. 'Major, you can if you will, get ready and leave here in thirty minutes. The moon is shining and the night air will give us cool travelling. Suppose you pull right out from here and cross over into Mexico before halting again.' He said he would confer with others of the party and if they thought as I did the march would be resumed as quickly possible. But when he broached the subject to Kuechler and Degener, both expressed themselves as being in favor or remaining in camp until morning."

Sansom asked to be put on guard duty. Called by the sentry before dawn, they started for the outpost. Within sixty seconds the guard was killed by a surprise shot. Sansom first returned the fire, then crept closer to learn the strength of enemy. Caught between two fires for a time, he finally rejoined his party, fighting until its rout, when he escaped. During the following months he took several squads of recruits into the Federal service, where he rose to a captaincy.

As stated on the monument, nineteen men – all Germans except Pablo Diaz – were killed in the Nueces battle. It's bloody aftermath disposed of eight more. A Confederate estimate placed their own dead at twelve and the wounded at eighteen.[16] Their troop total is variously stated as 100 to 125, while the Unionists (estimated by Captain Sansom at sixty-five) seem to have been but forty, according to the statements of both Schwethelm and Hoffmann concerning the number who left camp, believing their officers bull-headed in refusing to push on to the border. Probably this exodus was unknown to many. Checking various accounts, the number who escaped as did Mr. Hoffmann, after hearing their part in that dawn fight beside the water hold seems to have been seventeen.

## Some Swam the Rio Grande

Direful experience met those who tried to flee across the Rio Grande. Schwethelm, tramping by night to a ranch, had just sat down to dinner when his appétit was ruined by the arrival of Duff and Dr. Downs, surgeon who had been brought from Fort Clark to attend the wounded. (This doctor, according an article published by Albert Schutze, later said that when he suggested looking after the German wounded, certain of Duff's men replied, "Never mind: we will attend to them.")[17] Escaping by a ruse, the fugitive and two others succeed in swimming the Rio Grande. In this they were lucky. For instance, there were the Weiss brothers and the Fetterlein [Veterleins]. The latter – one badly wounded in the wrist – were in a "woeful sight," according to men encamped near El Paso: grotesque too, for their own clothes were fluttering from thorns upon a thousand chaparral bushes and they had substituted cast-off fodder sacks which marked the trail of Sibley's cavalry brigade!

## The Skull on the Pole

War's symphony of pain and terror has always certain notes that vibrate beyond the others. So – muted, yet rasping barbaric as a tom-tom – persist the following. Cut where the sunshine falls always upon the upon it, the third death roll of that Comfort monument names seven men, "Killed at The Rio Grande, Oct. 18, 1862." Last are Moritz and Franz Weiss. With lowered voice, sons of their contemporaries mention them dismiss the memory in briefest phrase. For it doesn't do to dwell overmuch on past atrocities. R. H. Williams, writing of his recruiting trip along the border, says of a certain outpost, "High up on a pole, on the top of their commissary store hut, grinned a human skull. I was told it had belonged to an unfortunate German, who, with others of his countrymen, had been killed when attempting to cross the Rio Grande some months before. They were quite indignant when I suggested it would be more seemly to bury the poor remnant of humanity."

## Lived on Prickly Pear Apples

Such the tale that drifted back to the hills after weeks or months – even as the battle refugees had crept in traveling on foot through the brush. Says August Hoffmann: "It took me five or six days to get back to Gillespie County. I was not wounded, but three in our little party were. They suffered, and we were weak from fever, caused by too steady a diet of prickly pears!"

Mr. Hoffmann smiles and strokes his neat, snowy goatee. Those lifesaving but prickly-slickly salads of castus (sic) apples and beargrass crop up in these narratives like raw beets in the stories told by A.E.F men who escaped from German prison camps!

## Slipping Through the Cordon

"I remember how glad we were to find some flour which had been lost off a pack horse. We pounced on it and at the next water hole had a grand baking on a flat rock. It was a good thing we had matches, for next day somebody shot a deer. This gave us strength and we could travel better, but were obliged to spread out, as we discovered the enemy was following. Nearing the Guadalupe, we took toll from a potato field, also were given a bucket of milk and two loaves of bread at a farm house. Our great concern was to slip through the cordon. Duff and Davis had a camp beside the Pedernales waterfall: However, most of us slipped to safety. One man was forced to run the risk of consulting a doctor. Under martial law, the physician had to report this to the authorities – but gave the name of a German he knew to be dead.

## The Rhinish Folk Worked On

"A friend must be fireproof, then," says the quiet voice. The veterans' kindly eyes shadow, as he tells of two were caught and hanged when closed to home – one a boy under 18. A farmer discovered molding bullets was taken prisoner, told to run – and killed by a shot in the back. (Lev Fuego!) "Things went on so until the spring of 1863. I had been in hiding most of the time. At last we heard that one of the State legislators, named Hamilton, I think, had secured passage of a bill – April 5 or 6 – which granted humanity to all who would agree to haul freight, etc., for the Confederacy."

And so the harassed people went again about their business. Self-supporting they had been and more, through all the stress. Texans owed more than she knew to those Germans who kept the wheels turning while so many of her own worthwhile men were away. Imports and exports – except a certain amount through Mexico – ceased. Says the Old Alcalde, O. M. Roberts, "By the first of 1862 the people in most parts of the State set about providing themselves with the necessaries of life." Those Rhinish folk who had come in tossing, masted ships to old Indianola, were, mostly, trained industrialists.

\* \* \*

### Brinkman's Strange Quest

"But in '65 he took a strange and solemn journey. With Charles Brinkman and others, he set out along that abhorred trail which led to the Nueces' fork. By day and night those bleaching bones had cried to mothers, wives, kinsmen. Now the time had come when upon the anniversary of the battle they might be brought back for burial.

"Although then a boy of 5, I can remember well the great express box, made so carefully its purpose. I was told that two uncles – my father's [friend] Henry [Steves] and his brother-in-law, William Boerner had been killed; but of course could not realize all that the trip up the country meant."

Mr. Brinkman, whose father also accompanied the party of sixteen, speaks of the difficulties encountered. With wagons drawn by mules, they proceed as far as possible, then with pack animals followed the river bed. Guided to the fatal camp site by [Henry] Schwethelm, they did their grim work, loading the packs for transit over terrain which was impassable for wagons. Reaching the latter, the return was made in a week's time over the main road leading back through Uvalde and San Antonio.

So came home at last that belated funeral train. So ends this story of the men commemorated by the shaft at Comfort. Foursquare it stands, bearing citations: northward, names of those massacred (with two who escaped, only to meet the same fate near home); southward, those killed beside the Rio Grande; westward, those fallen in the battle; eastward, their confession of faith to the Nation they had adopted.

ENDNOTES
Blackest Crime in The History of Texas Warfare

01. This is it! This is the one document that most "histories" and writers use to demonize the Confederate forces and James Duff in particular. From the very first the article is slanted and biased towards establishing how innocent the insurgents were and how horrible were the Confederates. This article has often been quoted as a primary source document, collecting several "first-hand" accounts. The fact is that the writer's bias is clear and many of the events she claims were first-hand accounts were not! The writer interjected in the body of the article things she thought were said by other sources. The following endnotes will explain these falsehoods and exaggerations; for example, the headline itself. Even if everything she claims was true the event was far from the "Blackest Crime in the History on Texas Warfare." One immediately thinks of the massacre of Colonel Fannin's men after they surrendered to the Mexican Centralist Army at Goliad. In that case, 342 men were executed on Palm Sunday, March 27, 1836. Other such blackest crimes also took place around Goliad. Santa Anna executed twenty-eight Americans on December 14, 1835. On March 15, 1836, Centralist General Urrea executed fifteen Texian prisoners. This document, like to the preceding one is often quoted as a primary document. This is not true. While it contains parts of several so-called "first-hand" accounts, Raley presents her interpretation of what she believed had happened – and not the actual story.

02. The author has written another book that deals with this so-called Waldrip Gang. Waldrip was a Texas State lieutenant of the Third Frontier District in command of a squad of men in western Gillespie County. This unit never took part in any atrocities. During the period from late 1863 until late 1864 there were a great many atrocities committed in Gillespie and surrounding counties. This was during the period termed by the author as *Haengerbande* [Hanging Gang], or the Bushwhacker War. The Bushwhacker War was between two groups: pro-Union and pro-Confederate vigilantes. Because of a breakdown of law and order these two vigilante groups began taking justice into their own hands and became known locally as bushwhackers. Which side one supported determined if a certain band of vigilantes were or were not bushwhackers. If the group supported your side, they were just loyal citizens trying to protect family and friends. If the band supported the other side, they were bushwhackers or outlaws.

03. David Sloane Stanley was born on June 1, 1828, in Cedar Valley, Wayne County, Ohio. He graduated from the U. S. Military Academy in 1852. He served in several western posts and participate in several Indians campaigns. At the outbreak of the Civil War he was a captain at Fort Washita in Indian Territory. He quickly led his command to Fort Leavenworth, Kansas. He

quickly rose in rank and was promoted to brigadier general by September, 1861. He was awarded the Medal of Honor at the Battle of Franklin on November 30, 1864. After the war, Stanley was appointed colonel of the 22nd Infantry Regiment. By 1879, he and his command were assigned to the Department of Texas. In March, 1884, Stanley was promoted to brigadier general in the regular army and assigned command of Texas in 1884. David Sloane Stanley died on March 13, 1902, at Washington, D. C.

04. It is certain at least part of this story is correct. When Stanley was invited to meet with a leading club, he learned that James Duff was a member. He was aware that Duff was court-martialed as an enlisted man. Duff was sentenced to receive forty lashes on his back and to be drummed out of the service. However, Duff's sentence was remitted and he received an honorable discharge after five years of service. Stanley was obviously not aware that Duff's sentence had been remitted and he was returned to his company. It is also very likely that while commander of the Department of Texas, he was told that Duff was a monster and did not check the facts but believed the stories Texas Unionists told him. Shortly after this incident Duff left Colorado and returned to Scotland.

05. Here Raley's article refers to Second Lieutenant Edwin Lilly who was in command of the party that executed the wounded insurgents after the Nueces battle. Lilly was promoted to captain and made quartermaster of the regiment. He did not leave the unit.

06. Riley's article here is referring to the "great myth" that the Texas governor or some other official issued a proclamation giving anyone who did not want to live under Confederate rule thirty days to leave under this authority the insurgents were leaving Texas. No such proclamation was issued. It is a trick of words by Raley and others attempting to show the insurgents were not a threat of Texas or The Confederacy. There were two such proclamations; one in June, 1861, when the Texas governor gave anyone not wishing to remain in Texas twenty days to leave the state. *(See Document Number 2, p. 23.)* The second was in August, 1861, when the Confederate Congress passed two laws stating that those not wishing to remained in the Confederate States had forty days to leave the bounds of the Confederate States of American. *(See Documents Numbers 4 and 5, pp.29 and 31.)*

07. Henry Schwethelm was never an officer in the Union Army. He deserted the army after the Battle of Las Rucias on June 24, 1864, and never returned to his unit. He was later a Texas Ranger captain.

08. The Schwethelm article is talking about the insurgents that left the camp after the opening shots were fired before the Confederate ground assault. In his reply, Hoffmann is apparently talking about those who left while at Turtle and Bushwacker Creeks; not the same men.

09. Here Hoffmann expands on the number that he is speaking of, when he says two men had visited the camp, saying that it would be all right to go back. He is clearly taking about those that left the party prior to the insurgent group leaving for Mexico.

10. That myth about the governor or someone issuing a proclamation that they had thirty days to leave Texas raises its head again. In this version it goes so far as to say the proclaimation had expired. Not so: the Confederate proclaimation had expired in September, 1861.

11. Here the Hoffmann article uses the name Bachman as the 'spy' who informed on the fleeing insurgent group. It seems for all the accounts referring to this 'spy' it was hard for them to determine his real name. The two most common names used are Burgmann or Bergmann.

12. This is the only account that says that Burgmann was killed in Mexico by a Seminole Negro. It is known that Burgmann fled to Mexico after the war.

13. The reason Lieutenant Lilly ordered the wounded insurgents executed is unclear. It was not because he assumed command after Lieutenant McRae was wounded, as some accounts state. There were five State or Confederate officers, all senior to Lilly and all had previously served as captains. A junior office would never commit such an act without the approval of more senior officer. It is the author's hypothesis that the officers had a council of war to decide what to do with the wounded insurgents. There were just enough Confederate troops to transport their own nineteen wounded plus the about seven wounded insurgents. The Confederates constructed hand litters which required four men to carry each of the wounded. That would require up to fifty-two men to transport all the wounded. The Confederate force consisted of about ninety-six men. Subtracting the two killed and nineteen wounded leaves only seventy-five men to take care of the eighty-three animals, equipment and the wounded; not enough able-bodied men to carry the wounded insurgents out. The council of war likely decided to execute the wounded insurgents and had the junior officer and volunteers carry out the execution.

14. Louis Ogi was born on October 17, 1826, in Alsace. The family arrived in Texas about 1846. By 1847, both his parents were deceased. Ogi went to work on a ranch on the Medina River. He enrolled in Duff' Company on May 4, 1862, at San Antonio. He was a member of the pursuit force. Ogi was promoted to second lieutenant in April of 1863 and to first lieutenant before the war ended. He married Elizabeth [Bettie] Letitia Newton on June 3, 1869, in Atascosa County. They were the parents of four children. Louis Ogi died on July 26, 1915, in San Antonio.

15. The Raley account is the only one which tells of a wounded insurgent was saved by a Confederate. This story is very likely correct. It is known that William Vater was seriously wounded and left near the battle site. Both the Kuechler and Hoffmann accounts tell of finding and treating him, but they left him near the battle site.

16. Many pro-insurgent accounts that claim something like T. R. Fehrenbach does in his book *Lone Star*. He says, "McRae rode down upon the camp while the Germans lay sleeping. He surrounded it and opened fire indiscriminately. The result was massacre." Yet these accounts also tell how the insurgents put up such a strong defense that they inflicted heavy casualties on the Confederates. Here Raley says her information is based on Confederate reports that show the Confederates lost twelve killed and eighteen wounded. The only Confederate report of the battle is that of Lieutenant McRae. He says the Confederate casualties were two killed and eighteen wounded. Of the wounded, four died from their wounds.

17. This information by Raley was taken from the Schwethelm account, Document 43. It takes place at least the day after the battle and is supposedly told by Dr. Downs, a contract physician. The execution of the wounded insurgents took place about 4:00 p. m. August 10th.

## 45. John W. Sansom – *Hunter's Magazine Article*– November 1911

## THE GERMAN CITIZENS WERE LOYAL TO THE UNION

Leaving Austin on February 5th, 1861, I returned to my home mountains to find the people there is a state of excitement and divided in belief – the American population, as a rule, approving the action taken by the Secessionists; the Germans, as a rule disapproving – both classes, however, knowing they were powerless to change the current ways. The exceptions were young men whose adventurous spirits could ill block (sic) the monotony of staying at home, while so many of their friends and acquaintances elsewhere were enlisting and taking active part in affairs. As for the Germans, they had come to Texas to shelter themselves from oppression and tyranny and the compulsory military service of the Fatherland, under the broad folds of the American flag, and it was not to be expected they would join in or have much sympathy with any effort to overturn the goverment which has treated them so kindly. And believing the secession movement a mere rebellion that would be quickly suppressed, they deemed neutrality their course. American Unionists were of pretty much the same mind, and so adopted a like course; none knew the depth of rebellion. As for myself, although the reports of all that was going on which penetrated our mountain fastnesses, orally and through occasional newspapers, stirred by blood and tempted me to open align myself on the Union side, the conviction that I was but one against many, the attractions of a home blessed by a charming young wife and the work I had to do as a farmer, stockraiser and occasional surveyor; sufficiently curbed my patriotism and kept me neutral in action, if not in speech.

I am not writing a history of the Civil War, or of all that took place during its continuance. Only those incidents and events in which I took more or less active part, or which throw light upon my movements, will claim my attention. 1861 was a year of changes and surprises. The Confederate armies were so uniformly victorious in the first battles as to seemingly justify the belief that the Union was doomed, and that the Southern Confederacy would become an accomplished fact. Influenced by this belief many pronounced Unionists in my section of the country were persuaded into a more or less honest recantation of former views and into seeming sympathy with the Confederates. The blare of martial music, the seductions of life in camp, the fund and excitement of soldiering, and in frequent cases the desire to be counted on the winning side, led a considerable number of our young men, Germans as well Americans, into enlisting in Confederate commands. That in choice of company they selected those not likely to be ordered into active and dangerous service out of the Sate is as true as that a large number of shouting secessionist were equally as cautious. To that caution, by the way, is attributable the circumstances, that of nearly 100,000 troops which, according to the late Governor Frank Lubbock, Texas put in the field, not half of them ever even smelled the powder of battle and only about 20,000 went east of the Mississippi where all the hard fighting was done. In addition it is not known generally but it is true nevertheless that when the Confederates east of the Mississippi, after the battle of Gettysburg insisted upon immediate reinforcement by the then-idle army west of the steam, preparations were at once and completed for the transportation across of Walker's large division. It was marched to place of embarkation and there the men rebelled, not only absolutely refusing to go on board the boats, but so many deserting that scarcely a corporal's guard we left under command of their officers.

One of the first things that created any feeling of insecurity in the minds of our mountain Unionists was a spirit of proscription that, not content with shining marks for its exercise, threatened to give trouble to everybody not a pronounced secessionist. The feeling of insecurity became alarm when it was known that the Hon. A. J. Hamilton and other prominent citizens of the State had deemed it wise to retire from public view and make their home for an indefinite period on the ranch of Guy Hamilton, situated on the Perdenales River, 30 miles west of Austin. A few days later the news came that Hamilton and his party had deemed their liberties, if not lives, in so much danger that they decided to leave the State, and under the guidance of one John Mackey they rode across the country to Laredo and crossed over into Mexico. The party consisted, as well as I can remember, of A. J. Hamilton, Capt. Buck Roberts, Theodore V. Copeland, Alfred Langley, Francis A. Vaughn, Jeff G. Lilly, James Speed, Jesse Stance, John Swearingen, Wm. Montgomery and Clung McLane, citizens of Austin, Lockhart, and Prairie Lea.[1] The fleeing of Hamilton – then a member of congress and but lately returned from Washington – and others to the safe side of the Rio Grande called the attention of the Confederate military authorities to the fact that there were many other self-confessed Unionists whom it might be well to watch and punish for their failure to leave the State, as by proclamation already issued all persons unwilling to take the oath of allegiance to the Confederacy had been commanded to do. The time allowed for their departure was short: nobody cared to pay a fair price for land and other property that when forfeited to the Confederacy would be auctioned off and sold for a song. Without money in Mexico, the nearest place to which he must go, what could a refugee hope for? If he took his family with him, how could he support it? If he left, what hope had he that it would escape the scalping knife? All things considered, he resolved to stay, not to abandon his property, not to desert his family and leave it to the prey of the savage. Certainly if he stayed quietly at home attending to his business and doing nothing against the Confederacy, he would not be molested. Arguing thus, very few of those to whom the proclamation applied obeyed its commands. But although we were no doubt kept under strict surveillance and spies were surely among us, no vigorous campaign was undertaken against us until June, 1862.

At the instance of Gen. H. P. Bee and other officers who never during the war gave the dust of battle a chance to settle on their brilliant uniforms, G. P. O. Hebert, then in chief military command in Texas, issued an order proclaiming martial law, which although applying to the whole State, was specially aimed at the counties of Kendall, Kerr, Gillespie, and Edwards, these counties being declared in open rebellion against the authority of the Confederate States of American. This "order" contained the essence of one-man that was repugnant to most of the people of Texas. It clothed provost marshals of his own appointment with despotic power and intended to weaken the cause for which Texas was contending. Among other things he said: "All orders issued by provost-marshals in the execution of their duties shall be promptly obeyed. Any disobedience of summons emanating from them shall be dealt with summary punishment. All officers commanding troops will promptly comply with any requirement made upon them by provost-marshals for aid or assistance." It opened, as was intended, a way for Gen. Bee and one Colonel James Duff to serve the Confederacy and win laurels for themselves for safely than by going where cannons roared, musketry rattled with shot, and shell sought victims by the thousands and right gladly they must have entered upon it. For Gen. Bee to have gone from Texas would have left the Lone Star State without a strategist to operated against Unionists and put them to death, or to have it done under Confederate might, also the great cotton interest then flowing to the Rio Grande country and into the pockets of the speculators who where gathering thee like vultures after the spoil. As soon as the hero and murderer, Col. James M. Duff, could leave the carnage house where Union men were slaughtered by him and his aides, he joined his friend and comrade, Gen. H. P. Bee, in the cotton and other money-making trades, and then crossing into Mexico, kidnapped and put to death Union patriots of the U. S. Goverment. Gen. Bee's and Col. Duff's first share of patriotism was began (sic) in the county mainly below and situated northwest of San Antonio. Duff was by birth and raising, a Scotchman. He came to American before the Civil War, joined the U. S. Army, committed a crime while in the service for which he was court-martialed, whipped at a whipping post and drummed out of the service.[2] Gen. D. S. Stanley told me that he witnessed the whole affair.[3] Gen. Stanley further stated that while he was in command of the Texas Military department in the 90's he was called to Denver, Colorado on official businesses and while there he was invited by the Denver Club to meet with them, which he failed to do for the reason that Col. Duff was a member of the club and army rules regarding official standing did not permit it. He was a second time called upon by club members to learn the why of his non-attendance; he informed the club of his reasons. Col. James M. Duff had reaped a large sum of money in the cotton business in Texas. He went to Denver when Confederacy collapsed, made money there, but when Gen. Stanley told his knowledge of the whipping post, it caused Duff to go to France, where he later died[4].

In language as eloquent in sound as he was himself General Bee ordered Col. Duff to take immediately steps to crush the rebellion in Kendall and other counties. Duff appointed a provost-marshal for each county[5] and stationed a large detachment from his regiment, the 33rd Texas Cavalry, within easy call of them[6]. It was Kendall County's good fortune to secure as provost marshal one of its own citizens, Mr. Joseph Graham, and his deputy J. G. O'Grady, both good men, who seceded in restraining the soldiers under one Lieut. Holmes from acts of violence, but his influence did not extend to the detachments regiment that rode over the country. These put to death during the last days of July 9 good men to wit: Gustav Tegener, Young Turnette, Rev. Tom Scott, Frank Scott, Rev. Jim Johnson, Hiram Nelson, Warren Cass, Wm. Schultz, [and] Ephraim Henderson.[7] The usual excuse for killing was that the victim resisted arrest. A number of old men of the younger ones took the oath to escape persecution. This war upon the people declared in open rebellion defeated its own objects. Up to the date the persecution not a citizen had joined the Union army and engaged in the fight against the South. It was their _____ and in it lined their people, and were (sic) all their interest. When however, troops came into their neighborhood that sought in force them into an espousal of the Southern side, they could no longer be neutrals and so went into the Federal Army. Let alone they and the Confederates living among them would have remained firm friends – proscribed hunted and driven to the woods, who can blame them for joining the Northern Army, which if successful would restore to them homes?

ENDNOTES
The Germans Were Loyal To The Union

01.  Many of these individuals had been members of the Austin Company of Unionists.

02.  This account of Duff's court marital is another of the myths. Duff did "go over the hill' for several days. He was captured, returned to his unit, court martialed, and sentenced to received forty lashes and be drummed out of the service. However the sentence was remitted and he returned to duty. He was quickly promoted to corporal and at the end of his five year enlistment was the regiment quartermaster sergeant. Duff received an honorable discharge.

03.  This Sansom statement that General Stanley supportable witnessed "the whole affair" just is not true. Stanley witnessed none of the Duff court martial. In his *Personal Memories of Major General D. S. Stanley* related what the Texas Unionists had told him about Duff; his U. S. Army court martial and how Duff "stood them [the wounded insurgents] in one rank and shot down seventy of them – killed the wounded and marched back to the settlement, a hero." Since Duff was not even at the Nueces battle, is all untrue. Why Sansom felt compelled to claim that Stanley told him this story is unknown. Perhaps Sansom felt this would add authentic detail to his story, but it hurts his credibility.

04.  This incident described by Sansom about Duff is essentially correct. After Stanley repeated the untruth of Duff's court martial, Duff did leave Denver and returned to England and Scotland.

05.  James Duff was only a captain at this time. General Bee appointed provost marshals in each county. Normally Bee appointed the chief justice of each county.

06.  The 33rd Regiment Texas Cavalry was not organized until May of 1863. Duff's official duty was a kind of super provost marshal, stationed at Fort Martin Scott. He was not in command of any troops, not even of his own company. Captain John Donelson was the troop commander of a task force that number about 350 soldiers. This is an example of just how truthful Sansom is in this article.

07.  This is another example of how incorrect the Sansom article is. Most of these men were killed in late 1863 and early 1864, long after Duff left the Hill Country. One, William Schultz, was not even killed. Four were executed on August 22, at Spring Creek by Captain Henry Davis' company, after Duff had left for San Antonio and John Donelson was the provost marshal.

## 46. Letter Extract–August Hoffmann – September 1, 1925

Bankersmith, Texas
September 1, 1925

I, August Hoffman, living at Bankersmith, Gillespie County, Texas will as I have been asked by many of my friends, try to describe and relate my experiences of my life as it presents itself to me.

I was born in Silesia, Germany, in the village of Lichtenau on December 9th, 1842.

My father was Traugott Hoffmann, my mother Christine nee Simten Hoffman.

\* \* \*

My mother died when I was nine years old. My father's trade was textile work. He weaved such articles as he could sell. I had to make four napkins a week and had to fill shuttles.

By that time several of my father's friends had left for America, so he realized that the future for him and me there in Germany wasn't too bright, so he sold everything and decided to look for a new home in America. I was then twelve years old. In August 1854 we left Germany on a sailing ship. There were 365 passengers on board besides the captain and sailors. There was considerable crowding when the time came to eat, but after a few days everything was adjusted. Those that were first one day were admitted to the table last the next day, so it didn't take long until everybody knew when and where to go. My father got work in the kitchen, and I helped the cook by carrying the lanterns when he went down into the hold to get provisions to eat. There I had the opportunity to get an extra bun once in a while. The food was plentiful and good, but the water was rationed. On Fridays, we always got herring, but as they were very salty most of them were thrown overboard, because [the] water supply was too scarce.

After nine weeks and experiencing lots of rough weather, we landed at New Orleans, Louisiana. After spending three more days on board the ship we were permitted to land. If the present immigration law would have been in effect we would not have been allowed to enter the U.S.A., because our total finances consisted of 15 cents. We spent five cents to buy a bottle of vinegar to mix with the Mississippi water, for we just couldn't drink it without it.

* * *

We stayed in New Orleans two months, when we had saved enough money to take us on another small ship to Indianola, Texas, which was at that time the biggest land[ing] place on the mainland of Texas. When we stepped off the ship a man asked us where we were going, and when my father told him to Fredericksburg, he said, I wish you very good luck but I am afraid you will be scalped by the Indians. We hunted around to see if we could find transportation. We found a man named Klamberg. Where the people that came or went to Fredericksburg handling freight, we had a place what we now call a camp yard. He told us that, that morning three men and their wagons had left for Fredericksburg and that we might be able to overtake them, so father and I started out with nothing else but the clothes we had on, and a blanket apiece. We left all our other belongings at Mr. Klamberg's to be brought up to Fredericksburg later. After marching for some hours, we met some men; they weren't black nor white. At first we thought they were Indians; later we met more of the same color and found out they were Mexicans.

Later that evening we caught up with the Fredericksburg-bound caravan of wagons and the trip took three weeks.

*(August Hoffmann's father died in 1858)*

The Fellers accepted me and treated me like one of their own children. I felt like at home at the Fellers. There I had the first home-like life since my father and I came to America.

\* \* \*

When the Civil War broke out in 1861, when Gillespie County voted on secession they voted against it about 85%.[1] The main reason for doing so, that they did not believe in slavery, besides the most of them left Germany to get away from the slavery work they were doing over there. The first year the county didn't suffer much as there [were] very few who volunteered for military service (18 to 35 years was the age). The people who had voted about 85 percent against secession and did not want to take up arms against their newly-adopted country. There was considerable trouble, so finally about 33 from Gillespie County and about 34 young men from Kendall County decided to go to Mexico,[2] and if possible work their way to Brownsville which at that time was still in hands of the Federal Government.[3]

They gathered at a designated point and proceeded on their way. We all had taken the pledge "one for all, and all for one"[4] but by some way it had leaked out[5] and they were ambushed on the banks of the Nueces River. Water and grass for their horses, the few they had, was scarce. It was in August 1862. We had stopped at a small opening amongst cedar. It was the 9<sup>th</sup> of August. That night we had a good time singing and doing acrobatic acts, not thinking that by daylight the next morning half of us would be lying dead where they had slept. On the east bank of the river there was a high bluff from where followers who had reached the spot that day also could see everything. We had put out guards but by daybreak as the[y] rest[ed] peacefully they heard shots and in a few minutes our camp was a battlefield.

We defended ourselves until the sun came up over the mountain which was about 9 a.m. There were about 30 of us left.[6] We ran but we had to cross a clearing where several more were shot down. There would have been more killed but the enemy kept on shooting on those that were dead or wounded. There would have been more killed if they would have seen us leaving. Those that could walked up and down the Nueces River to find water. It was the 10<sup>th</sup> of August and the heat was insufferable. No water and nothing to eat. Mathias Pehl[7] and I went to high bank our though we would find some water. The others wanted to wait there but on our return they were gone but had found them later hiding in the brush along the river, so we decided that two at a time we should to go [to] the water. It was close to [our] abandoned camp. Will Graf[8] had been able to hide in a thicket and had notice[d] where the other side had placed their guard. He advised us to take our shoes off so we wouldn't make any noise walking on the rocks. So we notified all the rest. One time as we were walking along the water we noticed a ripple in the water and as we were always prepared for emergency, we looked and say a man sitting under a willow bush in the water with just his nose out of the water. He raised his head just enough so he could see. When he saw us he said, "Oh, God, it is you." It was Adolf Vater.[9] He had lain there the whole day halfway between the camp and the water and finally had got into the water. He was shot through one arm and through the breast. We dried his clothes and took him along for a distance, where we made him as comfortable as possible on a bed of cedar branches. There he lived for three weeks on prickly pears and bear grass. He later surrendered to a scout who took him to San Antonio.[10] We others found another water hole about two miles from the other one where finally about 20 came together. From there about 14 wended their way home. On the way we found a place where our followers had camped and had left a small package of flour which we made into dough by adding a little water. We baked [it] on a stone and each one got a piece about an inch by half an inch. The next day we came to a house on the Guadalupe and asked for something to eat. They gave us two large loaves of bread and [a] bucket of milk. We didn't leave very much.

The next day we killed a hog and cooked some of it but no salt nor bread but found a patch of sweet potatoes on Johnson's Fork, so we fared pretty well again but as we were on our way again we noticed a man coming toward us on horseback. He was riding fast, he wanted to warn us that the Duff's and Davis' Company and others had their camp on the Pedernales, and others had their camp close to the Pedernales falls. But we all got home.

ENDNOTES
August Hoffmann's Letter

01. The actual vote in Gillespie County was 16 for and 398 against secession.

02. The actual number of in the party has been a point of dispute among 'histories' and writers. Major Tegener, the commander of the group gives the correct number as 65 because, "I remember the list, for I had all the names of our people in pocket notebook in order to assign the guards for each evening. *(See Document Number 9, p.105.)* The Confederates captured the notebook and Lieutenant McRae in his report says there were 64 insurgents, plus the five Anglos. The difference between Tegener's number of 65 and McRae's report is that Tegener included John W. Samson, the guide.

03. Brownsville was not in the hands of the Union, so Hoffmann is incorrect on this point. However, the ultimate destination for the insurgent group was New Orleans which <u>was</u> in Union hands.

04. This pledge was in fact a blood oath to kill anyone who betrayed them.

05. It is interesting that Hoffmann does not say they were betrayed by the so-called 'spy' Charles Burgmann. Nor does he say anything about a proclamation giving the insurgents 30 days to leave Texas. Likewise, there is no mention of anyone who turned back.

06. The total number in the insurgent force at the Nueces River was sixty-nine. Here Hoffmann is close to the correct number after those 28 two 'left early'.

07. Mathias Pehl was born on December 30, 1838, at Holler in the Duchy of Nassau. The family arrived in Texas on the *Hercules* in 1845 and settled in Gillespie County. Pehl was a member of Braubach's home guard company from February, 1861, until February, 1862. He was a member of the Gillespie Company of the league's military battalion. Pehl survived the Nueces battle and returned to Gillespie County. On February 9, 1864, he married 16-year-old Ernestine Ferch in Gillespie County. They were the parents of two children. Pehl was a member of Krauskopf's Company, Third Frontier District, of May, 1864. Mathias Pehl died on January 22, 1867, in Gillespie County.

08. Johann Friedrich Wilhelm Graff was born about 1841 in Prussia. The date he arrived in Texas is not known, but by 1860 he was living in Gillespie County. Graff married Emma Geoegel on July 15, 1860, in Gillespie County. They were the parents of at least six children. Graff was a member of the Gillespie Company of the league's military battalion. He survived the Nueces battle and returned to Gillespie County where he hid for the remainder of the war. William Graff died on February 3, 1905, in Gillespie County.

09. This was not Adolf Vater. He was killed at the battle site. Instead it was William Vater who was born about 1838, likely in Leignitz, Prussia. William Vater was a member of the Gillespie Company of the league's military battalion. He is likely the wounded insurgent Louis Ogi helped escape, who had been treated by his comrades, but still left at the battle site. Callimense Beckett of Uvalde rescued Vater about three weeks after the battle and took him to Brackettville for treatment. It is not known what eventually became of William Vater.

10. This scout was Callimense Beckett from Brackettville. He arrived at the battle site in early September, where he found William Vater.

## 47. German Unionist in Texas – *Harper's Weekly* - January 20, 1866

The engraving on our first page illustrates an interesting and affecting episode in the history of the rebellion in Texas.

In the summer of 1862, when an attempt was made by conscription to drag into the rebel army the Germans of West Texas, a number of these gathered from the mountain counties of Kerr, Kendall, Llano, and Gillespie, with the determination to proceed to Mexico, and, if possible, to join the Union army. Without any obstacle they had arrived on the evening of August 9, in the neighborhood of Fort Clark, where they encamped in a little cedar grove situated in an open prairie. After having posted some pickets to guard the approaches, the sixty young patriots lay down upon the ground, confident of security. At 3 o'clock a.m. they were awakened by a volley of musketry. Two of their pickets, wounded, came running in and gave the alarm. A group of men, whether white or read men it was impossible to say, was advancing upon the camp. Two pickets, Ernest Beseler and Louis Schieholz[1] had been killed.

The small and badly-armed band of Germans prepared for resistance. Daylight now at hand, disclosed that they were assailed by a band of a hundred strong. Their own ranks had been thinned by desertions[2], but the fight was stubbornly maintained. After the struggle had lasted an hour and a half all but twelve or fourteen of the Germans were wounded and the others exhausted. A retreat was resolved upon, but while withdrawing from the field they twice repulsed their assailants, who then desisted from pursuit. The band now numbering thirty-two, of whom eighteen were wounded[3], fled to the mountains, where they found shelter in a cave, and relief for wounds in cactus leaves. Some of them got astray and were captured, some were murdered by the rebels.

The bodies of the Union men who had been killed were left on the battle-field, and so long as the rebel flag floated over Texas no parent or friend ventured to afford them a resting place. As soon, however, as the United States had re-established its Government in the State, E. Degener, the father of two of the victims, accompanied by twenty-five men, relatives and friends of the slain, went to the battle-field, collected their remains, and brought them to Comfort, where they received the honors of Christian burial on the 20th of August, 1866. The funeral ceremony was an imposing and touching character. A procession of about three hundred loyal people, headed by the fathers of four of the victims – old men of sixty and seventy years – preceded the funeral car, drawn by four white horses. Under the Union banner lay the remains of the Martyrs of Loyalty. A detachment of Federal troops, sent by General Merritt, accompanied the cortege. At the grave E. Degener pronounced an oration which brought tears of grief to the eyes, and stirred with invigorating patriotism the hearts of the loyal mourners. He concluded thus:

"The sacrifice that we, the fathers of the slaughtered, made to our county and to liberty is great and dolorous. We shall, however, console ourselves, we shall be proud of having offered our sons to the Union, if the glorious victory of its arms bear all the fruits that this nation and the whole of humanity justly expects to reap!"

The detachment of the Federal troops fired a salute over the grave, and the liberated soil of Texas inclosed the remains of its brave and faithful sons. The little remote spot where they rest must be to the nation as sacred as those places where thousands of her fallen defenders are deposited. Small in numbers, far away from the patriotic heart and the strong arm of the loyal North, surrounded by fierce enemies of the Union, those brave and devoted Germans offered their lives as a holy protest against the treason of the recreant rebels.[4]

ENDNOTES
Harper Weekly, January 20, 1866

01.  This is the only source that states Louis Schieholz was killed while on guard. As best that can be determined there were four guards on the night of August 9-10. Two, Leopold Bauer and Ernst Beseler, were on the north side of the insurgent camp and killed in the opening exchange of gunfire. All other accounts say the other two guards came running back into camp. It is a fact Schieholz was killed at or near the battle site. It may be he was one of the other two guards and killed later in the battle. Louis Schieholz was born about 1833 in Hanover. He arrived in Texas on December 25, 1855, and settled in Comfort. The 1860 Kerr County census shows him as 27 years old, single, a wagoner by trade. He was a member of Kuechler's company of December, 1861, and took the oath of allegiance to the Confederacy on February 17, 1862. In any case, he was killed at or near the battle site.

02.  Many of the insurgent's descendants deny that some of the Unionists 'deserted' or left before the Confederate ground assault. Almost all of the battle survivors who wrote something about the battle confirm that some twenty-eight left early. The source for this article was survivors – so again this confirms the fact that some Unionists 'left early'.

03.  There were a total of 69 insurgents at the start of the battle. Twenty-eight 'left early.' This left about forty-one, of whom at least three were already dead at the time of the Confederate assault. Beside the 19 dead and wounded left on the battle site, another 10 wounded made good their escape. These ten were; Conrad Bock, August Luckenbach, Adolph Ruebsamen, August Ruebsamen; Karl Itz, Henry Kammlah, Fritz Tegener, Gottlieb Vetterlien, Franz Weiss, and Adolphus Zoeller. Another two wounded also survived; the Confederate captured Ferdinand Simon a few days after the battle, and Union sympathizers found William Vater about three weeks later.

04.  It is of special interest to note this article was written very shortly after the war ended. No mention is made of any proclamation giving the insurgents thirty days to leave the state. This article was written well before the myth regarding the proclamation was started. Likewise check Document No 8: Ernest Cramer Letter of October 30, 1862, and Document No. 33, Letter Julius Schlickum, December 21, 1862. Neither of the letters written shortly after the battle tells of any proclamation: there were written before the myth became a part of the story. This is also true of another document which fails to mention any such proclamation; R. H. Williams' account, *With the Border Ruffians*. Williams was very critical of anything to do with James Duff. Had such a proclamation been issued, Williams would have included it in his criticisms of Duff.

# 48. Lieutenant McRae's Report – August 18, 1862

San Antonio, Texas
August 18, 1862

Maj. E. F. Gray,
A.A.A.G., Sub – Military District of the Rio Grande.

Sir;

I have the honor to report, for the information of the general commanding, the result of a scout under my command, consisting of detachments from Captain Donelson's company, Second Regiment Texas Mounted Rifles; Captain Duff's company, Texas Partisan Rangers; Captain Davis' company of State troops, and Taylor's battalion; amounting in the aggregate to 94 men, rank and file.

I left camp on the morning of the 3d instant on the Perdenalis [sic] and proceeded up the South Fork of the Guadalupe River.

On the morning of the 6th instant struck the trail of a party of horsemen, numbering, as I suppose, from 60 to 100; pursued the trail in a southwesterly direction four consecutive days, and on the evening of the 9th instant, about 3 o'clock, my advance guard reported a camp in sight on the headwaters of the Western Fork of the Nueces River. I immediately diverged from the trail to the right, secreting my command in a canyon about 2½ miles from the enemy, and at once proceeded, in company with Lieutenants Homsley, Lilly, Harbour, and Bigham, to make a careful reconnaissance of the position of the enemy's encampment, which we were fortunate enough in effecting without being discovered. Returned to camp, and proceeded to make my dispositions for an attack at daylight, on the following morning.

According, at 1 o'clock that night, I moved my command to within 300 yards of their camp, where I divided my command into two equal divisions, placed one under the command of Lieutenant Homsley, whom I directed to take position on the right of the enemy, in the edge of a dense cedar brake, about 50 yards from their camp, which he succeeded in doing without detection. In the mean time I had had equal success in obtaining another cedar break with my division within about 40 yards of the enemy, on their left. These movements were accomplished about an hour before daylight. Shortly after having secured our positions a sentinel on his rounds came near the position of Lieutenant Homsley's division, which he had the misfortune to discovered; whereupon he was shot dead by Lieutenant Harbour, which caused an alarm in the enemy's camp, and a few shots were exchanged between the parties, and all became quiet again for the space of half an hour, when another sentinel hailed us on the left, and shared the fate of the first. It being still too dark for the attack, I ordered my men to hold quietly their positions until daylight. The enemy in the meantime were actively engaged preparing to resist us. The moment it became light enough to see I ordered the attack to be made by a steady and slow advance upon their position, firing as we advanced until with in about 30 paces of their line, when I ordered a charge of both divisions, which was executed in fine style, resulting in the complete rout and flight of the enemy.

They left on the field 32 killed. The remainder fled, scattering in all directions through the many dense cedar brakes in the immediate vicinity. From the many signs of blood I infer many of those escaping were seriously wounded.

We captured 83 head of horses, 33 stand of small arms, 13 six-shooters, and all their camp equipage, and provisions for

100 men for ten days. The arms I turned over to the commanding officer at Fort Clark. The horses are *en route* to this place. The provisions were consumed by my command.

Although the surprise and route of the enemy was complete, I regret to state it was not unattended with loss on our part. We had two killed on the field and 18 wounded.

The fight occurred about 20 miles north of Fort Clark, to which point I sent for assistance, both surgical and transportation, for my wounded, which was promptly forwarded by the commanding officer, Captain Carolan[1], and Assistant Surgeon Downs[2], to whom I am greatly indebted for many kind attentions to myself and command, as also to Mr. D. H. Brown[3]. My wounded are all well provided for and are doing well.

I have learned from one of the party whom we fought, captured some four or five days subsequent to the fight, that the party was composed of 63 Germans, one Mexican, and five American (the latter running [at] the first fire), all under the command of a German by the name of Fritz Tegener. They offered the most determined resistance and fought with desperation, asking no quarter whatever; hence I have no prisoners to report.

My officers and men all behaved with the greatest coolness and gallantry, seeming to vie with each other in deeds of daring chivalry. It would be invidious to attempt to draw any distinctions when all did their part most nobly and gloriously.

Enclosed find a list of killed and wounded of each company[4]
I remain, with great respect, your obedient servant,
C. D. McRae
First Lieut., Second Regt. Texas Mounted Rifles,
Comdg. Scout

ENDNOTES
McRae's Report

01. John M. Carolan was the commander of Company H, 32nd Regiment Texas Cavalry at Fort Clark. He was born about 1814 in Ireland. The date he arrived in Texas is not known, but he was living in San Antonio by 1850. He was the Bexar County district clerk for a long period of time as well as mayor in 1853-1854. Carolan married Catharine Conrad on September 30, 1852, in Bexar County. They were the parents of at least two children. Carolan enrolled in Company H on May 15, 1862, and was elected its captain. John M. Carolan died on May 2, 1863, at Ringgold Barracks, Texas.

02. Dr. Downs was the contract surgeon at Fort Clark. He is the individual that Schwethelm and others claim told them when he offered to treat the wounded insurgents, the Confederates said, "Never mind we will take care of them." As has been pointed out, Dr. Downs did not arrive at the battle site for at least a day afterwards. The wounded insurgents were executed about 4:00 p. m. the day of the battle.

03. David H. Brown was a merchant at Brackettville. He provided wagons to transport the wounded Confederates. Brown was born about 1824 in Coventry, England. The date he arrived in Texas is not known, but he likely arrived with the U. S. Army. Brown enlisted in Company G, First J. S. Infantry Regiment on October 3, 1850, and was discharged at Fort Duncan, Texas on October 1, 1855. Brown married Maria Antonio Patino, date and location of marriage not known. They were the parents of at least two children. David H. Brown enlisted in Duff's Company B on October 1, 1862, and served until the end of the war. He died about August, 1866, in San Antonio.

04. The Official Records of the Civil War show McRae's causality list was not found. However, a copy was located at the National Archives, see Document No. 49, p. 302.

## 49. McRae's List of Killed & Wounded[1]

Killed:

| | |
|---|---|
| L. Stringfield | Capt Donelson's Co |
| W. E. Poe | Taylor's Battalion |

Wounded:

| | | |
|---|---|---|
| Lt. C. D. McRae | Flesh wound in the arm. | Commdg |
| Albert Elder | Dangerously in head | Capt Duff's Co. |
| Robert Eder | Right arm broken | Capt Duff's Co. |
| Gregory[2] | | Capt Duff's Co. |
| Frank Robinson | Severely in thigh | Capt Duff's Co. |
| John Hill | Right shoulder severely | Capt Donelson's Co. |
| Wm Martin[3] | Right shoulder breast & Knee | Capt Donelson's Co. |
| Ben Rosser | Left arm severely | Capt Donelson's Co. |
| Dan Yarboro | Flesh wound in hip | Capt Donelson's Co. |
| Wilborn | Right breast severely | Capt Davis' Co. |
| Name not known | | Capt Davis' Co. |
| Morris | | Taylors Battalion |
| Name not known | | Taylors Battalion |
| Name not known | | Taylors Battalion |
| Name not known | | Taylors Battalion |
| Name not known | | Taylors Battalion |
| Name not known | | Taylors Battalion |
| Name not known | | Taylors Battalion |
| Charles Bergmann | Wounded three places Both thighs arm | Vol Guide |

A true copy
E. F. Gray
Major & A.A.A. Gen

ENDNOTE
McRae's List of Killed & Wounded

01.  The detailed biographies and correct names of the killed and wounded are included in Document Number 50 and end notes.

02.  The muster rolls of the Duff's Company shows no individual named Gregory. A search of the muster rolls of the other units does not show a man with the given name of Gregory. It is not known of whom McRae was thinking when he wrote the name Gregory.

03.  William Martin's Complied Service Records do not shown him as wounded. It is almost a certainty that the Martin which McRae listed as wounded the right shoulder, breast and knee was Emanuel Martin. Emanuel Martin's Compiled Service Records show he was wounded in the shoulder, breast, and knee.

# 50. Compiled List of Confederate Casualties at Nueces Battle[*]

| # | Sur Names | Given Name | Type of Wound | Unit |
|---|-----------|------------|---------------|------|
| **Killed in Action [KIA]** | | | | |
| 01. | Poe,[1] | William | Unknown | Co. E, 8th Bn |
| 02. | Stringfield,[2] | Littleton | Unknown | Co. K, 2nd Regt. T.M.R. |
| **Did of Wounds [DOW]** | | | | |
| 03. | Elder,[3] | Albert J. | Head | Duff's Co. P.R. |
| 04. | Elder,[4] | Robert G. | Right Arm | Duff's Co. P.R. |
| 05. | Martin,[5] | Emanuel | Shoulder & Knee | Co. K, 2nd Regt. T.M.R. |
| 06. | Morris,[6] | John K. | Unknown | Co. B, 8th Bn. |
| **Wounded in Action [WIA]** | | | | |
| 07. | Allen,[7] | Frost | Unknown | Duff's Co. P.R. |
| 08. | Barker,[8] | Henry W. | Unknown | Co. E, 8th Bn. |
| 09. | Benson,[9] | William Thomas | Unknown | Davis' Co. |
| 10. | Burgmann[10] | Charles | Both Thighs & Arm | Vol Guide |
| 11. | Edmonson,[11] | Latimore | Multiple Wounds | Co. A, 8th Bn. |
| 12. | Erwin,[12] | Stephen L. | Unknown | Co. A, 8th Bn. |
| 13. | Hill,[13] | John | Right Shoulder | Co. K, 2nd Regt T.M.R |
| 14. | McRae,[14] | Colin D. | Arm | Co. K, 2nd Regt T.M.R. |
| 15. | Robinson,[15] | John Frank | Thigh | Duff's Co. P.R. |
| 16. | Rosser,[16] | Benjamin | Left arm | Co. K, 2nd Regt T.M.R. |
| 17. | Singleton,[17] | Thomas J. | Unknown | Co. A, 8th Bn. |
| 18. | Welch,[18] | John | Unknown | Co. A, 8th Bn |
| 19. | Wilborn,[19] | Albert L. | Right Breast | Davis' Co. |
| 20. | Williams,[20] | Wiley | Unknown | Co. A, 8th Bn. |
| 21. | Yarboro,[21] | Dow | Hip | Co K, 2nd Regt T.M.R. |

[*] List is complied from three sources; McRae's List of Casualties, the Compiled Services Records of the individual soldiers, and from various newspaper accounts.

ENDNOTES
Compiled List of Confederate Casualties

01. William E. Poe was born in 1836 in Missouri. The family arrived in Texas by 1862. He enrolled in Captain J H. Combs' Company E, Taylor's 8th Battalion Texas Cavalry on July 6, 1862, at Fort Mason and was in the composite detachment from the battalion sent to Fredericksburg on July 23, 1862. He was killed in the Nueces battle and buried at the battle site. At some point his family recovered his body for reburial in the Johnson Station Cemetery in Tarrant County, Texas.

02. J. Littleton Stringfield was born on September 23, 1843, in Limestone County, Texas. He enrolled in the McMullen County Home Guard Company on August 17, 1861. Stringfield enlisted in Company K, 2nd Regiment Texas Mounted Rifles on September 23, 1861, at Fort Brown, Texas. Stringfield family members removed his body from the battle site about 1880 for reburial in the Tehuacana Cemetery in Frio County, Texas.

03. Albert J. Elder was born about 1839 in Kentucky. He was a brother of Robert G. Elder, below. The family arrived in Fayette County prior to 1844. Albert J. Elder enlisted in Duff's Company, Texas Partisan Rangers on May 4, 1862, at San Antonio. He was 'dangerously wounded in the head' during the Nueces battle. Elder died from his wounds on August 17, 1862, at Fort Clark.

04. Robert G. Elder was born about 1835 in Kentucky. He was a brother of Albert J. Elder, above. The family arrived in Fayette County prior to 1844. Robert G. Elder enlisted in Duff's Company, Texas Partisan Rangers on May 4, 1862, at San Antonio. Elder died from his wounds on September 17, 1862, at Fort Clark.

05. Emanuel Martin was born about 1828, location of birth not known. He enlisted in Company K, 2nd Regiment Texas Mounted Rifles on September 23, 1861. Martin died of his wounds on October 18, 1862, at San Antonio.

06. John K. Morris was born about 1841 in Missouri. The date he arrived in Texas is not known, but by 1860 Morris was living in Bell County. Morris enlisted in the 1st Regiment Texas Mounted Rifles in July, 1861, and re-enlisted in Company B, Taylor's 8th Battalion Texas Cavalry in May 1862. Morris died of his wounds on September 1, 1862, at Fort Clark.

07. Frost Thorn Allen was born on March 20, 1831, in Nacogdoches County, Texas. Allen enlisted in Duff's Company, Partisan Rangers on May 7, 1862, at San Antonio. His last entry in his compiled service records shows him as sick at Corpus Christi in December of 1863. Frost Thorn Allen died on January 28, 1880, in Nueces County.

08. Henry W. Barker was born in May, 1839, in Texas. His family lived in Walker County. He enrolled in 1st Regiment, Texas Mounted Rifles in May of 1861 at Camp Colorado. He re-enlisted in Company E, Taylor's Battalion in May,

1862, and remained with the unit until the end of the war. Barker married Emily Caroline Dannelly on December 12, 1865, in Walker County. They were the parents of ten children. Henry W. Barker died on July 13, 1917, at Mullin in Mills County.

09. William Thomas Benson was born on April 10, 1840, in Indiana. The family arrived in Texas about 1854 and settled in what became Kerr County. Benson enrolled in Davis' Company, Frontier Regiment on March 4, 1862, at Fort Martin Scott. He was in the pursuit force and wounded at the Nueces battle. Benson re-enlisted in Hunter's Company, Frontier Regiment on December 23, 1862, and remained in the company until the end of the war. He married Nancy Isabelle Holloman on January 8, 1866, in Gillespie County. They were the parents of ten children. William Thomas Benson died on August 20, 1907, in Gillespie County.

10. Charles Burgmann, as has been previously stated, is somewhat of a mystery man. His date of birth is not clear. The 1860 Bexar Census shows a Charles Burgmann as 29 years old, born in 'Germany', which would mean he was born about 1831. The first known record for him in Kerr County is the 1862 Kerr Tax Roll which shows he paid a poll tax of $1.25. He is also shown on the James Starkey's 1862 List of Kerr County Males Not in Military Service which shows him as 36 years old, which would mean he was born about 1826. It is a fact that he was a guide for the pursuit force and wounded in several places in the Nueces battle. On October 1, 1862, Burgmann enlisted in Duff's Company B, 14th Battalion Texas Cavalry. His late entry in the complied service records shows he was on detached service to the Confederate Quartermaster Department in April, 1863. It is also known he fled to Mexico after the war. Don Biggers in his book *German Pioneers In Texas* says Burgmann was killed by a Seminole Negro Indian and his body was thrown into the Rio Grande, but there is no confirmation of this account.

11. Latimore Edmonson was born in April, 1840, in Arkansas. The family arrived in Texas by 1860 and lived in Brown County. He enlisted in Company G, 1st Regiment Texas Mounted Rifles on May 12, 1861, at Camp Colorado. Edmonson re-enlisted when the company became Company A, Taylor's 8th Battalion, Texas Cavalry and remained with the company when it became a part of the 1s Regiment, Texas Cavalry. He was wounded in the Nueces battle; in the body, right hand, left ankle, and in both legs. Edmonson married Margaret [maiden name not known] about 1871, likely in Texas. They were the parents of five children. Latimore Edmonson died on June 6, 1915, in Coleman County.

12. Stephen Lowe Erwin was born on September 3, 1835, in McMinn County, Tennessee. The family arrived during the 1850s and settled in Parker County. Erwin married Susan Withrow Vardy on November 22, 1860, at Carterville in Parker County. They were the parents of at least six children. Erwin enlisted

in Company A, Taylor's 8<sup>th</sup> Battalion, Texas Cavalry on July 3, 1862, at Fort Mason. Erwin received a medical discharge on October 31, 1862, as a result of his wounds. Stephen Lowe Erwin died on December 8, 1917, at Weatherford in Parker County.

13. John R. Hill was born about 1823 in Ireland. He had arrived in Texas by 1850, as on February 17, 1850, Hill married Elizabeth Fraley in Guadalupe County. They were the parents of at least three children. Hill enlisted in Company K, 2<sup>nd</sup> Regiment Texas Mounted Rifles on September 23, 1861, and was elected or appointed first sergeant. He received a medical discharge due to his wounds on April 23, 1863. John R. Hill died on September 17, 1880, at Pleasanton in Atascosa County.

14. Colin Dickson McRae was born on September 22, 1835, near Clarksville in Red River County, Texas. By 1855 McRae was living in Bexar County, Texas. McRae enrolled in Company K, 2<sup>nd</sup> Regiment Texas Mounted Rifles in February, 1861, and elected the company's first lieutenant. In February, 1862, the company was re-organized and McRae remained the first lieutenant. He was the commander of the pursuit force. After the Nueces battle, McRae returned to San Antonio where on October 1, 1862, he married Margaret D. Haw. On the same date he was promoted to captain. He and his company took part in the Battle of Galveston on January 1, 1863. On November 3, 1863, McRae's wife gave birth to a son who died on June 26, 1864. Colin D. McRae died on September 10, 1864, of typhoid fever.

15. John Francis [Frank] Robinson was born in October 7, 1837, in Sabine County Texas. By 1860 he was living in Uvalde County. Robinson enlisted in Duff's Company, Partisan Rangers on May 4, 1862, at San Antonio and elected or appointed fourth corporal. He was elected second lieutenant of Duff's Company B, 14<sup>th</sup> Battalion Texas Cavalry. On August 8, 1863, he was elected captain of Company B, 33<sup>rd</sup> Regiment Texas Cavalry and remained with the company until the end of the war. Robinson married Mary P. Allen on February 14, 1866, in Uvalde County. They were the parents of eight children. Robinson was the Uvalde County judge from November, 1898, until November, 1906, and from November, 1912, until August, 1913. John Frank Robinson died on February 20, 1917, in Uvalde County.

16. Benjamin Franklin Rosser was born on March 4, 1838, in Alabama. By 1860 he was living in Bowie County. Benjamin F. Rosser married Martha Louise Russell on April 10, 1861, and they were the parents of least nine children. He enlisted in Company K, 2<sup>nd</sup> Regiment Texas Mounted Mounted Rifles on September 23, 1862, at San Antonio. Rosser received a medical discharge due to his battle wounds on May 15, 1863. Benjamin Franklin Rosser died in 1914 in Elk City, Beckham County, Oklahoma.

17. Thomas Jefferson Singleton was born on March 20, 1840, near Houston in Harris County. By 1860 he was living in Brown County. Singleton enlisted in

Company G, 1st Regiment Texas Mounted Rifles on May 12, 1861. He relisted in Company A, Taylor's 8th Battalion Texas Cavalry in May 1862. He recovered from his wound and remained with the company when it became a part of the 1st Regiment Texas Cavalry. Thomas Jefferson Singleton died on August 7, 1919, at Fort Worth, Tarrant County.

18. John Thomas Welch was born on March 11, 1839, in Pickens County, Alabama. By 1860 he was living in Caldwell County. Welch enlisted in Company G, 1st Regiment Texas Mounted Rifles in July, 1861, at Camp Coronado. He reenlisted in Company A, Taylor's 8th Battalion Texas Cavalry in May of 1862 at Fort Mason. Welch recovered from his wounds and remained with the company when it became Company G, 1st Regiment Texas Cavalry. He married Sara Jane Crenshaw on February 10, 1864, in Caldwell County. They were the parents of at least two children. His date of death is not known, but it was after 1912 when he was living in Bexar County.

19. Albert L. Wilborn was born in 1828 in South Carolina. He arrived in Kerr County in 1859. He was a member of Harbour's Minuteman Company from February, 1861, until February, 1862. He enlisted in Davis' Company, Frontier Regiment on March 4, 1862, at Fort Martin Scott. Welch received a medical discharge in May, 1863, because of wounds received in the Nueces battle. He married Virginia J. Moore on May 6, 1864, in Kerr County. They were the parents of three children. Albert L. Wilborn died on March 6, 1873, in Kerr County, likely as a result of his wounds.

20. William A. [Wiley] Williams was born on September 3, 1838, in Arkansas. The date he arrived in Texas is not known. He enlisted in Company F, 1st Regiment Texas Mounted Rifles in May of 1861 at Camp Colorado. He relisted in Company A, Taylor's 8th Battalion Texas Cavalry in May, 1862, at Fort Mason. He recovered from his wounds and remained with his company when it became Company G, 1st Regiment Texas Cavalry. He transferred to Company E, 21st Regiment Texas Cavalry on December 2, 1863, and remained with the unit until the end of the war. Wiley Williams married Ann Rosa Gammantaler on June 25, 1865, at Wallace Creek in San Saba County. They were the parents of at least 13 children. Wiley Williams died on September 24, 1901, at San Saba in San Saba County, Texas

21. Lorenzo Dow Yarbrough was born in January, 1840, in Texas. He enlisted in Company K, 2nd Regiment Texas Mounted Rifles on September 23, 1861, and relisted in June, 1862, at Helena. He recovered from his wound and rejoined his unit. Lorenzo Dow Yarbrough married Nancy White on November 30, 1863, in Live Oak County. They were the parents of nine children. Yarbrough transferred to Captain Tobin's Company F, 2nd Regiment Texas Cavalry on January 1, 1864. Yarbrough died on January 5, 1907, in LaSalle County.

## 51. *Neu Braunfelser Zeitung[1]* -
## August 29, 1862

Fort Clark, 15 August. As you know, on August 10, detachments of several troops pursuing the abolitionists or Hamilton-People[2] discovered they had fortunately caught up with them as they were encamping in a wild, mountainous region on the Nueces about 15 miles north from here (Fort Clark). The enemy was positioned in a cedar-brake which left us no choice but to assault them from the open side [3]. After the horses of the enemy (which was, by the way, 68 strong[4]) were secured, the sentries posted, and before any sentries were shot, the dance began. People's shared opinions were that the battle began at dawn and lasted until 9 o'clock that morning[5] and ended with the defeat of the enemy who had 30 men killed[6] besides two later in the day[7], compared to our losses of two dead and 16 wounded.[8] They enemy fought like the Devil incarnate; it had been ordered that "no prisoners will be taken"[9]. It is a wonder our side came through it. Among the enemy killed were the 2 sons of Degener[10] of Sisterdale, even so for Itz and many others from the area of Fredericksburg, this fight is just another affirmation of the duplicity of the Americans triumphing over the Germans. The entire Bande (people who engage in guerilla warfare) stood at 5 or 6 Americans[11] and many Germans. And letters, etc. that were found among the dead will reveal many more names of scapegoats before days end.

Our wounded, (the two dead I do not know) are the brothers Elder[12] and McCraig.[13] Robert Elder's right arm will probably have to be amputated[14]. A bullet striped his brother's forehead and laid his brain bare.[15] I believe him the most severely wounded, with the exception of one who is shot through the belly. Most of them were shot through the chest or legs, yet our Doctor believes all will survive. Overall the people are of good humor and ready to fight again; one can scarcely keep them in bed. In a few days the people will set out, one group will go to Eagle Pass to "clean house"[16] there.

The wounded are anticipating enduring great suffering during the transportation; we can give them only one wagon and one carriage in which we will transport them over hill and dale. We would have been the poor unfortunates if the fight had taken place 2 days earlier.

I have through examination, recalled a muster roll[17], since I knew so many of the people.[18] There are the names: Capt. Tegener, two Degener, two Schreiner,[19] Graf[20], three Schwethelm,[21] Simon, Leyendecker,[22] two Gold[23], Pass[24], Vater[25], ie.

## ENDNOTES
*Neu Braunfelser Zeitung*, August 29, 1862

01. The author of this letter is not known. It must have been a German as it was written in German. In the book *Lone Star And Double Eagle*, compiled by Minetta Altgelt Goyne, is letter written by Rudolf Coreth, a Confederate soldier from Sisterdale. In it he says a man in Captain John M. Carolan's Company which was stationed at Fort Clark, told him about the Nueces battle. There were several Germans in Carolan's company. The most likely writer among them was a man from Medina County named Louis Heickeman.

02. It is interesting to note that the writer of the letter claims the insurgents were part of Andrew J. Hamilton's Abolitionist party.

03. Here the writer is talking about the Confederates attacking from the open side, or in front of the high cliff behind the insurgent camp.

04. As has previously been pointed out, the insurgent group numbered sixty-nine men.

05. The opening shots of the battle were fired just after 3:00 a.m. However, the writer is correct; the actual battle started at dawn and lasted until about 9:00 a.m.

06. Most accounts of the battle say that about 30 insurgents were killed, which is incorrect; a total of nineteen were killed at the battle site. The number of 30 likely comes from Ferdinand Simon, captured by the Confederates several days after the battle. This belief was based on the number of survivors who came together after the battle. They were not aware that some 28 men had 'left early,' assumed they were the only survivors, and that anyone not with them was dead.

07. These two men are very likely the ones captured on August 9th and hanged because they would not lead the Confederates to the insurgent camp.

08. The actual number of Confederate wounded was nineteen.

09. The insurgent descendants have consistently claimed that orders were issued to take no prisoners. This is the only contemporary account which lends credence to this belief.

10. The two Degener sons were Hugo and Hilmar.

11. The total number of Americans was five; Sansom, Hester, Williamson, and the two Scott boys.

12. The two Elder brothers were Albert J. and Robert G. *(See Document Number 47, Endnotes 3 and 4.)*

13. This is Colin D. McRae.

14. Robert G. Elder died on September 17, 1862, at Fort Clark.

15. Albert J. Elder died on August 17, 1862, at Fort Clerk.

16. This is the only reference found indicating that the Confederate pursuit force had plans to go on to Eagle Pass and conduct anti-insurgency operations there. On October 17, 1862, Confederate or State forces attacked a second group of insurgents attempting to flee Texas and killed several

17. A small notebook kept by Fritz Tegener containing the names of the insurgents was captured. It is not known what became of this notebook.

18. This statement indicates that the author of this article knew many of the insurgents personally, which would mean he was familiar with the Hill Country German community.

19. This comment that there were more than one [the German word used is zwei] Schreiner with the fleeing insurgency group would mean that the second Schreiner was Charles Armand Schreiner, the brother of Amil, who was killed at the battle site.

20. This was Carl William Graff, who survived the battle and went on to join the Union Army.

21. There were not three Schwethelm men, only Henry Joseph Schwethelm.

22. This was Franz Joseph Leyendecker who was born on December 21, 1829, in Nassau. He arrived in Texas on the *Riga* in 1846 and settled in Gillespie County, where he married Maria Ann Klein on September 30, 1853. They were the parents of at least eleven children. Leyendecker was a member of Braubach's home guard company between February, 1861-November, 1861, a member of Kuechler's Company in December, 1861, and a member of the Gillespie Company of the league's military battalion. Leyendecker survived the battle and returned to the Hill Country. He was a member of Schuetze's company of November, 1863, who were likely pro-Union vigilantes. Leyendecker fled Texas in early 1864. On April 24, 1864, he enrolled in Company I, First Regiment [Union] Texas Cavalry. He remained with the regiment and was mustered out of service on October 31, 1865. Joseph Leyendecker died on November 8, 1889, in Gillespie County.

23. The Gold brothers were Jacob, Jr. and Peter, Jr. They arrived in Texas on the *Estafette* in 1850 and settled in Gillespie County. They were both members of Braubach's home guard company between February, 1861-February, 1862, members of Kuechler's company of December, 1861, as well as members of the Gillespie Company of the league's military battalion. Jacob Gold married

Johanna Kallenberg about 1871, likely in Gillespie County. They were the parents of nine children. Jacob Gold died on May 18, 1914, in Gillespie County. Peter Gold married Auguste Danz on November 13, 1866, in Gillespie County. They were the parents at lease five children. Peter Gold died on February 10, 1918, in Gillespie County.

24. 'Pass' is Joseph Poetsch [Petsch] who was born on November 4, 1838, in Nassau. He arrived in Texas on the *Washington* in 1845 and settled in Gillespie County. Petsch was a member of the Luckenbach Bushwhackers. *(See Document Number 26, endnote #6, p.1.)*

25. There were three Vater men in the insurgency group: Adolph and Fritz; who were both killed, and William, who was wounded and left at the battle site.

## 52. Letter–J. M. Seal[1] – September 8, 1862

Sept. the 8, 1862
Camp Davis

Dear friends

I once more seat myself to pen you few lines informing you that I am well at present. I hope those few lines may find you all enjoying the same.

You must excuse me for not writing sooner & oftener paper is scarce & hardly ever have any time to spare. I now write in haste I fear that I have nothing to write that will be likely to interest you much as you probably heard all that I could write.

The health of our company is generally good. We have a great deal of rain lately grass is very good. The tories in this part of the country is getting somewhat scarce; that is today, those that are living. It would be a hard matter for me to give anything like a definite account of those that have been shot or hung in this vicinity. They are lying & hanging all over the woods. We had a big battle with them 3 or 4 weeks ago on the neweses (sic) in which we was successful. We killed 33 dead on the ground. A good many was wounded which made there (sic) escape from the Battle ground. Several of which has since been captured & executed. Out of 70 we have got about 50 which was in the battle. We had 94 men engaged. Loss 2 Killed 17 wounded 2 of which has since died. We got 80 head of horses 50 guns 15 six shooters. In short we got nearly ever thing they had. I had the pleasure of shooting one of the poor devils a few days ago myself.[2] We have one more drive to make which I think will clear this part of the country. There is 40 or 50 on the head of the lanno (sic) river at least They was there not long since.

I have no Indian news of interest to write. We have not seen an Indian. Till yet some of the companies on the line have had several small brushes with them. I believe there has been only 5 or 6 killed. We had 11 men out a few days ago on a trail but they did nothing. The indians out run them. It rained nearly every day while they was gone. We have had a great deal of Sport at confiscating property of all kinds. We are now living on the fat of the land. We have plenty of beef pork chicken turkey mutton & goat & c to eat Which has been confiscated here.

When we ride up to dutchmans house now they are the worst scared people you ever saw. They don't know how youd to treat us. They invite us to lite take something to eat drink or smoke or chew more expecially if they see an extra rope. We are all very busily engaged how a building our winter quarters. We will have ours done in a few days. We have received no pay for more than 3 months. I was in hopes that I could pay for my horse at the expiration of 6 months but I new see that I can not as the time has done expired. I am well pleased with my horse. He has proved to be better than I anticipated. I am coming down some time this Fall. I want you to be certain to save me some leather to make me some shoes. So I must come to a close. Give my respects to all of the old folk & children and love to the girls. Tell them I want to see them all very bad.
Yours forever.
J. W. Seal

PS. Please write on receipt of this or at least when you get time.
To Mr Speed and J. C. Johnson

Editorial note: Every effort has been made to keep the original spelling and grammar on the source document.

ENDNOTES
J. M. Seal's Letter

01. John W. Seals was born in July, 1832, in Madison [now Iron] County, Missouri. He arrived in Texas about 1861 and settled in Hays County. He enlisted in Davis' Company, Frontier Regiment in March, 1862, at Fort Martin Scott. Seals reenlisted in Davis' Company F, Duff's 14th Regiment Texas Cavalry. He remained with the company when it became part of Duff's 33rd Regiment Texas Cavalry and served until the end of the war, at which time he settled in Fannin County. John W. Seals never married. He died in November, 1919, in Fannin County.

02. The individual Seals shot and killed was likely to have been either Theodore Bruckisch or Heinrich Stieler, about September 1, 1862, at Goat Creek, northwest of Kerrville.

# 53. Jacob Kuechler's Letter – August, 1887[1]

August, 1887

James Newcomb[2]
San Antonio

Dear Sir;

Complying with your request, I furnish you with a brief sketch of the Nueces affair. A party of about 62 Union men met in Camp on Turtle Creek[3] to leave Texas and join the Federal army by way through Mexico. We set out August 3, 1862[4], and intended to cross Rio Grande below the mouth of Devils River, where a good crossing was known to me. I guided the party as I was acquainted with Western Texas. We traveled very slow on account of the rough country we had to pass though and the heavy loads our pack animals had to carry.[5] Under the proclamation[6] we had plenty [of] time to leave Texas and did not expect to be molested by military force. We rather did not guard our trail by keeping a scout in our rear, as we would have done, had we apprehended danger in that quarter. On the 9th of August we reached the West prong of Nueces and took camp in an open Cedar grove near a spring in the riverbed. On the 10th about ½ an hour before daylight our guard near the spring was shot and at the same time a volley was fired into our camp. We suffered a severe loss as Fritz Tegener was among the troops' severely wounded men, he had a great influence and would have done a deal during the fight. After the enemy pulled back we prepared for the coming fight.[7] Our position was not good and could not be improved. We were crowded in a little Cedar grove with no under growth and had not sufficient shelter against the heavy fire of the rebels, which outnumbered us a great deal. After their 2nd attempt to take our camp about half of our men could not stand the fight any longer and left us.[8] The rebels noticed it. I heard one [of] them cry out "boys, they are running. Let us take the camp," and soon the 3$^{rd}$ attack was made. The rebels entered our camp but after a fierce conflict had to give ground [and] fall back.[9] This attack reduced our fighting force to about 6 men, which were still unhurt. We could not expect to stand another charge with success and the time had arrived to give up. The wounded men, who could walk, left camp first and we followed without being molested by the enemy. We found shelter in the cedar brake on the east side of Nueces. I selected a camp for the wounded men near a spring in Sycamore Creek about ½ mile from [the] Battleground.

On the 13$^{th}$ the Rebels left the Battleground. Soon afterwards I visited our old camp. I stood pale and shuddering at the sight of the fate which befallen the poor wounded, which could not follow us, all mutilated and murdered by a cruel foe. I met Mr. Vater[10], of our party, severely wounded – he had arrived in camp a little while before me and said, "I came back to camp to die by my dead comrades." He was hid in a dogwood thicket near the spring. I could not take him over to our camp and went twice a day to dress his wounds and provide him with water and something to eat. During our stay three scouts were hunting for us. I lost sight of Mr. Vater after the 3$^{rd}$ scout had left. I could not find him and was afterwards told that he had been rescued by a Union man from Uvalde.[11]

We did under the circumstances very well. All the wounded recovered and we reached the settlements after enduring great hardship.

Jacob Kuechler

Editorial note: Every effort has been made to keep the original spelling and grammar on the source document.

ENDNOTES
Jacob Kuechler's Letter

01. This letter of Jacob Kuechler was written to James P. Newcomb in early
    August of 1887. Newcomb was to be the main speaker at the *Treue Der
    Union*'s 25th anniversary of the Nueces battle. Newcomb had asked Kuechler
    to provide him details on the battle. Newcomb used this letter as the major
    source of his remarks. See Guido E. Ransleben's *A Hundred Years of Comfort
    in Texas*, Pages 96 – 98 for Newcomb's remarks.

02. James Pearson Newcomb was a newspaper editor in San Antonio. He was
    born on August 31, 1837, in Amherst, Nova Scotia. The family arrived in San
    Antonio by 1847. His parents died by 1850, and Newcomb went to work for
    the *San Antonio Western Star* and the *San Antonio Ledger*. In 1851,
    Newcomb and F. M. Whitemond started the *Alamo Star*. In 1854, Newcomb
    and a new partner, J. M. West, changed the name of the newspaper to the *San
    Antonio Herald*, a pro-Union paper. In 1860 Newcomb established the *San
    Antonio Alamo Express*, another pro-Union paper. In May, 1861, the Knights
    of the Golden Circle destroyed the paper, and Newcomb and other Unionists
    fled to Mexico. In 1867, Newcomb returned to San Antonio and purchased a
    part-interest in the *San Antonio Herald* which supported E. J. Davis, the
    reconstruction governor. In 1872, Newcomb married Antoinette Hitchcock in
    Vermont. They were the parents of four children who survived to adulthood.
    James P. Newcomb died on October 16, 1907, in Bexar County.

03. The insurgent meeting at Turtle Creek was more of an assembly area than a
    base camp.

04. The date the insurgents departed for Mexico has been of misunderstood by
    many 'historians' and writers who claim they left on August 1st. Here
    Kuechler gives the correct date – August 3. John W. Sansom confirms this in
    a letter of August 14, 1907, to James T. DeShields. In the letter Samson
    states, "We started from Turtle Creek August 3."

05. Another point that many of the historians and writers ask is why the insurgents
    travelled at such a slow pace. Here Kuechler provides an answer: *"We
    traveled very slow on account of the rough country we had to pass thought
    and heavy loads our pack animals had to carry."* The insurgents had to stop
    each night where they did because of available waterholes.

06. Finding the proclamation has taken a long time. After several years of research
    I began to wonder if there really had been a proclamation giving the insurgents
    thirty days to leave Texas. I searched when the proclamation was supposed to

have been issued. I rechecked the sources that stated that there had been such. The first mention of insurgents travelling under the authority of a proclamation is Kuechler's letter of August, 1887. He wrote, "Under the proclamation we had plenty [of] time to leave Texas and did not expect to be molested by military force." However, most sources referred to the 1905 John W. Sansom pamphlet, where he said, "Having read a proclamation from the Confederate Government announcing that all persons not friendly to it might leave the country, we believed we had a right to go in large or small bodies, as best suited our convenience." Another document often quoted as evidence of a proclamation was Albert Schutze's 1923 interview with Henry Schwethelm. In the article *Was a Survivor of the Nueces Battle*, Schutze says, supposedly quoting Schwethelm, "Consequently when the governor of the State issued a proclamation that all persons who would not take the oath of allegiance to the Confederate States would have to leave the State within thirty days, a group of the younger men met at a certain place and after a conference agreed to leave the state for Mexico." Likewise, the Helen Raley article in the *Dallas Morning News* of May 5, 1929, where she interviewed August Hoffmann clearly states there was a proclamation. In her article/interview titled *The Blackest Crime in Texas Warfare* she supposedly quotes Hoffmann, saying the men "who were unwilling to take the Southern oath of allegiance were given thirty days to leave the country. Complying with this order, sixty-five or sixty-eight men set out for the Rio Grande." No writer has every quoted an actual proclamation. But here we had what seem to be three survivors of the Nueces battle saying there was a proclamation issued, giving them thirty days to leave the state and that they were travelling under the authority of that proclamation. A fourth source is the 1913 Henry Schwethelm letter to his grandson. In it he says, "The Governor of the State issued a proclamation that all that would not take the oath of aligians (sic) [allegiance] to the Confederate had to leave the State within 30 days so we left." I spent several days in the Texas Archives searching for a copy of the proclamation. None was found in the Governor's Proclamation Book, or in any department records. I reasoned that in order for citizens to find out about such a proclamation, it had to have been published in a newspaper. Another several days were spent reading every newspaper available to them in both English and German, looking for the proclamation. None was found. It began to appear that no proclamation was ever issued. The next step was examining letters and articles written shortly after the battle – not what an interviewer said long afterwards. The first such letter was written by Ernest Cramer on October 30, 1862, to his parents from Mexico. Cramer did not refer to any proclamation. The second was Julius Schlickum's letter of December 21, 1862, written on an English frigate. Schlickum did not refer to any such proclamation. The third was the Fritz Schellhase journal, date unknown. This document mentions a friend of his, Gottlieb Saur, who told Schellhase, "He was going to escape and go to Mexico with the bushwackers (sic)." There was no reference of any proclamation or their intent to travel under its authority. Fourth was R. H. Williams, a Confederate private in Duff's company. In his book *With the Border Ruffians*, he was extremely critical of Duff. However, Williams did not refer to any proclamation. A deeper search of Sansom's writing revealed an article from 1911 in which he talked more about the proclamation. Sansom said, "As by proclamation already issued [prior to June 1862] all persons unwilling to take the oath of allegiance to the Confederacy had been commanded to do. The time allowed for their departure was short; nobody cared to pay a fair price or land and other property that when forfeited to the Confederacy would be auctioned off and sold for a song." Sansom further stated, "Without money in Mexico, the [nearest] place which he must go, what could a refugee hope for?" Earlier in the article Sansom said, "That I was but one against many, the attraction of a home blessed by a charming young wife and the work I had to as a farmer, stockraiser and occasional surveyor." His conclusion was; "All things considered, he resolved to stay, not to abandon his property, not to desert his family and leave it to the prey of the savage. Certainly if he stayed at home attending to his business and doing nothing against Confederacy, he would not be molested." As with Sansom, looking at other writing by Hoffmann revealed a letter he wrote to his children on September 1, 1925, telling about his life and the Nueces battle. There is no mention of any proclamation. *(See Document 45, p. 281)* Likewise, there is another account by Kuechler contained in Adolf Paul Weber's book *Zur Geschichte des Deutschthums in Texas*. In it he says, "It is not to be forgotten that the Confederation at the outbreak of the war granted each citizen who did not want to stay under the stay under the Confederate flag, 90 days to leave." I conclude that the only source except Schwethelm who historians and writers cite as a source in was the President Davis proclamation of August, 1861 – over a year earlier.

07.  The opening shots occurred about 3:00 a. m.

08.  The group was not the twenty-eight who 'left early.' Instead, this was the Hoffmann group which had run out of ammunition.

09.  It was Lieutenant Harbour of Davis' Company who saw the insurgents attempting to withdraw and urged his fellow soldiers to turn and attack again.

10.  This was William Vater, wounded too badly to move, and left at the battle site.

11.  The man from Uvalde who rescued William Vater was Callimense Beckett.

## 54. The Old Dutch Battleground of Kinney County

### by Byrde Pearce Hamilton

FIVE OAKS RANCH
Montell, Texas.

A little more than a year ago it was my good fortune to hear "The Old Dutch Battleground" mentioned by Roy Luca, a Nueces canyon rancher and native of this section. As I am interested in history and legend, I asked him particulars. He referred me to Sam Beckett of Uvalde, who he said was a native of Kinney County and was familiar with the history of West Prong County. I went to Uvalde shortly afterward and saw Mr. Beckett, to whom I am indebted for much of the following very interesting story.

### Young German Refused to Be Conscripted

When the Civil War, or War Between the States, broke out in 1861, there were many residents living in Texas who were neither in sympathy with the Confederate nor Federal sides. Among those neutrals was a colony of German people living in Fredericksburg, Texas. Following the secession of Texas from the Union, and the conscription of soldiers to fight for the Confederate or Southern cause, there were those who rebelled and refused to be drafted in the army.

Among these were 82 young Germans of Fredericksburg. Their parents were said to be opposed to their taking up arms and fighting, and secured for them a pass into Mexico, in order they escape the conflict. Now, at this time there were many splendid soldiers of a high character, as also there were renegades and others who were supposed to Southern sympathizers, who donned the uniform of the gray, in order to deprecate, rob and otherwise bring discredit on that grand old uniform, worn so proudly by many of our ancestors. To those supposedly Southern sympathizers is credited a very deplorable deed, which will be related in the following paragraph:

## Mr. Sansom a Guide

The story of the Dutch battleground is interestingly told by Sam Beckett of Uvalde, whose grandfather, Callimense [sic] Beckett, rescued one of the German boys three weeks following the battle.

Mr. Beckett said that a Mr. Sansom, for who North Uvalde was at one time named, we employed as a guide to pilot the young Germans over this, at that time untrodden [sic] path into Mexico.

The Germans with their guide, travelled southwest to a place in Northern Kinney County where they camped. This spot, located on the West Prong of the Nueces River, and near what was called the Kickapoo springs (named for the Kickapoo Indians who before this time had inhabited the spot), is the place were the tragedy occurred.

## Boys Unaware of Their Danger

Not knowing that any danger lurked near, some of the boys went out from camp to hunt deer and wild turkey, and some others, in order to play a prank and scare them, hid themselves behind Spanish daggers, and planned to spring from behind these flimsy hiding places as dark approached and make believe that they were Indians or soldiers.

Some of the boys who had strayed further away camp came in with the report that they had seen soldiers upon some of the peaks surrounding the Germans – they had seen them through field glasses. As the captain and guide knew that some of the boys had gone out to play pranks on the hunter, they laughed and said that it was only a joke.

## Sansom Wanted to Move Camp

The story goes that Sansom felt ill-at-ease as they were in the territory where a Confederated camp was located (at Brackettville). He proposed that to safeguard the German boys who he was guiding into Mexico that it would be better to move camp. But the captain was in his "No." He said that there was nothing to be afraid of – that it was just boys trying to play a joke on them. So they stayed in camp over Sansom's protest. But guards were placed on duty as a precautionary measure.

The next morning just before daybreak, one of the guards called Sansom to come and said: "I want you to see what I found." It proved to be a blanket the soldiers had left as they had run away from the camp. The guard and Sansom went to where the blanket had been dropped. On the way back, the soldiers who were concealed in the underbrush shot the guard. Then the vicious battle began.

## Sansom Made His Escape

When the fight started Sansom was caught between the soldiers and the German boys, and had trouble in getting back to his own companions. The fight continued on until after daybreak, the soldiers killing all they could. Sansom escaped and went up on the backbone between Sycamore Creek and the Nueces River. The soldiers had captured several of the German boys and were scouting around to see if they could find more. It was an awful sight, when from his hiding place Sansom saw the boys lined and mercilessly shot down.

## Carries Wounded to Post

In all warfare things happen that are regretted by those fine characters who are usually in command, and this deplorable incident was one of those occurrences which makes every war a horrible thing.

Some of the German boys escaped and went down to the lower country. These boys came before the Confederate captain and talked straight, telling of the terrible wholesale massacre. The Confederate captain thereupon carried many of the wounded into the army post, leaving some behind. The soldiers claimed they gave out and could not bring the wounded in.[1] The army doctor strongly reprimanded them, saying: "Yes, it would be bad to leave the crippled boys out in the hills to die alone."

## Rescues Germany

Mr. Beckett said that three weeks later his grandfather, hearing of the tragedy, made up a scouting party and went to the scene of the battle. The dead lay scattered around, and all of the valuables were gone, supposedly stolen, either by the soldiers or others. He found one of the German boys in the water hole near camp with a broke leg. He was almost dead from hunger and his wounds. He had bandaged his broken limb as best he could by tearing off some of his clothes. He was brought into Brackettville and doctored.

Mr. Beckett told of a cave right across from the Dutch battleground containing the skeletons of ten or fifteen people, which skeletons have been there since long before the Civil War. It is supposition that they were killed Indians in older time. The cave might give up important secrets if thoroughly explored by archeologist. Also Mr. Beckett told of the Indian butchery of some of his ancestors and relatives, which will be used in an exclusive historical story at some future time.

ENDNOTE
Dutch Battleground

01.  Of all the stories dealing with the execution of the wounded insurgents this one comes the closest suggesting the real motive; the Confederates just did not have the manpower to carry their own <u>and</u> the wounded insurgents to Fort Clark.

02.  Callimense Becket was born on October 20, 1820, in Harrison County, Kentucky. Harriet Bell and John Beckett were his parents. Callimense Becker married Eliza Jane McInturff about 1837, likely in Missouri. They were the parents of fourteen children. The family arrived in Texas about 1844 and first settled in Kaufman County. They moved to Kinney County about 1862. Beckett enrolled in First Lieutenant Thomas Riordan's home guard company on September 21, 1863, and served until the end of the war.

## 55. Letter #1–John Donelson – August 21, 1862

August 21<sup>st</sup> 1862[1]

August 21$^{st}$ 1862[1]

A. A. A. Genl.
San Antonio, Texas

Sir:

Desiring to visit San Antonio, about the first of Sept. on business connected with the reorganization of our Regiment as also in regard to the office which I now fill, I hereby make an application, for a furlough for twenty-days.

This I do more particularly as most of the business connected with the office of Provost-Marshal is now finished & the affairs of the country nearly settled.

Please return an answer to this application at the earliest convenience

Respectfully
Your Obedient Servant

Jno Donelson
Capt. Commanding Battalion
& Provost Marshal

ENDNOTES
Captain Donelson's Letter of August 21, 1862

01. The date of August 21st shows that John Donelson and not James Duff was the provost marshal. The seven insurgents were hanged on Spring Creek on August 22, 1862. This clearly establishes that the deaths took place while Donelson – not Duff – was the provost marshal in Fredericksburg.

## 56. Letter–Leonard Pierce, Jr.
## U. S. Consul at Matamoras, Mexico

Consulate of the U. S. of America

At Matamoras September 22, 1862

Sir;

A party of Union Men numbering sixty-eight[1] left the Country of Guadeloupe[2] in Texas to cross to this city from whence they intended to embark for the Northern States – when about one hundred and forty miles from San Antonio they were attacked by three Companies of rebel soldiers to the number of about two hundred.[3] A desperate fight ensued which resulted in the massacre[4] of nearly all of the Union Men, but seven[5] of them having reached here, to this date.

They left thirty-two [6] dead on the spot and many wounded who were afterwards killed. The fight took place about the tenth of August.

Most of killed were Germans who have relatives in the Western States. As yet I have been unable to obtain a complete list of the names of those missing, but as soon as I can do so, I shall transmit it to the Department.[7]

I have now under my charge fifty loyal Americans from Texas and from the Vice Consul at Monterey I learn that he has fitted out and started on the road for this city another party numbering thirty-four who are entirely destitute.

I have sent already by the *U. S. S. Montgomery* one hundred and thirty and by a small schooner going to New Orleans, I sent six U. S. Soldiers who were prisoners at San Antonio. As I had been under the necessity of supplying them with clothing, Mr. H. C. Jordan[8] a refugee who was fortunate enough to escape with his money, kindly volunteered to pay their passages in the vessel and turn them over to the Military Commander of that city.

I could send many men from this place who are willing and anxious to join the army, if there were any means by which I could get them on, but since the departure of the *Montgomery* there had been no ships here until last week, when the *Albatross* arrived, and is now blockading the Texas coast. I have communicated with her commander who says that it will be impossible for him to take any on his ship but that he will do all in his power whenever a Supply ship may arrive, but when those ships come they stop but a few hours and as it is twenty-seven miles to the shipping I do not have time to send them down.

So I have done all in my power to aid them until I am nearly as destitute as the refugees themselves.

I am Sir, very respectfully
Your Most Obedient Servant
L. Pierce, Jr.
U. S. Consul


Hon H. H. Seward
Secretary of the State
Washington, D. C.

ENDNOTES
Letter Leonard Pierce, Jr., September 27, 1862

01. The actual number in the insurgent group was sixty-nine. Sixty-five left for Mexico and another four joined them on the trail.

02. The insurgents left from the Guadalupe River, not Guadalupe County.

03. The Confederates numbered ninety-six men, not two hundred.

04. It is interesting that the term "massacre" was used by the insurgents to tell the story of what took place on the Nueces River. Thus the event would come to be known as the Nueces Massacre.

05. The seven included two groups of survivors: four Anglos and three Germans. The Anglos were the ones who joined the group on the trail: Thomas Scott, Warren Scott, Howard Henderson, and William Hester. The three Germans were Carl Graff, Jacob Kusenberger, and Henry Schwethelm.

06. The insurgents lost nineteen at the Nueces battle. Pierce got the number of insurgents' casualties from survivors. Ferdinand Simon, who was captured shortly after the battle, told the Rebels that they had lost thirty-two.

07. No record has been located showing Pierce ever sent the names of the missing to the State Department.

08. No further data on H. C. Jordan has been located

## 57. The Bonnet Brothers
by
F. W. Schweppe

In 1856 Charles Bonnet[1], who was in the cattle business and somewhat of a hunter himself, joined the Beversdorf brothers[2] and took up a piece of ground just above theirs on the creek. As Indians did not molest the brothers, Bonnet thought he would share the same good luck. But the first night he moved up there the Indians slaughtered one of his fat work oxen only a few yards from where he slept and he did not discovered his loss until the next morning. On the whole this Joshua [Creek] settlement prospered until the Confederate War broke out. The men were of military age and were required to enter the Confederate army. They refused; because living in an Indian country their entering the army meant the loss of all they possessed. Besides, Bonnet had a family, a young wife and six little children, two sets of twins. Like others on the frontier they kept on the dodge from the Confederate soldiers that were after them.

These frontiersmen were looked upon as deserters and they were treated with cruelty that cannot be explained. Here is one example; Mr. Bonnet had a young man working for him, who was not overly smart, somewhat simple-minded. One day a squad of soldiers suddenly appeared at the house. Mrs. Bonnet, in order to save the young man, gave him a bucket and told him to go to the spring and get drinking water. She expected that the boy would stay away and hide. He, however, foolishly returned with the water and was taken away as a prisoner and next day was found hung to a limb of a live oak tree, three miles northwest of Boerne on the Cibolo.[3] Finally the Beversdorf brothers and Charles Bonnet concluded to leave for Mexico. They were joined by three of Mr. Bonnet's brothers, Daniel[4], William[5] and Peter[6], in the spring of 1862.

Mexico itself was then in the toils of war. The men left to escape the Confederate Military Company which had been in search for them for the months. They were well-armed and well-mounted. Of course they could not follow the regularly traveled road from San Antonio and Eagle Pass. They had to avoid all settlements for fear of being betrayed and hunted down. They had to keep from being seen by other traveling parties even if they might be traveling like themselves, for the purpose of escaping death. In those days "nobody trusted anybody." While the true Confederate soldiers were sorely pressed and daily under shot and shell in the trenches around Richmond and Atlanta, regiments of men busied themselves hunting down a few harmless people.

On reaching the Rio Grande they found the river well-guarded and decided to evade the guard by crossing at night. In this attempt they attempt they found themselves suddenly right in the midst of soldiers. Taking advantage of the confusion their sudden appearance caused they rushed on until they reached the edge of the water before a deadly fire was open upon them. They found the river swollen and unfordable. Using the river bank as a breastwork, they fired back and held their pursuers at bay until they could prepare for swimming across. In crossing the firing was increased and Peter Bonnet was shot through the body and had to be dragged along, making it still more difficult to get across. After being carried down the river for several miles they finally reached the opposite shore bare-headed and bare-footed, scantily clothed, without food or arms and one of them in a dying condition.

They wandered about for two days without food except prickly pear before they came to a Mexican settlement. In the meantime Peter Bonnet had died. In due time they reached Matamoras. Mexico was also in a state of war and Matamoras was at that time in possession of the French who were neutral toward the United States and the Confederacy. The party was shipped to New Orleans, then in possession of the United States forces, as refugees. Here there was nothing to do but to enlist in the army. They joined the First U. S. Texas Cavalry Regiment. Dan Bonnet obtained the rank of captain and Charles a lieutenancy. The war soon ended and they all returned to San Antonio.

ENDNOTES
The Bonnet Brothers

01.  Johann Charles Bonnet was born on July 10, 1828, at Charlottenberg. The family arrived in Texas on the *Harriet* in 1846, and first settled near San Antonio. Bonnet married Anna Louise [Elisa] Kleme about 1848. They were the parents of at least ten children. The Bonnet family arrived in the Joshua Creek area below Comfort, about 1860. Charles Bonnet was likely a member of the Kendall Company of the League's military battalion. He was a member of the Comfort Home Guard in February, 1862. In mid-October of 1862, the four Bonnet brothers decided to flee Texas and go to Mexico, where they would take a ship to New Orleans and join the Union Army. On October 18, 1862, the group was attacked by Confederate troops when they reached the Rio Grande. Charles was seriously wounded, but reached the Mexican side of the river safety. In late 1862 or early 1863, he joined Philip Braubach's guerrilla company and operated along the Rio Grande around Eagle Pass. On February 1, 1864, Bonnet enlisted in Company H, First Regiment [Union] Texas Cavalry at Brownsville, which was in Union hands at that time. He was appointed first lieutenant. Charles Bonnet resigned on February 3, 1865, because 'rebels' were operating near his home at Joshua Creek and there was no one to take care of his family. Anne Louise Kleme Bonnet died on March 25, 1878, and on November 10, 1880, Charles Bonnet married Mrs. Catherine Forschen, the widow of Sebastian Forschen. They were the parents of five children. Johann Charles Bonnet died on January 22, 1892, in Kendall County.

02.  The Beversdorf brothers were Albert H. and August. Albert was born about 1828 at Koeplin in Prussia. August was born on March 28, 1834, at Koeplin, Prussia. The date the two brothers arrived in Texas is not known, but it may have been in 1853 on the *J. W. Buddecke*. They settled in the Big Joshua Creek below Comfort, in Kendall County. They were likely members of the Kendall Company of the League's military battalion. In mid-October of 1862 they decided to flee Texas and go to Mexico where they would take a ship to New Orleans and join the Union Army. On March 30, 1863, they enlisted in Company C, First Regiment [Union] Texas Cavalry. Albert remained with the company until the end of the war and was mustered out of service on October 31, 1865, in San Antonio. August was captured at Cairo Crown Bayou, Louisiana and was exchanged on December 26, 1863. He remained with the company until the end of the war. Albert Beversdorf married Wilhelmina Schube on December 13, 1878, in Bexar County, but later divorced. The date and location of the divorce is not known. Albert married Agnes Wenck, the date and location of marriage not known. Albert was the father of at least four children. He died on May 4, 1898, location is not known. August Beversdorf married Maria Spitzer on March 27, 1869, in Kendall County. They were the parents of ten children. August Beversdorf died on August 16, 1921, at San Antonio, in Bexar County.

03.  Who this individual was is not clear. The 1860 Kerr Census shows a Henry Tiedemann, twenty-three years old, a farm laborer, born in Hanover, and living in the Bonnet household. At first glance it would appear this was the man. However, on November 20, 1873, a Henry Tiedemann who was born about 1837 in Hanover began his naturalization process in Bexar County.

04.  Heinrich Daniel Bonnet was born on August 18, 1835, in Charlottenberg, Prussia. The family arrived in Texas on the *Harriet* in 1846, and first settled near San Antonio. He very likely moved to the Joshua Creek about 1860. Daniel Bonnet was likely a member of the Kendall Company of the League's military battalion. Along with his brothers, Daniel Bonnet safely reached the Mexico side of the river. On October 27, 1863, he enlisted in Company A, First Regiment [Union] Texas Cavalry. Daniel Bonnet was commissioned a first lieutenant of Company A on July 16, 1863, and on March 15, 1865, was promoted to captain in command of Company G, First Regiment [Union] Texas Cavalry. He was mustered out of service on October 31, 1865, in San Antonio. He married Mary Josephine Breitenstein about 1865, location not known. They were the parents of at least seven children. Heinrich Daniel Bonnet died on May 9, 1926, in Val Verde County.

05.  William Jacob Bonnet was born on October 28, 1848, in San Antonio, Texas. By 1860, the family was living in the Joshua Creek area of Kendall County. He was likely a member of the Kendall Company of the League's military battalion. In mid-October he joined a group of Unionists heading for Mexico and than on to New Orleans to enlist in the Union Army. On October 18, 1862, when the group reached the Rio Grande River a Confederate force attacked them. Jacob's brother Peter was seriously wounded, and Jacob helped care for him until he died on January 12, 1864. Jacob remained in Mexico, where he likely was a member of Philip Braubach's guerrilla company that operated along the Rio Grande near Eagle Pass. It is not known when he returned to Texas; however on January 5, 1876, he married Francisca H. Kleck in Bexar County. They were the parents of ten children. William Jacob Bonnet died on March 22, 1904, in Bexar County.

06.  John Peter Bonnet was born on February 9, 1833, in Charlottenberg Prussia. The family arrived in Texas on the *Harriet* in 1846, and settled first near San Antonio. By the mid-1850s they were living in the Joshua Creek area south of Comfort. On March 22, 1855, Peter Bonnet married Sophie Katharine Dorothea Tays in San Antonio. They were the parents of four children. Peter Bonnet was likely a member of the Kendall Company of the League's military battalion. In mid-October he and his brothers decided to join a group of Unionists heading for Mexico and than on to New Orleans and join the Union Army. On October 18, 1862, Confederate troops attacked them at the Rio Grande. While crossing the Rio Grande, he was wounded in the shoulder. His brothers helped him reach the Mexican side of the river and nursed him until he died on January 12, 1863, at Piedras Negras.

## 58. Extract From Mary McDonald and Charles Frank Scott Story[1]

By
Rose Ann Harper

Mary Ann McDonald was born in the State of Arkansas. In 1840 her father moved to Lavaca County, Texas, where he ran a cider press, saloon, eating house, and dance hall combined.[2]

\* \* \*

At the age of seventeen she married Frank Scott[3] in Gillespie County, [he was] a hunter and Indian fighter. He had come home to see his people who lived in the same settlement [Spring Creek]. They met at a dance, fell in love, and married. He had one horse, saddle, lariat and a blanket. She had a bed and quilts, a pot to cook in, a coffee pot and a skillet to bake in. As the country was settling up fast, they took what they had and her father have her a yoke of oxen, an axe, a saw, and an old cart and they moved to Kerr County on what is the present site of Kerrville. He went to work for Capt. Chas. Schreiner[4], making shingles and cutting timber. Since it was hard to get supplies, Capt. Schreiner got two freight wagons and eight yoke of oxen and sent Frank on one wagon and a man named Russell[5] on the other and they hauled freight from San Antonio.

\* \* \*

Two of Frank's single brothers fought for the Southland – The Confederacy – belonged to Hood's Brigade.[6] It was during this time that Captain [Donelson[7]] and his "Cutthroats" were sent out to round up and bushwhack the Union men, but the main thing they did was to rob and steal and kill innocent men, steal their womenfolk and ravage and mistreat them.

About this time there were a lot of Union men who had families who were depending upon them for protection. [Donelson's] men would make a raid looking for these men who were hiding out. Frank Scott had accidentally shot himself in the foot – had shot his big toe off – consequently he was at home when [Donelson] made the raid.

By this time another boy had been born to them named Frank, who was four months of age now.

Well, [Donelson] took Frank Sr. and old man Henderson – a man about 60 years old – with two more men as prisoners[8], out to the camp at a water hole on the Divide about 3 miles west of Fredericksburg. They took the women and children to Headquarters in Fredericksburg where they were kept in a one-room hut; would not permit them to leave this hut unless they would ride out with them.

Meanwhile Mother and the children had the measles. There were ten people in that one room. Mother later said she almost lost her mind with her three children sick and she had not heard a word in all that time from or about her husband.
Now, there were some good men in the bunch that had taken the oath or had joined the band to save their lives or their families. These men would help the women when they could do so without detection. They were sorry for the women and children and were kind to them as they could possibly be but they could not do very much for them.

One man named [Banta[9]] told Mother that the Captain had ordered those four men killed as they would not take the oath, and that they killed them and threw their bodies into Dead Men's Hole[10], and that the renegades had moved their camp nearer to Fredericksburg. The women begged to be allowed to bury their dead, so [Donelson] told them that if they would join the band they could go and bury their "Damned Men", but Mother and her cousin[11] would not do that so the men would come one at a time and make proposals to them. Finally, Mother told them that the next time one came for that purpose, she was going to scald him. The women were not bothered for hours, then near dark a man slipped up to the window and said. "Come on out, Mary, and go walking with me." Mother asked him to leave, but he refused to go. Again, she said, "Go away." But he would not. He told her that he would give her a fine horse, but she still said, "No." He then asked, "Why not? Your man is dead." She had the water hot and she was so mad when he started to climb through the window that she dashed the scalding water in his face. He fell back howling. The others came running. Mother said she thought they might kill her, but they just laughed and howled and took him away. Two of the women gave up, but Mother didn't. Finally, the women were released.[12]

*  *  *

Although sick with the measles, the women buried their men. They, and their six children, had only two jugs of water with which to quench their thirst. They selected the place for burial and dug all night. They would take turn about. They finished the one big grave late the next evening. They waded into the water hole up to their armpits, slipped sheets under each body, carried them out, and rolled them into the grave. They said a prayer and filled the grave. The bodies were so swollen and black that they could not identify them except for the body of Frank Scott, as his big toe had been shot off.[13]

*  *  *

When she recovered enough to know what has happening, she was at old man Scott's, her father-in-law.[14] Her cousin told her that [Banta] had brought them there and that

[Donelson] was sending most of his men up on the Pecos to fight the Indians, but there [was] enough left to worry the settlers. They would watch around old man Scott's house to see if he was feeding any "hide-outs" or men they were after. Mr. Scott told them that he would feed any hungry man. Mr. Scott was quite old and had a lot of friends. As time passed Mother grew stronger.

When the Captain, with his bodyguard, took Mr. Scott everybody feared he would be killed, but he was only questioned. Now here is where Captain Temple[15] comes in. I just can't remember who he was. I don't know if he was Confederate or just who he was but I know he was a brave man and a Captain and a man of fair education. He sent word to [Donelson] to free Mr. Scott – that he would kill him if he harmed Mr. Scott in any way. [Donelson] must have feared him because he brought Mr. Scott to home. He ordered Mother to get dinner for him and his men. Mother got the dinner for them, but as she had seen Captain Temple slipping up behind the brush, she feared he would shoot [Donelson] and there would be a fight in the house among the children and some innocent person might be led. She had hurried up to put dinner on the table. [Donelson] sat at the table with his back toward the door, his bodyguard facing the door. Mother sent [Donelson] a knife by Chloe. He told the child he already had a knife, but childlike she stood there offering him the knife. Capt. Temple motioned to Mother to get Chloe out of the way, but Mother shook her head "no." The men had left their guns on their saddles on the horses in front of the door. When Mother saw that Capt. Temple was going to the horses, she walked to the door, stood there looking on in a casual sort of way, looking back at the men at the table as if who was looking to see if she could get something form them. All the time she knew that Capt. Temple and the men were stealing the guns. Capt. Temple got four guns but the fifth hung in the scabboard [sic] and the horse reared up and snorted, but he succeeded in getting it out in time to throw his gun on the men as they rushed out the door.  Mother grabbed two of their pistols as they rushed past her on their way to see what was disturbing their horses.  When they saw it was Capt. Temple, they did not even try to shoot, but put their hands up high.[16]

[Donelson] was scared and cursed his men for letting Temple get the best of him. He begged Temple not to kill him. Capt. Temple said he would kill them all – [Donelson] first. He told Mother to hold the men with her pistol but she said she was so scared that she would be sure to miss if she had to shoot, so [Donelson] said he would leave Mr. Scott alone and move his men entirely away from there. Capt. Temple then got on [Donelson's] horse and had Mother take the other men's pistols, then he made [Donelson] trot ahead of them–with the other men riding ahead of [Donelson].  He made [Donelson] trot for about a half mile to where he had his own horse hidden in the brush. He got down and mounted his own horse and made [Donelson] get on his own horse. He then told [Donelson] to get going and stated, "If you ever bother those people again, I'll kill you."  As they started off, he started to shooting and [Donelson] and his men fairly flew.

They did not bother the people there any more, but they ran all the stock off and they burned Mother's house down to the ground. There was nothing to go back for.

She, with her father-in-law, then moved and settled a place on Onion Creek [in Travis County].  They had for neighbors a Mr. Harper[17] and Mr. Gregg and some others I cannot recall. Austin was the nearest trading place.  It was there my Mother met my Father, Jeremiah Gregg[18], a widower with five children. This was his third marriage. His children by his first marriage were either dead or married. The children with him were by his second marriage. The youngest was a half-starved baby. The oldest was 15.

So they married and settled down.

## ENDNOTES
### Mary McDonald and Charles Frank Scott Story

01. Frank F. Koepke provided a copy of this article to the author in March 1977. The story is much longer than what is present here. It has been edited down to contain just the relevant information about Mary and Frank Scott during the Civil War. One paragraph has been added, which is identified, to fill in the events about the burial of Frank Scott and the other three Unionists executed on August 22, 1862.

02. Mary Ann McDonald was born on February 13, 1838, in Arkansas. Her parents were Nancy "Polly" Clover and Augustus Baldwin McDonald. The family arrived in Gillespie County about 1853.

03. Charles Franklin Scott was in 1836, likely in Illinois. His parents were Mary Ann Brady and Benjamin Franklin Scott. It is not clear when they arrived in Texas, but by 1855, they were living near Spring Creek in western Kerr County. He and Mary McDonald were married on September 16, 1855, in Gillespie County. They were the parents of three children.

04. Charles Armand Schreiner was born on February 22, 1838, at the Castle of Reichenstein, in Alsace. The family arrived in Texas in September, 1852. The parents died shortly after arriving in Texas. Charles settled on Turtle Creek in southern Kerr County. He married Mary Magdalena Enderle on October 1, 1861. They were parents of eight children. During the Civil War Charles enlisted in S.G. Newton's Company, 3$^{rd}$ Regiment Texas Infantry and served until the end of the war. He established the Charles Schreiner General Mercantile Company in 1869. It grew into a business empire that included banking and ranching. Charles Schreiner died on September 7, 1905, in Kerr County.

05. Unable to identify Russell.

06. The Scott family identifies these two brothers as Tom and Ike. The compiler spent numerous hours trying to identify a Tom and Ike Scott serving in Hood's Brigade. The Compiled Service Records of the units that served in Hood's Brigade did not list men with the surname of Scott and the first names of Tom and Ike. There <u>were</u> two sets of Scotts, likely brothers who served in the brigade; the first beingThomas B. and John F. Scott. Both served in the 5$^{th}$ Regiment Texas Infantry. Thomas B. Scott enlisted on August 2, 1861, near Harrisburg in Company G. He was wounded at Malvern Hill, Virginia on June 27, 1862, and received a medical discharge on October 30, 1862. John F. Scott enlisted on August 20, 1861, near Harrisburg in Company D. A surgeon certificate discharged him on July 20, 1862. The second set of Scotts was J. B. Scott and Garrett Scott. Both enlisted from Grimes County in early 1862, in Company G, 4$^{th}$ Regiment Texas Infantry. J. W. was wounded at Gaines'

Mill on June 27, 1862, and died on July 5, 1862. Garrett Scott was killed at Sharpsburg on September 17, 1862.

Finally it was determined that Tom and Ike did not serve in Hood's Brigade, nor in any Confederate unit. They both served in Union units. It turns out that Tom was Thomas Jefferson who had joined the insurgents on the trail and was at the Nueces. He enlisted in Company A, First Regiment [Union] Texas Cavalry in New Orleans on October 27, 1862, and mustered out of service on October 31, 1865, at San Antonio. Thomas Scott died on January 2, 1907, in Bexar County. The Ike was Isaac Shelby Scott he remained in Iowa when the Scott family came to Texas. Scott enlisted in Company A, 4th Regiment Iowa Cavalry on March 16, 1862. He was mustered out of service on March 20, 1865, in Chickasaw, Alabama. Isaac Scott died on February 26, 1911, in Harris County, Texas.

07. The original version of this story uses the name Duff in naming the captain of the Confederate troops, obviously referring to James Duff. However, Captain Duff was neither the provost marshal nor the commander of troops in Gillespie County when these incidents occurred. Duff had departed by August 21, 1862, and Captain John Donelson was the provost marshal and the commander of troops. This contradicts all the folk stories of this time period, which blame James Duff for committing atrocities. But military records and official correspondence clearly prove it was either Henry T. Davis, commander of the state company or John Donelson, the commander of the Confederate force who perpetuated or permitted abuses and atrocities during that period.

08. The other three men captured were Sebird Henderson, Herman Nelson, and Gustav Tegener.

09. William Banta was born on June 23, 1827, in Warrick County, Indiana. The family arrived in Texas in late 1839. He married Lucinda Hairston on March 4, 1850, in Burnet County. He enlisted in Davis' Company on March 4, 1862. On December 24, 1862, Banta re-enlisted in Hunter's Company of the Frontier Regiment and he was elected first lieutenant. He was promoted to captain on January 12, 1864, when Hunter was promoted to major and given command of the Third Frontier District. Banta was one of the leaders of the *Haengerbande* [Hanging Gang] and committed many of the atrocities later blamed on Duff. Banta was indicted for the April, 1864, murder of Warren Cass. He was arrested and placed in the Fredericksburg jail. Pro-Union bushwhackers attacked the jail in May, 1864, and he was wounded in the ensuing fight. Banta was released from Confederate military service in August, 1864. Banta was arrested several more times but never tried. He died in 1898 in Lampasas County.

10. Dead Man's Hole is located on Spring Creek west of Fredericksburg. It obtained its name from the four bodies thrown into it on or about August 22, 1864.

11. The itentity of Mary Scott's cousin is not known.

12. The two women who 'gave up' were likely Mary Jane Payton, the widow of Gus Tegener, and Susan Ann Benson, the wife of Fritz Tegener. Mary Jane married John W. Helms, Jr., on Oct. 5$^{th}$, 1862. Mary Jane believed that Fritz was dead and married Frederick Schladoer on July 27, 1863

13. This is the section added to the Mary Scott's story.

14. Benjamin Franklin Scott was born about 1792, in Illinois. He married Mary Ann Brady. They arrived in Texas about 1854 and settled in the Spring Creek area. Benjamin Scott moved in with Mary Scott to Orion Creek in Travis County in 1862. He likely died there by 1870.

15. Captain Temple is Philip G. Temple who was born in 1835 in Ohio. After his service in the Mexican War he remained in Texas, settling in the Spring Creek area. He was the lieutenant in the Kerr [American] Company of the League's military battalion. He fled to Mexico in late August or early September and went on to New Orleans where he enrolled in Company A, First Regiment [Union] Texas Volunteer Cavalry on October 27, 1862. Temple was elected first lieutenant of the company on November 6, 1862, and was promoted to captain on January 21, 1864. He was mustered out of Union service on October 31, 1865, in San Antonio. He returned to Gillespie County where he lived until ill health forced him to return to his Ohio home in 1896 where he died on February 28, 1903.

16. This is very similar to a story involving Captain Frank Van der Stucken. The Van der Stucken version says he was ordered to apprehend some of the more "dangerous American Union men." Complying with his orders, Van der Stucken attempted to arrest some of these Unionists. He selected a few of his more trusted men and went to the home of one of the Unionists. They left their horses outside and went inside to search for the owner. The Unionist and some of his friends had been warned and were waiting outside. When they saw Van der Stucken and his men go inside they took Van der Stucken's horse and rode away firing Van der Stucken's pistol, which had been left hanging on the saddle horn, shouting, "Hurrah for the United States."

17. Mr. Harper has not been identified.

18. Jeremiah George Gregg was born on March 24, 1813, in Coppers Fort, Missouri. He married Polly Alexander Smeltzer on October 28, 1835, in Clay County, Missouri. They were the parents of four children. Polly Smeltzer died in 1849. Gregg married Margaret Bratton on October 12, 1850, in Travis

County. They were the parents of five children. Margaret Gregg died in 1856. On June 5, 1863, Jeremiah Gregg married Mary Ann McDonald Scott in Travis County, Texas. They were the parents of three children. Jeremiah George Gregg died on December 16, 1905, in Travis County, Texas.

## 59. Captain Donelson's Letter #2

Office of Provost-Marshal
Fredericksburg, Texas
September 8<sup>th</sup> 1862

Office of Provost-Marshal
Fredericksburg, Texas
September 8th 1862

Brig. Gen. H. P. Bee
San Antonio, Texas

Sir:

Since my last report nothing has occurred within this jurisdiction worthy of notice.

This disaffected citizens opposed to the Confederate government have generally yielded obedience by taking the Oath of Allegiance.

Some twenty – or thirty – Unionists are still concealed in the cedar brakes, near this place. It is difficult to capture them, as their friends & hiding places are numerous.

Fifty men would now be sufficient to hold these counties in subjection. They would also be necessary in rendering assistance to the Receiver while securing & selling the confiscated property in this section; a large amount of which is on hand.

As before stated my opinion is confirmed that this population – principally Germans – will remain peaceable & not again commit an overt act of Treason, unless the State is invaded by our enemies, in which event most of them will join the foe.

Nearly every male citizen here is armed with a good six-shooter & rifle. Would it not be best to press these arms into the service before an opportunity could be afforded for having them [used] against us?

I understand the second Regiment is to rendezvous near San Antonio on the 10th of this month, for the purpose of reorganization. If such is the case I would wish to be present with my company. This request I made the more especially as my name has been presented to fill one of the Field Officers. Part of my company who were in the Nueces fight, under Lt. McRae are in San Antonio & those remaining here would like to join the balance in consultation as to the selection of their superior officers. Consequently if consistent with your approbation I would like to be relieved of my command here for a few days in order to be present at the reorganization of our Regiment at San Antonio.

Hoping the policy Capt Duff & myself have pursued here has met your approbation.

I have the honor to be your most obedient servant

Jno Donelson
Provost Marshal
& Capt Commanding Post

# 60. Extract Thomas C. Smith's Diary[1]

**Tuesday Aug 19th 1862.** Captain T [Taylor[2]] started home yesterday on a furlough. Lieut. Kelso[3] in command received an order for Co. "G" to take 20 days rations and repair forthwith to Fredericksburg about 75 miles distant.

Several of the Company had to go to Lockhart to get their horses shoed myself among the rest.

While at Lockhart I bought me a Colts Six Shooter Navy Size (No 70731) for which I paid the mere sum of $70.00! Seventy Dollars.

I am now the owner of a Six Shooter & will hereafter always keep one if able.

**Thursday morning 21st.** We had all our horses shod and started to camp.

**Friday 22nd.** At 2 o'clock we all was at and the train started All that were going drew Six Shooters from the Commis. sarg (sic) [commissary sergeant] before they started.

I drew one and left mine with Joe who did not go, as all the married & disable men were exempt.

We camped that night on the San Marcos or rather in San Marcos Town.

No. of Company along; 44 privates, 7 non commissioned officers, & 2 commd. Officers. I was Sargt. Guard tonight.

**Saturday 23rd August, 1862 3 o'clock in the morning.** Charley blowed his horn and all hands was aroused, got breakfast, fed horses and was off. We now came to a mountainous country. Road very rough on account of rocks.

Going on a little farther we came to what is called the "Devil's Backbone". This is a long and winding ridge of hills & bluffs, very rough traveling. Deep ravines and almost bottomless pits lie on either side, while as far as the eye can see hill after hill meets the view.

Here having passed over the "Devil's Backbone" we came to "Purgatory." This is a stream which by its name seems to be entitled to it. We made about 20 miles or more and struck camp. Found a very cool spring which afforded water for man and beast.

Camped here for the night. Some of boys being hungry went out in quest of fame and returned with large loads of meat which proved to be the meat of the celebrated "Mountain Buck." (Beef).

\* \* \*

**Sunday 24<sup>th</sup> August 1862.** Aroused all hands early as usual and left camp as the sun was making his way up. Still mountainous country, rough roads, hard on the teams.

Camped on a creek near the residence of H. F. Kelso[4] whom we left back at Camp Clark. The place looks desolate and lonely among the mountains.

The boys, not regarding the day which we are commanded to keep holy, produced a pack of cards and went to gambling as usual. Camped here for the night.

\* \* \*

**Monday 25<sup>th</sup>.** Arrived at town of Fredericksburg and camped in the superbs. (sic) No grass for our horses. Some got fodder at 21 per bundle.

\* \* \*

**Tuesday 26<sup>th</sup> August 1862**.  Lt. Kelso in command having reported & consulted with Capt. Donelson[5] and procuring a guide we started to his camp about 15 miles distant.  Got dinner at a spring about 2 miles from the camp and then went on and got there about 2 o'clock p.m.

Found a camping place and struck camp.  Rainy evening. Our camp is surrounded by mountains, but there is plenty good grass for our horses. Some talk of our having to stay here a month or so.

* * *

**Wednesday August 27<sup>th</sup> 1862**.  An order came for 8 men to go on a scout.  Everyone was excited and "where & what are they going to do?" was the question.  It was not necessary hardly to make a detail for several volunteered.

Camp Perdenalis (sic) in the mountains 15 miles from Fredericksburg.  No tents and rain!  Rain rain it has been every day since we came; wet blankets and bad fires, half cooked victuals etc etc etc.  Glad enough to see clear weather once more.

There is now a daily guard around Fredericksburg.  The "bushwhackers" or traitors are plentiful in this country but keep themselves hid, and they had selected a good country for the business.

When one chances to fall into the hands of the C.S. soldiers he is dealt pretty roughly with and generally makes his last speech with a rope around his neck.  Hanging is getting to be as common as hunting.

The creeks in this vicinity are said to be full of dead men!! I witnessed yesterday a sight which I never wish again to see in a civilized & enlightened country.

In a water hole in Spring Creek (about two miles from camp) there are four human bodies lying on top of the water, thrown in and left to rot, and that too after they were hanged by neck and dead.[6] If they are traitors no doubt they deserved their reward but should have at least gave them a burial.

Scouting still continues and now and then a prisoner is brought in.

Capt. Taylor, Lt. Blair[7] & 1 or 2 others came to camp and staid awhile but have returned to Camp Clark. No telling when we'll leave this country.

\* \* \*

**Saturday 20<sup>th</sup> September 1862**. A detail of 18 men from our company and 15 from Taylor's Battalion were ordered to go on a scout, Lt. Kelso in command. Camped at Fredericksburg for the night.

Started a small scouting party of 8 men with a guide to go to 'Hudson Mound' about 20 miles distant, (tonight) and be there by daylight in the morning.

Next morning we were ready to start by 5 o'clock. We left town and traveled in a N. E. direction and finally went almost due East. Bushes plenty & thick; hills large and high, roads rough & rocky, horses hungry, morning cool & clear, men anxious and willing to encounter the enemy.

As the crown were riding cautiously along through the bushes, each one looking out for himself, a man was seen to cross the road on horseback and ride out into the bushes! The Lieut. and those in front immediately galloped up and the whole crowd went tearing through the bushes over rocks, etc. Several were seen to feel for their six-shooters (myself included) but at last we came up with the man and found him to be a solitary horse hunter and as some of the boys were acquainted with him we bade him good morning & struck out.

Got to the mound called 'Hudson's' Mound which is a large and very tall standing in the valley alone. We were to meet the other boys here but could not find their camp at first. The party rode up to the foot of the mound and suddenly we discovered one of our men placed up there as a sentinel.

He pointed out the direction of the camp, and after riding around and about, we finally found them. No signs of the "Bushwhackers" yet.

Eat dinner & concluded to camp here tonight. After dinner, prompted by curiosity I went with J. A. Middleton[8] up the mountain. Before I reached the top, I found it more fun than pleasure. The summit is covered over with a thick growth of bushes. The whole country below can be viewed distinctly.

Talk about hunting a man in this country! I had rather hunt a needle in a hay stack! There are hills here which it is impossible to climb, especially on horseback. Large rocks lie pile upon pile as though laid by some Stone Mason.

Placed out Guard of four men round camp tonight.

* * *

**Monday 22nd September 1862**. The Lieut. divided the Co. into two scouts, one to go with Sergt. Wms.[9] on the left of the mound, while the others with the Lt. went to the right.

We thought we had seen most of the rough country but it seems we are just getting into it. It is truly the roughest country I ever saw. We had to walk and lead our steeds most of the time, as it wouldn't be safe to ride down the hills or mountains we passed over. Some are covered with pure white quartz rocks and others with huge stone heaps as though constructed for a fortification of some sort.

A Californian that was with us gave it as his opinion that Gold abounded in this section, as every indication of it.

We saw no signs of any human and the only living creature is now and then an immense rattle snake or a frightened Fawn goes leaping from one hill to another.

The other party were to meet us at noon near an old house known to the Guide. Our horses being weary, ourselves hungry and our clothes nearly torn off, we camped here for dinner & allowed our horses to graze. The boys all said they must have some beef and the guide picking a young calf took aim, the next moment the poor little thing was lying dead & its mother looking at it gave a loud lament and fled. All now fell to skin it & get some to broil.

In less than ½ an hour nothing remained but the hide & a few bones! (etc.) Even the head was thrown in the fire and carefully cooked as a rarety by the fastidious.

The other party joined us here and no sign being discovered the Lt. said we would return.

Went three or four miles farther and camped for the night, our Guides left us here as there was no further use for them.

* * *

**Tuesday 23rd September 1862.** Started for Fredericksburg.

Stopped awhile at a spring on the road & let our horses graze. While here we found the mountain grapes in abundance & feasted on them. They are truly delicious, tasting almost like the tame English grape. Arrived at town and stopped long enough to get some Coffee & something to eat and then out to camp.

Now again comes the loneliness and laziness of camp life, intermingled with all sorts of vices such as Swearing, Card playing, stealing, etc. May I be able to resist them all.

\* \* \*

**Wednesday 24th September 1862.** The Vices of the camp is as much to be guarded against as the invasion of the enemy. Here we are thrown together with 40 or 50 men, all of different tempers and morals. Owning to the dullness of the camp some 3 or 4 propose a game at cards just for amusement. The game commences and soon they wish to play for something, say 25 cents to make it interesting. Thus they go on and while the game goes on a number of Spectators gather around. Ah! Those Spectators soon get interested and they propose a game, so soon the whole camp is taken up, divided in squads and each loses or wins as fortune frowns or smiles. Thus we see the Young Man who has been brought [up] in a different way is led off step by step and he is almost a confirmed Gambler. I found myself beginning to be fascinated with it until I played almost every day for amusement. But I was urged & invited to play for some small sum, but I have thus for resisted it and hope to do so henceforth.

Intermingled with every game is horrid oaths calling upon God to send their Soul to hell, etc, etc, while others use all sorts of Vulgarity Blackguard (sic) talk, which sickens me at once.

Oh! How can I withstand all? I will ask God daily to help me and lead me not into the way of temptations but deliver me from evil!

\* \* \*

**Thursday 25th September 1862**. Lt. Kelso informed me this morning that I must take the situation as Commissary Sergeant for awhile in Fredericksburg. Rode in with B. Lampley[10] and staid at the Hospital with Hays[11] who has the rheumatism.

Lt. Kelso came in later next day.

\* \* \*

**Friday 26th Sept 1862**. Lieut. Kelso arranged the business and is to take charge of the Commissary tomorrow. I staid at the Hospital and made arrangement with the Steward to eat & sleep there.

W. H. Webb[12] came in this evening. He is to stay in Town and help me in the Commissary. Staid in town and eat at the Hospital during the week. Bill Webb staid with me. The Hospital steward (Charles Ervay[13]) is a very pleasant fellow.

\* \* \*

**Thursday 2nd October 1862**. The dullness of the town was revived this evening by all hands getting on a big Spree (myself not included). The firing of pistols and yelling of men announced the fact. Going down to the Bar Room I found where it started for there was good Parish Wine selling at $3.50 per bottle. Amt. spent for wine in the spree not less than $200.00!!!

\* \* \*

**Friday 3rd October 1862**. Captain Josiah Taylor and the rest of the men from Camp Clark arrived this evening bringing our tents, clothes. I suppose we will stay here during the winter. Joe did not come up but will be up in a few days. Lieut. Blair took charge of the QMD.

\* \* \*

**Friday 10<sup>th</sup> October 1862.** In camp on the Perdenalis. (sic)

This morning a cold blowing Northern came up accompanied with a drizzling rain which made it a cold disagreeable day. Winter of 1862 has set in and now the Soldiers will suffer a great many times.

Our tents do some good by keeping off the wind but when it rains hard they leak badly. Joe has been unwell for the last week & this weather is bad for him.

I slept in the Captains Tent last night and had a very pleasant Dream which I here record for my own amusement. In my dream I was at Home (that was pleasant thought) and this unholy and deadly War was at an end! The Independence of the C.S.A. was acknowledged by U.S.A. and all Nations were willing to treat with us as one of the Nations of the World!! But that was not all. I was in the pleasant little village of Clinton; and what was no less strange, I loved!!

* * *

Smith and Company G were transferred to Fort Clark. They departed from Fredericksburg in early November and on November 17, 1862, arrived at Fort Clark.

Editorial note: Every effort has been made to keep the original spelling and grammar on the source document.

ENDNOTES
Extract Thomas C. Smith's Diary

01.   This portion of Smith's Diary is included because it shows the Confederate and insurgent activities around Fredericksburg after the Nueces battle. Thomas Crutcher Smith was born on December 12, 1843, in DeWitt County, Texas. Smith enlisted in Company G, 32nd [AKA 36th] Regiment, Texas Cavalry on April 3, 1862, in Clinton. He was a member of the Company G detachment sent to Fredericksburg on August 25, 1862. He remained with the company until the end of the war. Thomas C. Smith married Josephine Marietta Harrison Brown, the widow of Joseph T. Brown, on November 4, 1874, in DeWitt County. They were the parents of at least three children. Thomas Crutcher Smith died on May 17, 1913, in Waco, Texas.

02.   Josiah Taylor was the commander of Company G, 36th Regiment Texas Cavalry. He was born about 1822 in Alabama. The family arrived in Texas in 1826, and settled in DeWitt Colony. Josiah Taylor married Sarah Jane York on March 21, 1849, in DeWitt County. They were the parents of at least five children. Taylor organized a cavalry company known as DeWitt's Guerrillas on September 1, 1861. It was later redesigned as Company G, 36th Texas Cavalry in March, 1862. He was ordered to Fredericksburg with the remained of his company in September, 1862. Taylor replaced John Donelson as provost marshal in Gillespie County in September, 1862. Josiah Taylor died on March 27, 1864, as the regiment was on the march to Louisiana.

03.   John Roebuck Kelso was born about 1835 in Tennessee. The family arrived in Texas about 1850 and settled in DeWitt County. Kelso married Mary Ann Chisholm on August 14, 1856, in DeWitt County. They were the parents of eight children. John Kelso enrolled in Company G, 36th Regiment Texas Cavalry on April 3, 1862, and was elected first lieutenant. He was in command of the fifty-four man detachment sent to Fredericksburg on August 25, 1862. Kelso was promoted to captain on March 27, 1864, shortly after Josiah Taylor died. Kelso served until the end of the war. Mary Ann Kelso died about 1877. John R. Kelso married her sister Jane P. Jennie Chisholm Fore, about 1878, likely in DeWitt County. They were the parent of a son, John Clyde, born about 1880. John Roebuck Kelso died in 1910.

04.   Henry F. Kelso was born about 1828 in Tennessee. The date he arrived in Texas is not known. He married a woman identified only as S. [maiden name not known] about 1857, in Caldwell County. They were the parents of at least one child. Kelso enrolled in Company G, 36th Regiment Texas Cavalry on May 1, 1862, at Clinton. His date of death is not known, but it may have been as early as February, 1864.

05.   Captain Donelson was commander of Confederate troops at Fredericksburg. *(See Document 31, Endnote 2, p 164.)*

06. These bodies were those of Hiram Nelson, Gustave Tegener, Frank Johnson and Sebird Henderson. They were hanged at Spring Creek on August 22, 1862, by Davis' company.

07. James Francis Blair was born on November 1, 1826, in Dyer County, Tennessee. The family likely arrived in Texas in the late 1830s. Blair married Lensay Elizabeth Ainsworth on April 18, 1851, in DeWitt County, Texas. They were the parents of at least seven children. Blair enrolled in Company, G, 36th Regiment Texas Cavalry in March, 1862, in Clinton and was elected second lieutenant. He remained with the unit until the end of the war rising to the rank of captain. James Francis Blair died on December 17, 1901, in DeWitt County.

08. John A. Middleton was born on February 6, 1846, in Goliad County, Texas. He enrolled in Company G, on May 1, 1862, at Clinton. Middleton deserted on February 1, 1864, at Camp Hardimann. He married Mary Samantha Parker on November 26, 1865, in DeWitt County. They were the parents of at least two children. John A. Middleton died on January 8, 1876, in Goliad County.

09. Unable to identified this Sergeant Williams. No individual with this name appears on Company G's Muster Rolls.

10. Benjamin Lampley was born on July 3, 1814, in North Carolina. Lampley married Appeline Shipman on January 2, 1834, likely in Barbour County, Alabama. They were the parents of at least ten children. They arrived in Texas about 1858 and settled in DeWitt County. Lampley enrolled in Company G, 36th Regiment Texas Cavalry on April 3, 1862, at Clinton. Benjamin Lampley died about 1865, in DeWitt County.

11. Unable to identify Hays.

12. William Henry Webb was born on October 29, 1835, in Missouri. The date he arrived in Texas is not known. Webb married Jemima Ann Spearmen on July 29, 1858, in Grayson County. They were the parents of at least three children. Webb enrolled in Company G, 36th Regiment Texas Cavalry on April 3, 1862, in Clinton. He was promoted to corporal in March, 1863, and remained with the unit until the end of the war. Jemima Ann Spearman Webb died on May 5, 1874, in Sherman in Grayson County. Webb married Paralee Jane Allsup Bucks, the widow of George L. Bucks on January 10, 1875, in Grayson County. They were the parents of at least six children. William Henry Webb died on September 25, 1913, in Coleman County.

13. Charles H. Ervay was born about 1837, likely in Pennsylvania. No further data.

## 61. Letter, James M. Hunter

Office of County Surveyor, Edwards County, Texas
November 17, 1895

Captain J.W. Sansom, San Antonio, Texas:

Dear Old Friend: I have just had the good pleasure of receiving and reading your very truthful, impartial, and graphic account of the battle and massacre on the West Nueces, in August, 1862. I am as familiar with the details of that battle as Davis, company which was there, and Bill [Harbour], who opened the battle was Second Lieutenant. I had been transferred to regimental quartermaster's place. I saw and talked with many of the men of both sides who took part in that battle and massacre, whose head, like your and mine, is hoary with age, and who on that occasion was one of the Duff and Davis men that followed your party, and made the night attack which brought on the battle you so well describe. After the battle was over and the Union party vanquished, he[1] – Bill Wharton[2] – was one of the men detailed to murder the helpless wounded Unionists who lay upon the battle ground. This may be the reason why he is now allowed to carry a six-shooter; he no doubt fears that some relative of the murdered men might attempt to take his consecrated life.

That massacre was one of the most shameful acts remembered in the unwritten history of the Southern Confederacy, and I am glad that you, as an eye-witness have portrayed it as you have in your very neat little pamphlet which I most surely appreciate. It shows the guilty parties, who will not be indorsed by innocent Confederates.

Yours very truly,
JAMES M. HUNTER
County Judge, Edwards County, Texas.

ENDNOTES
Letter, James M. Hunter.

01. This letter is located in Guido E. Ransleben's *A Hundred Years of Comfort in Texas: A Centennial History*, Naylor Company, San Antonio, Texas, 1954. This copy does not name the individual who was one of the 'murderers'; it has a blank where the name has been left out.

02. J. Evetts Haley, *Charles Schreiner General Merchandise 1869 – 1969*, Charles Schreiner Company, Kerrville, Texas, 1969. This book identifies the murderer. It states; "Uncle Bill Wharton was an old-time Texan who, with Aunt Lou, his wife, finally settled half-way out on the Rock Springs road. Since it was a trip of two days between the towns, his home was the convenient stopping place for all travelers, who were hospitably received for as long as they wished to stay. On a morning Uncle Bill rose and buckled that heavy belt about his hemispheric abdomen, pushed his upbrimmed hat on his leonine head, and followed by his hunting hounds made the round of chores. It was no affectation with him; he could not milk without his gun. The numerous German settlers disliked him, because, rumor had it, he was with Duff's command when it overtook the German Union sympathizers who were leaving Texas during the Civil War, and killed most of them on the Nueces as they made their way into Mexico. The same source credits Uncle Bill with having volunteered to finish off the wounded, which was done, but as he was never one to talk, much less brag, about his exploits, this report goes unconfirmed."

## 62. Letter, Howard Henderson[1]

Ingram, Texas
October 16, 1908

J. W. Sansom, San Antonio, Texas

Dear Captain: I was in the Nueces battle, as you know, and while reading your pamphlet account of it, could see it just as it was. For goodness sake, write a book and tell more of those times.

I am now on my death-bed. I know that J. M. Duff and his company of murderers killed many of my neighbors and friends. My uncle[2] and cousins Schram Henderson[3], my wife's father[4] and brother[5], Turknette[6], were murdered, my neighbors, Hiram Nelson[7], Frank Scott[8] and his father[9] Parson Johnson[10] and old man Scott[11] were all butchered by Duff and his gang. Rocks were tied to their feet, and they were thrown into Spring Creek.[12] Many others of my neighbors were put to death[13], their houses burned, and their wives and children taken to the camps of soldiers where, when not otherwise insulted, they were compelled to listen to the foul tongues that denounced their husbands and fathers, all of whom, as you personally know, were first-class citizens.

Some of my relatives and friends as far away as far away as New Mexico and Colorado, have been to see me, and my children have been with me lately. I guess I will never see you again, my comrade, and now bid you God speed. My family has written for. Goodbye[14].

Howard Henderson

*Howard Henderson Letter*

ENDNOTES
Howard Henderson Letter.

01. This letter originally appears in Guide Ransleben book *A Hundred Years of Comfort in Texas.*

02. Howard Henderson's uncle was Sebird Henderson, who was born about 1805 in South Carolina. John Jasper Henderson was his father. His mother's name is not known, but it *may have been* Sarah Anderson. Sebird Henderson married Mary Ellen Blancett about 1827, likely in Morgan County, Tennessee. Sebird Henderson and his family arrived in Kerr County about 1859, as they appear on the 1860 Kerr Census. Sebird was arrested about August 5, and Davis' company hanged him on August 22, 1862.

03. Unable to identified Schram Henderson.

04. Howard Henderson's wife was Narcissa R. Turknett. Her father was Philip Brandon Turknett, who was born in Tennessee, in 1822. Ede Brannam and Jacob Turknett, Jr. were his parents. Philip Turknett married Hannah Culbertson about 1847, likely in Mississippi. The family arrived in Kerr County in early 1861. Philip Turknett was a pro-Union bushwhacker. He was shot and killed by Jonas Harrison [not by Duff or the Confederates] on July 13, 1864.

05. Narcissa Turknett Henderson's brother was John S. C. Turknett, who was born about 1845 in Neshoba County, Mississippi. Pro-Confederate bushwhackers [not Duff] captured him in January of 1864 and beat him to death because he would not tell them where his father was.

06. The third Turknett male who was killed was Jacob Turknett, Jr. He was born about 1788, in Wilkes County, Georgia. Barbara [maiden name not known] and Jacob Turknett, Sr. were his parents. Jacob, Jr. was the father of Philip B. Turknett and the grandfather of John S. C. Turknett. Pro-Confederates [not Duff] captured him in January, 1864, and beat him to death because he would not tell where his son, Philip Turknett, was.

07. Hiram Nelson was born about 1800, in Orange County, North Carolina. It is believed Martha Williams and Thomas Burton Nelson were his parents. Hiram Nelson married Mary Ana [Polly] Roundtree about 1832, in either Missouri or Illinois. The family arrived in Kerr County about 1859. Hiram Nelson was a pro-Unionist bushwhacker and was arrested by the Confederates on August 4, 1862. He was hanged on August 22, 1862, by Davis' company – not Duff's – at Spring Creek.

08. Charles Franklin [Frank] Scott was born about 1836 in Texas. Mary Ann Brady and Benjamin Franklin Scott were his parents. Frank Scott married Mary Ann McDonald on September 15, 1855, in Gillespie County. He was a

## 63. Court Martial of Private James Duff

Headquarters 7th Military Department
Fort Smith June 9, 1849

Orders
No 10

A General Court Martial to consist of nine members, will convene at Fort Gibson C. N. at 10 o'clock A. M. on the 15' of June 1849, or as soon thereafter as practicable, for the trial of such prisoners as may be properly brought before it.

Detail for the Court

Bvt. Brig Genl W. G. Belknap, 5 Regiment of Infantry
| | | | | | |
|---|---|---|---|---|---|
| Captain | Isaac Lynda | " | " | " | " |
| Captain | S. H. Fowler | " | " | " | " |
| 1st Lieut | J. C. Robinson | " | " | " | " |
| Bvt. Capt | F. T. Dent | " | " | " | " |
| 1st Lieut | P. A. Farrelly | " | " | " | " |
| 2' Lieut | T. H. Neill | " | " | " | " |
| 2' Lieut | B. Wingate | " | " | " | " |

Bvt. Major P. Lugenbeel, Adj '5 Regt. Of Infantry, is appointed Judge Advocate of the Court.

By Command of Brig Genl Arbuckle
F. F. Flint
A.A. Adj Genl

Headquarters 7th Military Department
Fort Smith June 23, 1849

Orders
No. 13

II At the General Court Martial which convened at Fort
Gibson C. N. on the 15th of June 1849 pursuant to "Orders"
No 10, June 9th 1849 and which Bvt. Gen Genl W. G. Belknap
5th Regt. Infy is president were arraigned and tried:

1st Private James Duff of "C" Company 5th Regt Infantry
on the following.

Charge "Desertions"

Specification.  "On this that the said Private James Duff of
"C" Company 5th Regt Infy did desert the service of the
United States at Fort Gibson, Cherokee Nation, on or about
the night of the 14th May 1849 and did remain absent until
apprehended and brought back on the 22nd of May 1849.
Thirty dollars paid for his apprehension"

To which the prisoner pleaded "Guilty"

The Court fined the prisoner "Guilty" as charge and
sentence him Private James Duff of "C" Company, 5th Regt
Infy to reimburse to the United States the expenses paid for his
apprehension: forfeit all pay and allowances now due him,
except just debts to Sutler and Laundress: be confine at hard
labor in charge of the guard, with a chain from two to three
feet long, attached to each leg with a shackle: for a period of
six months: at the expiration of the six months to receive fifty

lashes on his bare back, will laid on with a raw hide: be indelibly marked on the left hip with the letter **D** 1 1/2 inches long: have his head shaved and be drummed out of service."

\* \* \*

By Command of Brig Genl Arbuckle
F. F. Flint
A. A. Adjt Genl

## 64. Letter, National Archives

June 12, 1997

Reply to: NWDT/1-97-12107-DW

Mr. William Paul Burrier, Sr.
Post office Box 1085
Leakey, TX 78873-1084

Dear Mr. Burrier:

The following is in reply to your request form information concerning the military service of James Duff of the 5$^{th}$ U. S. Infantry Regiment following his court martial in 1849.

We have enclosed a copy of Special Order 9, which was dated October 29, 1849, and was issued by the 7$^{th}$ Military Department. This order, while it does not pardon James Duff, does remit the unexecuted portions of his sentence.

Duff was later transferred to Company K of the 5$^{th}$ U.S. Infantry on November 1, 1849, and was appointed corporal in this unit on December 1, 1849.

We hope that this information will be of assistance to you with your research.

Sincerely,
DAVID H WALLACE
Archives I Reference Branch
Textual Reference Division

Enclosure

Headquarters 7$^{th}$ Military Department
Fort Smith, October 29, 1849

Special Orders
No. 9

On the recommendation of their Regimental commander the unexecuted portions of the sentences against Privates James Duff, Joseph Bald, Edward Bald, and John Burns of "C" Company, 5$^{th}$ Regiment Infantry promulgated in Department orders no 13 of 1849 are remitted except so much as prescribes that their reimburse to the United States the expenses paid for their apprehension and they will be returned to duty with their company.

By Command of Brigadier General Arbuckle

F. F. Flint
A.A. Adjutant General

## 65. Extract James Duff's U. S. Army Service Records

10-06-49.  Enlisted in Company C, 5<sup>th</sup> U. S. Infantry at Boston, Massachusetts.
Age: 21.  Place of Birth: Perthshire, Scotland.  Color of Eyes: Gray.  Color of Hair: Light Brown.  Complexion: Fair: Height: Five Feet, Ten Inches.

05-14-49.  Deserted from Fort Gibson.

05-22-49  Apprehended and Return to Fort Gibson.

06-15-49  Court Martial and Found "Guilty"

10-29-49  Sentence Remitted.

11-01-49.  Transferred to Company K, 5<sup>th</sup> U. S. Infantry at Fort Gibson.

12-01-49  Promoted to Corporal.

06-01-51.  Promoted to Fourth Sergeant and appointed Commissary Sergeant.

05-05-54  Honorable Discharge as Sergeant at Fort McIntosh, Texas.

## 66. *Texas State Gazette*, May 10, 1865

We had the pleasure of a call this morning from our old friend, Col. Jas. Duff, of San Antonio, who is on way to join his command in Burleson County. We are pleased to see him in fine health and spirits. Few men in Texas have made more sacrifices for the Confederacy than Col. Duff. At the commencement of the war, he was engaged in a large and prosperous business, and having been a large contractor, for many years, for the old U. S. Army, he might still have been engaged in that capacity for the Confederate government, by which he might have realized an immense fortune, as many others have done; but after furnishing all the means within his control to support our cause, he closed up his business, and has not been for three years in active service in the field. Under ordinary circumstances we should not have made this statement, but in times like these, it is desirable we should know who are the patriots of the country.

www.ingramcontent.com/pod-product-compliance
Lightning Source LLC
Chambersburg PA
CBHW030512100426
42813CB00001B/14